THE MURDER OF
CLEOPATRA

THE MURDER OF
CLEOPATRA
HISTORY'S GREATEST COLD CASE

PAT BROWN

 Prometheus Books

59 John Glenn Drive
Amherst, New York 14228–2119

Published 2013 by Prometheus Books

Cover image © 2013 iStockPhoto
Cover design by Nicole Sommer-Lecht

Inquiries should be addressed to
Prometheus Books
59 John Glenn Drive
Amherst, New York 14228–2119
VOICE: 716–691–0133
FAX: 716–691–0137
WWW.PROMETHEUSBOOKS.COM

17 16 15 14 13   5 4 3 2

Library of Congress Cataloging-in-Publication Data

Brown, Pat, 1955-
    The murder of Cleopatra : history's greatest cold case / by Pat Brown.
        p. cm.
    Includes bibliographical references and index.
    ISBN 978-1-61614-650-4 (pbk.)
    ISBN 978-1-61614-651-1 (ebook)
    1. Cleopatra, Queen of Egypt, d. 30 B.C. 2. Cleopatra, Queen of Egypt, d. 30
B.C.—Death and burial. 3. Queens—Egypt. 4. Egypt—Kings and rulers. 5. Egypt—
History—332-30 B.C. I. Title.

DT92.7.B78 2013
932.021092--dc23

                                                                2012040641

Printed in the United States of America

CONTENTS

6 CONTENTS

ACKNOWLEDGMENTS

This exploration of the life and death of Cleopatra VII has been one of the most fascinating adventures of my life, and, once I decided there was a story to tell, I knew I needed others along with me who wanted the ideas I developed to get out into the world. The journey started in 2003 with Discovery Channel and Atlantic Productions, and if they hadn't selected me to analyze this part of history and be the host of *The Mysterious Death of Cleopatra*, this book likely would not have been written.

Next I have to thank my wonderful and incredibly supportive literary agent, Claire Gerus, who believed in this book and fought to find a publisher who would believe in it is as well. She brought me to Steven L. Mitchell and Prometheus Books, who took this book on and brought it to fruition. I can't thank Steven enough for choosing this story of Cleopatra for publication.

Finally, I want to thank the people of Egypt for making my two trips so enjoyable, and, especially I want to thank Dr. Zahi Hawass, who oversees everything archeological in Egypt, who saw me without an appointment, and who set up my wonderful trip to Tapasoris Magna. And my utmost thanks to Dr. Said Gohary, whose hospitality and conversation along with his lovely wife, Dr. Jocelyn Gohary, made both my trips to Egypt so very special and helped me immensely in my understanding of ancient Egypt and the times in which Cleopatra lived.

And, finally, my readers; thank you for having a mind that is open enough to read this new look at history and being willing to give Cleopatra the extra attention she has always deserved.

—Pat Brown

NOTE TO THE READER

This book is an examination of the life and death of the last Egyptian pharaoh, Cleopatra VII, with an aim to uncover what really happened to Cleopatra and why. What is not contained in this study is a detailed and complete history of Rome and Egypt. If I endeavored to include such a thorough account of all the events of those days, this book would be a very large tome and it would defeat the purpose of this work, which is to focus on the most relevant issues leading to the queen's demise. For this analysis of the death of Cleopatra, I have included the background information most pertinent to understanding Cleopatra and the Roman men in her life and the specific pieces of evidence that will illuminate what led to the final days of Alexandria. For more information about ancient times and the Roman and Egyptian world in which Cleopatra was born and died, I recommend Joyce Tyldesley's *Cleopatra* and her other books on the queens of Egypt; Michael Grant's *Cleopatra*; Anthony Everitt's *Augustus*; Jean-Yves Empereur's *Alexandria Rediscovered*; N. G. L. Hammonds's *The Genius of Alexander the Great*; Adrian Goldsworthy's *Caesar*; and Peter Green's *The Hellenistic Age*. Any of Zahi Hawass's books on Egypt and archeology or the books of Said and Joceyln Gohary on the Egyptian tombs and monuments will round out one's understanding of the world of Egypt until the end of the Ptolemaic Dynasty at Cleopatra's death in 30 BCE.

THE MYTH OF CLEOPATRA'S DEATH

When the sun rose over the city of Alexandria on the morning of August 12, 30 BCE, it did not shine down on the great Alexandria of Egypt, but the new Alexandria of the Roman Empire. The air was heavy with resignation and solemn respect for the passing of the queen and for the transfer of Alexandria into the hands of the Roman general Octavian. Cleopatra had provided a dignified conclusion to the great dynasty with her brave, if surprising, exit from the world.

The story was simple, yet awe-inspiring. Octavian had been in the palace, and Cleopatra in her tomb with her two favorite handmaidens. Somehow, a cobra had been smuggled into the mausoleum hidden in a basket of figs. A soldier delivered a letter to Octavian in which Cleopatra explained that she was about to take her life with a request that her body be buried next to her beloved husband and Roman general, Mark Antony, who had already committed suicide a few days earlier, dying in the arms of his wife. Octavian immediately dispatched his men to the mausoleum to intervene and stop the queen from this rash course of action. However, by the time the soldiers arrived, Cleopatra was dead. Word was sent back to Octavian, "We were too late."

Unwilling to believe Cleopatra was truly dead, Octavian hurried to the mausoleum. He was stunned and angered by the sight of the motionless queen. This determined woman who had refused to yield

11

at any time in her life, this enchantress who lured married Roman men into unfaithfulness and turned them against their countries, this queen who had refused to recognize his superiority in life, preferred death over submission to his sovereignty. He would now be unable to bring her back to Rome in shackles and parade her though the streets in his grand triumph—his final coup de grâce. Queen Cleopatra, the greatest prize in the entire world, had slipped out of his grasp.

Hoping she was perhaps in a coma, the sleep that mimics death, Octavian desperately sent for the physician and for specialists in snake venom who might still find a way to save her. But the snake-venom experts had no remedies and the doctor pronounced her dead. All of this was witnessed by the soldiers, and after they left, Octavian met with his advisors.

The story of Cleopatra's death did not take long to spread beyond the compound, and soon the city was in mourning. Later that week, a wealthy friend of Cleopatra's came to Octavian and gave him a large sum of money to maintain st'satues of the queen. Wishing to prove he was a moral leader who respected the sentiments of his new subjects, Octavian agreed.

This is the account of Cleopatra's death, a tale that has been dutifully retold for two thousand years. But the real story of how Octavian got away with the most perfect crime in history, the murder of Cleopatra, has never been uncovered until now.

CHAPTER 1

THE COLDEST CASE

"I won't be involved in any project just for the sake of it," I told Atlantic Productions. The call had come in from London on my cell phone, which I tried to juggle as I shifted gears in an attempt to keep my car from sliding backward down an icy hill in the midst of a Midwestern snowstorm. I wasn't sure I was going to make it to any hotel on this trip; the storm was pretty bad and I was driving a BMW that should have been sitting in a garage.

I was skeptical of the project. Yes, Cleopatra had always intrigued me as a child; the visuals of the scantily clad queen, a snake biting at her breast—these were powerful images that stayed in one's mind. As I grew older, I would come across artists' depictions of her death and wonder at the tawdriness of her final moments.

I had questioned why any queen would purposely allow herself to be seen in such a manner, half-naked and sprawled out lasciviously on display. The cobra wrapped around her body always seemed a tad ridiculous. And I felt there were simpler, more effective ways to commit suicide that a rational person would more likely have chosen. Perhaps, I thought, Queen Cleopatra was simply the hysterical type, a queen by default rather than one of intelligence and strength. I had put her out of my mind until that day in Ohio.

The project that Atlantic was calling about was part of the wave of television pitches that would pick a popular topic, find some issue to question or attack, whether or not there was really any valid reason to do so. Atlantic made quite a few Egyptian shows of this nature for Discovery Channel and now was probing the possi-bility of bringing up some new controversy about Cleopatra's death.

"I won't be involved unless I can determine there is a legitimate reason to doubt that Cleopatra didn't die by snake or didn't commit suicide. I don't make up stuff like a defense expert, just to get a payday." The producers got my point but told me they wanted an answer as soon as possible—like, that day. Television folks have little patience.

Looking at my map for the nearest, most populated location, I changed course and rolled into the nearest town with a large-enough bookstore, heading straight for the section on Egypt.

I wasn't expecting to come up with much, certainly not within the time frame given. I assumed I would read the very limited mate-rial by the early historians, skim some opinions of the modern-day historians, and call the network back with a "No, there is simply no evidence to determine anything; just a bunch of stories and conjec-ture." End of project.

But when I thumbed my way to the end of each Cleopatra book and read the story of her death, I became more and more intrigued. Not by the repetitive narration each historian seemed to parrot, but by the fact one basic story had been passed down through the centuries and had hardly been questioned by anyone, even experts in the field.

The death of Cleopatra, though two thousand years old, is like any other cold case with a suspicious death scene. There is a body, there is a crime scene, and there are witnesses (even if they are only testifying to what they found after the deceased was discovered). Any good crime analyst knows that what one might think to be true on first glimpse may turn out to be completely incorrect when the evi-dence is analyzed.

Scenes can be staged, family members might remove objects to cover up embarrassing facts or to ensure collecting insurance money, and the first people on the scene may disturb the evidence in their rush to help, or in their panic. Or they might be thieves simply taking advantage of the circumstances.

All of these possibilities must be taken into account when attempting to determine what actually happened to the victim. And even this is not enough. An investigator must look into the behavioral history of the deceased and all the people and events connected with him or her. The culture and the actions of the inhabitants of his time and location must be considered as well.

Finally, each aspect of the physical evidence must be factored in: the wounds, the position of the body, the time of death, the weapon, the location, the weather . . . every physical feature of the world encompassing the victim, and an assessment of how each feature might have affected the final moments of the victim's life.

The ancient crime scene of Cleopatra had to be treated in a like manner. One cannot simply accept the words of a few observers or "journalists" or politicians or later writers. What we think we know of a past event is often distorted, and unless we examine all the evidence to uncover the truth, the distortion will remain.

I was shocked at the number of red flags that popped up from the pages of the historical accounts of the Egyptian queen's final day. How was it that Cleopatra managed to smuggle a cobra into the tomb in a basket of figs? Why would the guards allow this food in and why would they be so careless in examining them? Why would Octavian, supposedly so adamant about taking Cleopatra to Rome for his triumph, be so lax about her imprisonment? Why would Cleopatra think it easier to hide a writhing snake in a basket of figs rather than slip poison inside one of the many figs? How did all three women end up dead from the venom? Wasn't it unlikely that the snake cooperated in striking all three, releasing sufficient venom to kill each of them? Why was the snake no longer present at the crime scene? Was a brand-new tomb so poorly built that holes remained in the walls of the building? Why did the guards not look for the snake once they thought it had killed the women? Why were the wounds from the fangs of the snake not obvious? Why did the women not exhibit the symptoms of death by snake venom or even by poison? Why did the guards not see any of the women convulsing, vomiting, or holding their abdomens in agony? Why didn't they see any swelling or paralysis of face or limbs or any foaming at the mouth?

Now filled with questions, I began to work backward in the texts. Did the behaviors of Cleopatra and Octavian support a suicide? As a criminal profiler, one of the important tasks of analyzing crimes is reviewing the behavioral history of the players; no one acts outside of one's own frame of thinking.

With each step back in time from the end of Cleopatra's life to the beginning, I discovered more and more evidence pointing to a radically different explanation of history than the ancients and Octavian wanted us to believe.

I made the call back to England. "I'm in. Cleopatra was murdered."

My interest didn't end with my work on the documentary *The Mysterious Death of Cleopatra* or my debunking of the death-by-snake theory or my assertion that Cleopatra was murdered. While I was in Egypt, Rome, and England working with Egyptologists, poison experts, archeologists, and historians of the ancient world, I began to piece together another, more credible story behind the death of Cleopatra.

I believed Cleopatra was tortured.

I believed Cleopatra was strangled.

I believed Antony was murdered.

I believed Cleopatra did not hide in her tomb with her treasure.

I believed Cleopatra did not bargain with Octavian.

I believed Cleopatra planned a brilliant military maneuver at Alexandria, her Actium Two, which this time would not have been an escape strategy from a failed naval battle, but a faux naval battle to permit a successful escape from a dire military position that offered little hope of survival.

I believed Cleopatra never loved Antony.

I believed Cleopatra never loved Julius Caesar.

I believed Cleopatra did not have Caesar's son.

I believed Cleopatra may have been one of the most brilliant, cold-blooded, iron-willed rulers in history and the truth about what really happened was hidden behind a veil of propaganda and lies set in motion by her murderer, Octavian, and the agenda of the Roman Empire.

Now I had to prove it.

CHAPTER 2

THE PHANTOM COBRA

The first place a criminal profiler goes when on a cold case is to the crime scene—or at least to where the crime scene had been. I traveled to Egypt in search of an archeological substitute for the tomb in which Cleopatra and her handmaidens supposedly committed suicide, and for the snake, the very kind of snake that could have struck down all three women in ruthless succession.

Cairo is a city that never sleeps, at least not for the men who inhabit the coffee shops, smoking incessantly, chatting, playing Parcheesi, an enviable world for male camaraderie if it weren't for the nearly 12 percent unemployment rate that allows for endless hours of leisure. The women of Egypt have certain constraints, but compared to the highly restrictive Muslim countries that surround them, they live in relative freedom. Head coverings are not required by law and in upscale areas of Cairo one can see Egyptian women sitting in cafés, hair cascading freely over their shoulders, tight jeans on their young bodies, arguing blithely with their male companions at their outdoor table, while both are smoking American cigarettes.

I was new to Egypt and wanted to hide my blond hair. I preferred not be offensive to anyone and I wanted to dull any of the harassment that American and European tourists often experience, mostly from men trying to sell something. So, after settling my bags in my inexpensive hotel room (a four-floor walk-up with an iron-barred elevator in the lobby encased in so many layers of dust I didn't even question the possibility that it was operable), I went shopping on the Talaat Harb, a spender's mecca of fashionable apparel in the heart of Cairo. This was my second trip to Egypt, but instead of moving about with a "fixer" (the Egyptian manager who made sure the Discovery Channel production team and I got where we were going in comfort and safety), I was on my own. Without cameras tailing my every move, I was female, alone, unprotected, and with no celebrity attached to my appearance in public.

After my whirlwind tour of a myriad of shops, I huffed and puffed to the high-ceilinged room of my hotel, carrying bags of long skirts, sleeved shirts, and a half dozen hijabs of assorted vibrant colors, and collapsed into my bed. I slept like a mummy, a dreamless sleep after the grueling flight in coach and the endless layover at Heathrow in London, content and unconscious under the heavy quilt that adorned the bed, unconcerned that it had not likely been washed in the last century.

If one can sleep late in Cairo, one has lived in the city for a long while or is luxuriating in a fine hotel along the Nile that serves alcoholic beverages to tourists, dead to the world from inebriation, sheltered from sound by the thick walls and airtight construction. At my fifteen-dollar-per-night hotel in the teaming streets of the city downtown, at far before the break of dawn, I woke to Adhan, the morning call to prayer that was emanating from a loudspeaker on a nearby mosque. It tends to raise the neck hair on the non-Muslim first-time visitor to Egypt, but is a comforting soliloquy for the start of day for those of the Islamic faith and for others who have become accustomed to the early-morning song of the city.

I threw open the massive window shutters and soaked in the lilting melodies floating above the courtyard, if one could call it that, a square trash dump with nondescript walls rising on its four sides. But, the magic held. I was in the land of Cleopatra, even if it had changed radically over the centuries from the days of the pharaohs to the Arab Spring, the about-to-begin 2011 revolution of Egypt. Each period of history contributed to the development of the region, the people, the religion, and the culture. The days of the Old Kingdom began in 2686 BCE, when the great pyramids of Giza were built. Three dynasties of indigenous rule held fast for almost seventeen centuries until the Libyan invasion in 945 BCE; followed by the Persian conquest of 525 BCE, under which the Egyptians were extremely unhappy; and the then most-welcomed liberation by the Macedonian general Alexander the Great in 332 BCE. His conquest set up the many years of pharaonic rule through the death of Cleopatra in 30 BCE. Then Egypt became part of the Roman Empire and was regarded as a large estate that Rome could plunder for its crops, cash, and cultural amenities. The polytheistic religion was allowed to continue with relatively little interference, and the priests were actually aided by the Roman rulers in the construction of new temples and the completion of unfinished ones; life was hard but one could still pray to one's own gods, those of human appearance and those in animal form.

Then came the spread of Christianity and the invasion of 324 CE, which resulted in almost three hundred years of rule under the thumb of Constantinople and the ravaging of the tombs, temples, and monuments. Today one can still see the breadth of their destruction at the temples where the noses of nearly every one of the ancient Egyptian deities has been lopped off in a mass cleansing of polytheistic worship. Christianity grew greatly during this period, in spite of disputes and offshoots fighting for power and survival like the early Coptic Church, which survives to this day. Presently, Christians make up 10 percent of the population; the many Christmas decorations I saw hanging in windows of businesses and in restaurants attest to this.

The next radical change came in 639 CE, when the Muslim general Amir ibn al-'As invaded Egypt and ended the Byzantine rule and Islam began to take root. Weathering the Ottoman, French, and British occupations from the early 1500s until the 1952 revolution resulting in the 1953 establishment of Egypt as a republic, the country remained an Islamic nation and an Arab culture. The next three presidents—Gamal Abdel Nasser, Anwar Sadat, and the recently ousted

Hosni Mubarak—brought a roller coaster of ups and downs to the struggling country, and now I was standing at my window listening to the call to worship in a land about to dramatically change yet again.

But, as I dressed that morning in my new Egyptian garb, I wanted to roll back through the centuries and see the vestiges of earlier times, work my way back to the world of the pharaohs and that fateful last day in which Cleopatra was to have died with her handmaidens within the cool recesses of her stone tomb.

Before I set off down the four flights of stairs to the hubbub of the streets below, I carefully concealed my hair in a bright turquoise scarf, wrapping it as properly as I could so that no wisp of hair escaped, no bit of my ears or neck might be observed. I positioned the scarf strategically so the embroidered flowers with their shiny mirror stigmas and tassels flowed down my left shoulder. I snuck a pair of earrings up into the holes in my covered lobes and studied my workmanship. I was pleasantly surprised to find that a tightly worn hijab offers a cheap and immediate facelift, even though my hearing was quite diminished from my ears being sealed off. I found, when I returned to the United States and no longer wore my hijab, that I was a bit sad because I had to style my hair again and there seemed a missing final touch to my outfit.

Down at the entrance to the hotel, I grabbed a cab and instructed the driver to take me to the Citadel, the massive walled fortress begun by magnificent Saladin in 1176 to defend against the Crusaders. This structure with its impressive stone walls and the domed Ottoman-style Muhammad Ali mosque, towers over the city on the high promontory, dominating the skyline of Cairo and reminding all below of Egypt's long history of invasions and military rule. As the taxi driver maneuvered his way through the traffic-snarled streets of Cairo, it was hard to believe, with all Arabic writing scrawled atop the entrances to businesses, women in black burqas and men in Muslim religious dress, that the people of Egypt once worshipped Anubis the jackal; Horus the hawk; or Hathor, the goddess of love, wearing the horns of a cow. Nor was it easy to imagine Queen Cleopatra swathed in a

Grecian gown, entertaining an entourage of Romans in her resplendent palace by the sea.

The taxi pulled in front of the entrance gate to the Citadel. I paid the driver and made my way up the steps. I removed my shoes and entered the Mosque of Muhammad Ali, walking silently across the red-and-gold carpet, staring up at the rings of chandeliers that lit the Turkish-style interior. It was beautiful. But then I had to smile at the irony of how this place of worship was built at the location where, seventeen years before its construction began, Ali gave a celebration in his palace with very little spirit of brotherly love. That night he held a banquet for 470 Mamluks, the powerful military caste that controlled the army and much of the politics of Egypt. They were a constant threat to Ali's governorship of Egypt. After an evening of festivities, the Mamluks poured out into the lane leading down the hill from the fortress, where they were ambushed and massacred. Ali achieved his goal of eliminating his opposition and gaining sole control of the country.[1] Cleopatra clearly wasn't to be the last of the ruthless rulers of Egypt.

I wandered back to the doorway, retrieved my shoes, and strolled over to the terrace, and, there spread before me was a spectacular view of Cairo, miles and miles of square and rectangular buildings, tin domes and minarets, smog submerging the mishmash of newly built high-rises, half-finished apartments, and older two-storied buildings in varying shades of grey and brown, a smattering of white mosques and occasional flashes of color as far as the eye can see, or at least distinguish under the film of dirty air created from the congestion below.

And then there, behind all the city tableau, was what I was longing to see. Two massive triangles, the greatest of the three Giza pyramids, so incredibly large that they seemed almost a mirage or a photographic trick that has been staged for the naïve tourist. But they are real. They are the essence of Egypt. They are the symbol of people of the desert and the Nile, the land before Europe encroached on the continent from across the Mediterranean Sea. It is the backdrop to the life into which Cleopatra VII, the last Cleopatra of the Ptolemaic line, was born.[2] It is evidence that would help me profile the life and death of Cleopatra more thoroughly and concretely.

I arrived at Giza early the next morning, far before the site was open to the public and when there was hardly anyone but the locals moving about, getting ready for their day. Giza is a bit of an odd site up close, not at all what one expects from the carefully shot photos of the three pyramids. There is a tendency to believe that one will need to travel miles from the city, and there in endless sands of the Western Desert, the pyramids will rise majestically on the horizon. In reality, one can jump on the metro and arrive at Giza in a matter of minutes. I took a taxi from downtown and passed by hotels and restaurants, and in less than fifteen minutes I was at my destination. Hardly far from the present-day world, the pyramids can be seen through a Pizza Hut window just a short walk down the street from the archeological site, the laser light show viewable from its roof, as a number of low-budget tourists (including myself) have discovered. The remainder of the 118 pyramids of Egypt spread west across forty-three miles of desert to Fayoum City, most of which are not visited by the majority of visitors to the country. It is easy to see why once one has viewed the Great Pyramid, the others pale in comparison, although they are still treasures to historians and archeologists.

Since it was still early, I decided that before I entered the Great Pyramid, I would take a visit farther down the road to nearby Dashur to examine a couple of smaller pyramids built earlier: the Red Pyramid and the Bent Pyramid. I grabbed another cab and traveled south along the canal until I came to the two pyramids, both built by King Sneferu (2613–2589 BCE), the pharaoh who ruled during the Fourth Dynasty; he preceded his son, Khufu (2589–2566 BCE), who built the Great Pyramid at Giza. It would be interesting to see the construction of these two pyramids and what kind of workmanship they displayed and what their burial chambers might have looked like. I was specifically interested in two things: (1) did burial chambers make good living spaces for a trio of women to spend time in, and (2) how tightly sealed were burial chambers back in those days? Were they too tightly sealed to let a snake slither out of them?

In my previous travels throughout Egypt, I had visited two other sites in which burial chambers were included in their structures. One location was in the Valley of the Kings, just east of the famous sites of Luxor and Karnak in Upper Egypt, an overnight trip by train straight south along the Nile River. The Valley of the Kings was on the West Bank of the Nile, a quick ferry ride from Luxor and twenty minutes into the desert by van. The site itself is rather unspectacular, just a drab entrance, a bunch of dirt hills with holes in them looming up behind it. It seems a rather odd setting for kings to be buried, but apparently at least sixty-three tombs were built to house the royals for eternity, so they had little issue with their finery being confined to burial chambers and elaborately decorated corridors hidden under the dirt rather than some large memorial seen from above the surface. The tombs were built in the Eighteenth Dynasty, and the pharaohs who would eventually be buried in them hoped to protect them from grave robbers, a centuries-old problem for royal Egyptian tombs built earlier. Considering the plundering of so many of these tombs not too long after the kings were ensconced in them, that wish did not exactly pan out over time; criminals always seem to find a way to break into wherever massive wealth is stored.[3]

I visited a half dozen of the tombs, including the small tomb of the boy-king Tutankhamen, the least interesting of them all in spite of the twenty-dollar charge. However, for the pleasure of saying one had been in King Tut's burial chamber and of seeing his mummy, it was oddly worth the expense. It was also quite thrilling to have been there and then to later go to the Egyptian Museum in Cairo and view King Tut's beautiful coffin and spectacular golden funerary mask inlaid with jewels, along with a supposed seventeen hundred items that were removed from his tomb; having been in the tomb made the museum experience more meaningful. And, like Tut's tomb, none of the other Valley of the Kings tombs retained any treasures, but their walls are covered with fabulous reliefs in many colors.

All these tombs were reached by descending a very long corridor into the earth until one came into a rectangular compartment (with the exception of King Tut's chamber, which was quite close to ground level). I noted during my visit to each chamber that all the edges of floors, walls, and ceilings inside the tomb were aligned perfectly, with no cracks or separating seams or holes. The burial chamber itself was quite small, providing only for the deceased in its coffin and a space to move around the platform upon which it rested with its mummy inside. There are some tombs that are larger, but, in general, the tomb was meant for one body to be ensconced in the chamber along with a pile of expensive possessions to keep the pharaoh company on his journey into the next world. Once the body was interred in the tomb along with the requisite royal treasures, the door was sealed and no one entered again. There was hardly a need to have a massive room for a corpse that was not going to be getting up and strolling about. If one were alive and spending any amount of time in the tomb, the only thought going through one's head would be to notice how stifling it was and to question how soon one could get out.

Now, I stood in front of the Bent Pyramid at Dashur, theorized to be second of King Sneferu's attempts at pyramid building. His first is believed to be the "Collapsed Pyramid," on the outskirts of Fayoum at the village of Maidum. That pyramid was built like the earliest ones, a step pyramid with simple layers of massive stone like the one built at Saqqara in the Third Dynasty. Each pyramid had four or six huge stone terraces, each of which was smaller than the one below it. But the Collapsed Pyramid was modified. It was encased with an outer shell of white limestone blocks to beautify the exterior and make it a true pyramid (with flat sides). Unfortunately, it was badly designed and fell down from the stresses of the poorly planned structural addition. Sneferu then tried again. His Bent Pyramid was a far better attempt, but the sides of the thing go up at a steep angle and then taper off toward the top, making it look rather like a schoolchild's poor attempt a drawing a triangle and failing to make a proper shape. It is supposed that the sides did not continue in the proper line because of unstable ground that caused cracks to appear in the walls of the burial chamber, and when they started leaning inward, the design was modified to prevent further damage. In all the burial chambers I have examined, I have never noted any problems with the walls, so it would appear that better design methodology was applied in future massive structures. The Bent Pyramid was abandoned and never used for its intended purpose. Sneferu gave it another shot and built the Red Pyramid (also at Dashur), and this time he got it right, a true pyramid that had its perfect geometric shape. Here the burial chambers were put to use.

The Bent Pyramid was not open to visitors when I was there, but I had the opportunity to observe the base areas, which no longer had limestone covering the stone blocks. It is amazing to see the craftsmanship that went into putting these blocks so closely together. Stonemasons did not fill large areas between the stones as one often sees today with traditional brick and stone walls; instead, the sand, gypsum, and lime mortar was scraped on in a very thin layer with one's hand and used as a lubricant to slide the next forty- or fifty-ton block into position right up against the neighboring one. It is dead weight or friction that keeps the stones together. Hence, unlike today, where you often see chunks of mortar having fallen out of some building or chimney that needs to be repointed to secure the structure, stones of these ancient Egyptian edifices stay solidly in place for centuries, barring manmade assault or catastrophic movement of the earth. While the limestone surfaces were often stolen from these monuments (which is why they aren't as attractive as they once were), those massive blocks of stone stayed put. As a matter of fact, the blocks are so tight that one couldn't even pour mortar between them, so it is doubtful a reptile of even the tiniest size could find a way through those walls.

The Red Pyramid was Sneferu's great achievement and, thereafter, pyramids were built in this manner, with the sheer sides we tend to associate with pyramids today, at least the most perfect ones in history, the trio of pyramids at Giza. In all of these structures, burial chambers were aboveground but located within the depths of the pyramid. The Red Pyramid required me to climb the outside stairs, which continued approximately halfway up the side of the pyramid; and then I descended via a tight inside passageway for what seemed an eternity until I made it into the burial-chamber area. Here the chambers, three of them, were larger than at the Valleys of the Kings, so one could imagine it more likely that it would be possible to spend a bit of extended time inside one, if it weren't for the darkness and the claustrophobia one feels while in the guts of the massive pile of stones. Keeping the light on, or shall I say the torch, for any length of time would prove problematic, as it would use up the available oxygen in the room and smoke up the place. The seams between walls, ceilings, and floors were just as tight as I had seen previously in tombs in the Valley of the Kings.

Then, I returned to Giza to visit the Great Pyramid, built by King Sneferu's son Khufu, also known as Cheops. The son outdid his father, building an even larger and more spectacular pyramid. I paid my admission price and entered the site, now being trampled by a number of tourists, though not as many as I would have expected to see.

The Great Pyramid is, well, great. What can one say about a structure that took twenty-two years to build and used around 2,300,000 limestone blocks that each weighed an average of 2.5 tons, with some weighing sixteen tons? Sadly, the beautiful, smooth, white limestone no longer covers the pyramid, as it was stolen to be used in constructing the modern-day Cairo. The massive stones are exposed, and one can see just how huge each one is. I entered the door to the sloping pathway to the burial chamber, this time climbing up inside the pyramid. Again, after a very long time, I reached the center. The room was simple and empty, with the exception of a massive stone box that had no top (into which the coffin would be placed). But the feeling of being in such an isolated and secret place built so long ago, with its smooth interior, its perfect dimensions, was amazing. Those guidebooks that advised me not to bother with the uncomfortable ascent into the tomb because it wasn't worth the trouble were dead wrong.

As I sat inside what would become my favorite burial chamber, deep inside the Great Pyramid in Giza, I envisioned what we've been told happened twenty centuries ago in a room supposedly just like this one. This square vault was so deep inside Cheops's magnificent structure, I felt I had truly crawled back in time to the cusp of the millennium. There was nothing painted on these walls of the room, nothing of beauty to be seen (the unadorned oddity of this interior room in the Great Pyramid has yet to be satisfactorily explained by historians). I felt as if I were alone in the center of Cleopatra's last days, a landscape barren of hope for the embattled queen. Although the stark room in which I sat was built many years before the birth of Cleopatra, the inside of this tomb would not be so different from one the last pharaoh would find herself ensconced, should she be laid to rest in proper Macedonian or Egyptian tradition. Wherever and whenever the queen's body was put to rest, it would be in a similar simple, fully sealed room with just enough space to fit a platform topped with a big stone box in which to secrete the casket. Around the platform, riches would be piled to travel with her into the afterworld. The walls would be adorned with colorful paintings, as likely would the narrow entranceway leading from the outside into the burial vault. It is a small, simple cubicle, not roomy and elaborate living quarters.

It is here that I needed to start my return trek into pharaonic times to pick up where I left off from my last trip to Egypt with the Atlantic crew, to dig even deeper into the mystery of Cleopatra's death.

I reviewed what I had learned from my visits to the various tombs and from the study of history leading up to the death of Cleopatra, purportedly taking place inside a tomb room like the one in which I was now sitting. In reality, Cleopatra's tomb would have looked more like a Macedonian tomb than an Egyptian one (the small subterranean alabaster tomb in Alexandria that may or may not have been the burial chamber of Alexander the Great would be a good representation of such a tomb); however, the burial vault inside would be very much the same. But, whether the origin of Cleopatra's mausoleum architecture was Macedonian or Egyptian, the one thing I noted for sure in all the tombs I visited was that *none* of them seemed a convenient place to store the *entire* Ptolemaic treasury or to burn up all the wealth of the pharaohs, as Cleopatra supposedly told Octavian she was planning to do. With the lack of much air in these places, I doubt a fire would burn terribly well or long, nor would hanging out for an extended period of time with the door shut be tolerable; it is terribly hot, dark, and airless in these underground or interior burial chambers. Burial tombs are nothing like the structures Plutarch describes.

> Now that she had a tomb and monument built surpassingly lofty and beautiful, which she had erected near the temple of Isis, collected there the most valuable of the royal treasures, gold, silver, emeralds, pearls, ebony, ivory, and cinnamon; and besides all this she put there great quantities of torch-wood and tow, so that Caesar was anxious about the reason, and fearing lest the woman might become desperate and burn up and destroy this wealth.[4]

Furthermore, none of these tombs appeared to be on the ground floor of large, square, aboveground buildings, as Cleopatra's mausoleum was described in the ancient texts. The other thing I learned after visiting tomb after tomb is that the construction was solid; no shoddy work or flimsy materials were used here. These tombs were intended to keep out all the elements.

The writings of Plutarch oddly describe the interior of the tomb as similar to that of a room in the royal palace or a large interior room of a grand temple. Indeed, in many paintings depicting Cleopatra in her mausoleum, we see a velvet bed upon which Cleopatra is draped and, around her, the decorations of a fine sitting room or a throne room. Yet, in each of the tombs I visited, no such comfortable ambience was present. The rooms weren't even large enough to accommodate more than the coffin and the ruler's selected possessions.

She begged Caesar that she might be permitted to pour libations for Antony; and when the request was granted, she had herself carried to the tomb, and embracing the urn which held his ashes, in company with the women usually about her.

After such lamentations, she wreathed and kissed the urn, and then ordered a bath to be prepared for herself. After her bath, she reclined at table and was making a sumptuous meal.[5]

Tombs have one thing in common: they are secure vaults. In the Valley of the Kings where one can actually see colorful artwork adorning the walls of the entranceways and the tombs themselves, there is still no question that this is a final destination. First, there is the long crippled-over or hands-and-knees crawl down, down, down, or up, up, up—inching along inside the tight tunnel walls, so encroaching that many visitors simply refuse to make the attempt. There is an odd feeling of air escaping from your chest as you make your way down the shaft, even though your brain is telling you that this is a tourist venue, that you will arrive shortly at your goal and be perfectly fine.

When you get there, finally, finally, you can stand up. You have entered the resting place of a god. And you feel alone, even with others. The weight of the earth above, or the massive stones above, below, and on all sides, causes an uncomfortable feeling of entrapment. This *is* a grave, albeit a slightly larger one than most of our bodies will ever reside within. In the middle of each room is a stone platform, with a stone outer casket placed on top of it. This, then, is it. A body encased in stone, upon stone, within stone. It is stifling and eternal and inescapable. This is no place to linger, to hide in, to bargain from within. It is no hotel room with furniture and bath and dining facilities. It is simply a storage unit for someone no longer needing to see the light or expend energy. It would not have been Cleopatra's choice of a hiding place or a holdout. Yet this is where the ancient texts claim Cleopatra spent her last days and chose to end her life.

The final moments of the last Egyptian pharaoh are the most

famous in all history, barring that of Jesus Christ's crucifixion at Golgotha outside of Jerusalem. Those last minutes of the great queen Cleopatra's life have been reenacted for centuries on stage in Shakespeare's famed play, *Antony and Cleopatra*. We have watched, mesmerized, as the beautiful pharaoh clutches the hissing snake, mouth wide open, fangs visible, and then presses it to her breast. We shudder as we hear her gasp loudly for breath, her throat muscles contracting in a vicious spasm, moaning as excruciating pain surges through her being.

Then, tears came to our eyes as the actress playing Cleopatra collapsed to the floor, artistically posing herself in as attractive a heap as she could muster for a lifeless body on display. It is a scene not easily forgotten.

As reported by Plutarch:

After such lamentations, she wreathed and kissed the urn, and then ordered a bath to be prepared for herself. After her bath, she reclined at table and was making a sumptuous meal. And there came a man from the country carrying a basket; and when the guards asked him what he was bringing there, he opened the basket, took away the leaves, and showed them that the dish inside was full of figs. The guards were amazed at the great size and beauty of the figs, whereupon the man smiled and asked them to take some; so they felt no mistrust and bade him take them in. After her meal, however, Cleopatra took a tablet which was already written upon and sealed, and sent it to Caesar, and then, sending away all the rest of the company except her two faithful women, she closed the doors.

But Caesar opened the tablet, and when he found there lamentations and supplications of one who begged that he would bury her with Antony, he quickly knew what had happened. At first he was minded to go himself and give aid; then he ordered messengers to go with all speed and investigate. But the mischief had been swift. For though his messengers came on the run and found the guards as yet aware of nothing, when they opened the doors they found Cleopatra lying dead upon a golden couch, arrayed in royal state. And of her two women, the one called Iras was dying at her feet, while Charmion, already tottering and heavy-handed, was trying to arrange the diadem which encircled the queen's brow. Then somebody said in anger: "A fine deed, this, Charmion!" "It is indeed most fine," she said, "and befitting the descendant of so many kings." Not a word more did she speak, but fell there by the side of the couch.

It is said that the asp was brought with those figs and leaves and lay hidden beneath them, for thus Cleopatra had given orders, that the reptile might fasten itself upon her body without her being aware of it. But when she took away some of the figs and saw it, she said: "There it is, you see," and baring her arm she held it out for the bite. But others say that the asp was kept carefully shut up in a water jar, and that while Cleopatra was stirring it up and irritating it with a golden distaff it sprang and fastened itself upon her arm. But the truth of the matter no one knows; for it was also said that she carried about poison in a hollow comb and kept the comb hidden in her hair; and yet neither spot nor other sign of poison broke out upon her body. Moreover, not even was the reptile seen within the chamber, though people said they saw some traces of it near the sea, where the chamber looked out upon it with its windows. And some also say that Cleopatra's arm was seen to have two slight and indistinct punctures; and this Caesar also seems to have believed. For in his triumph an image of Cleopatra herself with the asp clinging to her was carried in the procession. These, then, are the various accounts of what happened.[6]

And from Cassius Dio:

No one knows clearly in what way she perished, for the only marks on her body were slight pricks on the arm. Some say she applied to herself an asp which had been brought in to her in a water-jar, or perhaps hidden in some flowers. Others declare that she had smeared a pin, with which she was wont to fasten her hair, with some poison possessed of such a property that in ordinary circumstances it would not injure the body at all, but if it came into contact with even a drop of blood would destroy the body very quietly and painlessly; and that previous to this time she had worn it in her hair as usual, but now had made a slight scratch on her arm and had dipped the pin in the blood. In this or in some very similar way she perished, and her two handmaidens with her. As for the eunuch, he had of his own accord delivered himself up to the serpents at the very time of Cleopatra's arrest, and after being bitten by them had leaped into a coffin already prepared for him. When Caesar heard of Cleopatra's death, he was astounded, and not only viewed her body but also made use of drugs and Psylli in the hope that she might revive. These Psylli are males, for there is no woman born in their tribe, and they have the power to suck out any poison of any reptile, if use is made of them immediately, before the victim dies; and they are not harmed themselves when bitten by any such creature.[7]

And from Suetonius:

Cleopatra he greatly desired to lead as a captive in his triumphal procession and even had Psylli brought to her who were to suck out the venomous liquid—it was believed that her death was caused by the bite of an asp. He honoured them both with a joint burial, giving orders that the tomb which they themselves had started to build be completed.[8]

Through the writings of Plutarch, Cassius Dio, and Suetonius, the ancient historians who narrated the tales of ancient Egypt and Rome, I reconstruct the final episode of Cleopatra's life and visualize the scene inside the tomb where the figures of Cleopatra and her handmaidens lay still and unmoving on the cool marble floor. Yet, unlike Shakespeare, who used his stories to create an entertaining show, I choose to examine their accounts as a forensic investigator, using logic and science to determine what is true and what is not, piecing together the past until I have as truthful a picture of the events as possible.

From the corner of Cheops's burial chamber, I envision the scene.

The tomb is now empty save the bodies of the three women. The guards, the physician, and the snake charmers, purportedly sent to save the queen, have all left the mausoleum to report back to Octavian. From then until the moment the cleanup crew arrives to take care of the deceased, the crime scene will not change. It is this particular event I must examine before it is permanently erased, the evidence eliminated, and the tomb sealed for all time.

Cleopatra and Antony will disappear into the sands along with the building that encases them, leaving only fragments of evidence strewn about the region. The stories of their lives and deaths will undergo many modifications, and even this scene in the tomb is a questionable rendition. But by doing my best with it, examining the known evidence, both physical and behavioral, I can put together what really happened to Cleopatra and all those who had traveled the treacherous road through history with her.

At the very beginning of any death investigation, I know very little, usually only that a person, or more than one person, has met with some unfortunate turn of events that has led to their demise. I do not know if they met their fates through accident, suicide, homicide, natural causes, or, if there are multiple corpses, by any combination of these manners of death.

The same is true for Cleopatra and her handmaidens. All I know is that they are dead and here they lie in the mausoleum, unmoving in their final death positions as if someone had yelled out "Freeze!" and they had obeyed. That they are dead is my first verifiable fact, and as I begin collecting and analyzing the evidence, the picture begins to fill out.

First, I find there is the claim by Octavian that Cleopatra and her servants have committed suicide. The queen's physician, who visited the scene of the crime and pronounced the ladies dead, did not state the deaths were natural, so we can determine that their deaths were at least suspicious. The investigation is worth pursuing because in any death where there is a possibility that the deceased did not die from disease or old age, one should conduct an examination to determine the actual cause and manner of the fatality. If there has been foul play, the victim deserves a full exploration of the circumstances to bring the truth to light and to have the perpetrator or perpetrators who took his or her life brought to justice.

If too much time has passed for the guilty to stand trial for their crimes, it is never too late for the pages of history to be corrected to reflect a more accurate accounting of the events.

During the last trip I made to Egypt, I met up with Professor David Warrell, a poison expert with the University of Oxford. After a hair-raising taxi ride through the streets of Cairo, Dr. Warrell and I arrived at a secluded cobra facility and examined the various snakes found in the region. Only one snake turned out to be a candidate for the job of Cleopatra's killer, and that was the Egyptian Cobra, the Naja Haje. This was the only one with sufficient venom to do the job.

Standing within a couple of feet of that large hooded asp flicking its tongue at me, watching it rise in the air each time the old, grizzled snake handler ticked it off with the poke of a stick, I realized what the women in the tomb would have been dealing with (even if it had been a smaller asp, as some people think might have been smuggled in with the figs, the fact that it is so deadly makes even a tiny snake just as terrifying). I had moved quite near to the snake and, suddenly, it occurred to me that none of the production team was within twenty feet of the beast; just me, Dr. Warrell, and a man who was so up in years that he didn't likely have that much time left in the world anyway. Clearly, fear of deadly snakes is a natural deterrent that keeps people at a safe distance. To be willing to reach out and touch one would require great courage and an acceptance of death that few humans have; Cleopatra, perhaps, but her handmaidens, doubtful.

Dr. Warrell filled me in on the scientific facts of the cobra and its venomous ability to kill, and I inserted this knowledge into the tomb crime-scene scenario.

The beautiful and beloved queen of Egypt and her handmaidens had reached the end of their lives. It has been believed for over two thousand years that a snake of this sort—a cobra or an asp—was responsible for the deaths of all three ladies. The physician in attendance said there were two marks on Cleopatra's arm that resembled a snake bite, yet no tests were conducted to prove that venom was actually within any of these purported puncture marks.

Furthermore, there was never mention of similar marks on the bodies of the other two women. Nor is it mentioned that anyone actually examined the bodies of the handmaidens; perhaps they were of so little consequence that any information about their deaths did not rate worth mentioning.

But if indeed a snake was the weapon used to bring about the deaths of Cleopatra and her handmaidens, why was the reptile never reported to have been seen or found within the tomb? Why weren't Octavian's men afraid of being struck down by the deadly cobra? If they had passed the snake from victim to victim, wouldn't the last woman to die have dropped the snake to the floor? Or if all three had stuck their hands into the container to access the deadly snake, wouldn't it have been left in the basket of figs? Once it was "realized" that a poisonous snake caused the death of the three females, wouldn't it be natural for any human being to be unnerved at the thought of the creature slithering within the walls of the tomb, a building that was practically hermetically sealed?

Though still in the process of being built, the work in progress was supposedly on an upper floor or the roof, not the ground level. The brand-new floors and walls would yield neither a crack nor a gap where the perpendicular surfaces meet (and even in those most ancient of tombs I visited, I never saw a sliver of space where the floors met the walls).

The asp had nowhere to go except to circle around futilely. Surely the men would be unwilling to share space with the deadly snake. One would expect them to shout out warnings, walk cautiously about, fearing the cobra would suddenly strike from behind or emerge from under an object concealing its location. They would search the tomb thoroughly, prepared to crush the poisonous viper as soon as it was discovered.

Yet nothing is mentioned of this in the writings; the men entered the tomb and tended to business with not the slightest concern that they, too, could become victims of the deadly asp.

And what did Plutarch say? Only that someone saw an impression in the sand some distance from the tomb that resembled the swishing of a snake making its way to the sea. If none of the visitors to the crime scene felt the need to locate the cobra when its presence could cost them their lives, it seems rather contradictory to search for it at a later time and out somewhere on the beach!

I decided to play devil's advocate in my mind to further determine whether the cobra could have caused the deaths of these three women, even if there were no witnesses or evidence to prove it.

First, there is the question of how Cleopatra could have gotten possession of the deadly snake. She was already in captivity and under guard. Nothing would have been allowed into the tomb that Octavian did not give his approval for, and surely before the women were left unattended within the structure, a thorough sweep would have been made of the area to ensure no items were available to the queen to use in an unacceptable manner.

Once the area was secure and Cleopatra and her maidens each endured a full body search, the ladies would have been locked inside, and guards would be stationed to secure the area (one should think there would be competent guards placed outside the door and possibly a guard or two inside the door as well). Plutarch wrote that the snake was hidden among figs in a basket and that the guards barely glanced into it before they permitted it to be brought into the tomb. Either this is a fanciful story or the guards were later put to death by Octavian for their carelessness and stupidity. Any guard who wished to see the next sunrise would have thoroughly examined the basket and its contents. A snake is not something likely to be missed during such a search.

But, I allowed, suppose the guards were fools or drunks or stooges paid off by Cleopatra, and the basket, snake included, ended up inside with the prisoners. Cleopatra, the determined queen, would have been the one to remove the snake from its temporary lair and apply it to her body. In this first scenario, something goes wrong. The two handmaidens stare at Cleopatra. The snake has bitten the queen and she does not seem affected by the bite of the asp. Cleopatra, who has studied snakes and the effects of their venom in depth, realizes her attempt at suicide has failed due to what is called a "dry bite." When a snake bites its prey, a dry bite occurs a fair portion of the time since the venom does not always make it all the way to its fangs. Maybe she tries again, and this time the snake bites and she collapses. Then the women must each make an attempt or two or three. Passing around a cobra in a group suicide attempt is a version of reptile Russian roulette, the venom in the fangs of the snake like not knowing if there is a bullet in the right place in the cylinder of a revolver. It is likely one of the women simply would not have died.

I considered yet another possible scenario. Cleopatra applies the mouth of the creature to her body, the snake injects its venom, and she falls to the floor, the snake dropping alongside her. Which one of the remaining two women will have the guts and determination to chase after and pick up the vicious snake? Having just seen Cleopatra begin the dying process in front of them, it would take an unusual woman to follow suit and grab the snake to continue with the planned suicide. Cleopatra is already dying and she can no longer pressure her servants to commit suicide with her. Even if the next woman repeats Cleopatra's death dance, the third woman would also have to be equally as determined and brave to catch the cobra and allow its fangs to sink into her as well. It is highly unlikely for all three women to carry out this particular suicide method when there would be ample time from victim to victim to change one's mind. Finally, death from the venom of an asp or a cobra is not instantaneous; death is usually not achieved for thirty minutes to an hour, and sometimes longer. For Cleopatra to be dead and the other two women about to expire within moments of the guards' arrival, the letter Cleopatra sent off to Octavian announcing her intentions would need to have been sent a couple of hours prior to the suicide attempt, not only minutes before. For that matter, since Octavian was so close by at the palace and a suicide note would be delivered quite quickly to him, a queen with the intelligence of Cleopatra would never have given her captor any hint of her suicidal intentions; she would have simply committed the act and left the letter to be found alongside her body. Plutarch appears to have dramatized the events of that night with much artistic license, and the elements of his story about suicide by snake appear to be quite improbable and, more likely, impossible.

The story of the asp seems to have been created after the death of Cleopatra. Plutarch was the first writer to allude to its existence, but he also comments that perhaps the deaths of the women could have also been achieved by poison. Yet there is no container of any sort near the bodies. If a bottle of poison was passed from one woman to the next, by the time the third victim was ingesting the poison, Octavian's men would already be hurrying to the tomb. The last dying woman would hardly have had an opportunity to cleverly conceal the container in some hidden niche to remain undiscovered by future searches. No, such a bottle would simply be dropped to the floor, and upon entering the tomb, the men would quickly realize the women had used poison to end their lives.

Of course, one must stop to ask the question, did one of Octavian's men, or Cleopatra's physician, or Octavian himself, remove the cobra or the bottle from the scene, eliminating the evidence of the cause of death? What would be the point? It might make sense if one wished to cover up the manner of death, to hide a suicide, but it is illogical to take away the evidence and then attribute the cause of death to be the result of evidence that has been removed! This would be sense-less, and, therefore, if one believes Octavian's claim that Cleopatra committed suicide, it is clear that when Octavian's men came into the tomb, the women should have been simply lying on the floor with either a snake or a bottle of poison present.

So a crime scene without a tool of death present is immediately troublesome. If neither the asp nor the poison existed, then neither of these caused the deaths of the three women. There was also no mention of a knife or a ligature for hanging, so there appears to be no other possible implements for the women to have used in the commission of suicide. And, as mentioned previously, it is also physically impossible for Cleopatra to have sent a suicide note to Octavian and achieved three successful suicides within the next ten to twenty minutes, the amount of time it would have taken him to read the note and dispatch his men over to the tomb.

The stories told of Cleopatra committing suicide must then be untrue. If they are untrue, the witnesses' statements of what occurred within that tomb on Cleopatra's fateful last night on earth cannot be trusted. It would seem then that the only option left for the manner of death would be homicide and a conspiracy to cover up what really happened to the unfortunate Cleopatra and her equally unlucky handmaidens.

There is something clearly wrong with the explanation of the deaths of these three women that must be investigated further. Outside of the forces of nature, what happens to humans is not without some purpose, a purpose enacted by the individual himself or by some other individual in his realm. If the evidence within the tomb conflicts with the story of Cleopatra's demise that we have believed for centuries and her death cannot be ruled a suicide, a thorough investigation is the only way to uncover the truth.

The investigation must start at the end and then go back to the beginning to discover the truth about Cleopatra's death. Once all the other evidence has been gathered leading up to that pivotal moment in time, the investigation of the last crime scene will be analyzed once again in light of the new evidence that will lead us to a more complete understanding of the suspicious death of Cleopatra.

Inspired by my conclusions as to the implausibility of Plutarch's rendition of the death of the queen, I crawled back out of the ancient tomb to start on my exploration back into the early life of Cleopatra and her future killer, where the seeds of murderous thought were already being sown.

CHAPTER 3

THE STAGE:
ANCIENT ALEXANDRIA

I was thankful I set out early to catch my train to Alexandria, the next stop on my quest to learn more about Queen Cleopatra and the world she occupied. Arriving at Ramses Station, I was immediately lost in a rabbit warren of construction, tunnels, and platforms.

"Alexandria?" I asked at the ticket counter. "Platform 3." At Platform 3, I was told, "Alexandria, no. Platform 7." At Platform 7, I was told, "No, Platform 6." At Platform 6, I was told, "Platform 3!" After scurrying back and forth from wrong platform to wrong platform, I somehow ended up on the right one, just before the train was set to depart the station.

I settled gratefully into my seat and watched the city give way to the green delta, a pleasant change from the earth and cement tones of Cairo. I was heading west to Alexandria, the city that for centuries was the jewel of the Mediterranean established by Alexander the Great after his conquering of the country; before that moment, there was nothing to speak of at that location. The sleepy fishing village, Rhakotis, was not a place that caught the attention of the early pharaohs, those before the pharaohs became Macedonian. Barley fields made up acreage of flat land that bordered the sea, not a large congregation of people or temples. But then Alexander saw just how perfect a location the site would be to build a fabulous city—a crescent-shaped shore that would make a fine, protected harbor, gentle sea breezes to cool the land in the summertime heat, fertile fields, limestone for building, the Nile just thirty miles to the east and a fresh coastal lagoon, Lake Mareotis, to the south. Until Alexandria was built, the large and important Egyptian cities were the capital, Memphis, at the apex of the Nile River (just south of present-day Cairo), and Thebes (as Luxor down in Upper Egypt was called back then).

The plan set down by Alexander was quite grand. The streets were laid out in a grid pattern in the Hellenistic tradition with two main and very wide thoroughfares that intersected, one from north to south, the other from east to west.

But, to get a true feeling of the grandeur of the city at the time of Cleopatra, we can do no better than to read the description given by Strabo, the great geographer who traveled to many places in his day, enough to not be overly impressed with a city if it was not worth his admiration. He was clearly taken with Alexandria.

> The advantages of the city are of various kinds. The site is washed by two seas; on the north, by what is called the Egyptian Sea, and on the south, by the sea of the lake Mareia, which is also called Mareotis. This lake is filled by many canals from the Nile, both by those above and those at the sides, through which a greater quantity of merchandise is imported than by those communicating with the sea. Hence the harbour on the lake is richer than the maritime harbour. The exports by sea from Alexandria exceed the imports. This any person may ascertain, either at Alexandria or Dicaearchia, by watching the arrival and departure of the merchant vessels, and observing how much heavier or lighter their cargoes are when they depart or when they return.
>
> In addition to the wealth derived from merchandise landed at the harbours on each side, on the sea and on the lake, its fine air is worthy of remark: this results from the city being on two sides surrounded by water, and from the favourable effects of the rise of the Nile. For other cities, situated near lakes, have, during the

heats of summer, a heavy and suffocating atmosphere, and lakes at their margins become swampy by the evaporation occasioned by the sun's heat. When a large quantity of moisture is exhaled from swamps, a noxious vapour rises, and is the cause of pestilential disorders. But at Alexandria, at the beginning of summer, the Nile, being full, fills the lake also, and leaves no marshy matter which is, likely to occasion malignant exhalations. At the same period, the Etesian winds blow from the north, over a large expanse of sea, and the Alexandrines in consequence pass their summer very pleasantly.

The shape of the site of the city is that of a chlarnys or military cloak. The sides, which determine the length, are surrounded by water, and are about thirty stadia in extent; but the isthmuses, which determine the breadth of the sides, are each of seven or eight stadia, bounded on one side by the sea, and on the other by the lake. The whole city is intersected by roads for the passage of horsemen and chariots. Two of these are very broad, exceeding a plethrum in breadth, and cut one another at right angles. It contains also very beautiful public grounds and royal palaces, which occupy a fourth or even a third part of its whole extent. For as each of the kings was desirous of adding some embellishment to the places dedicated to the public use, so, besides the buildings already existing, each of them erected a building at his own expense.

In the great harbour at the entrance, on the right hand, are the island and the Pharos tower; on the left are the reef of rocks and the promontory Lochias, with a palace upon it: at the entrance, on the left hand, are the inner palaces, which are continuous with those on the Lochias, and contain numerous painted apartments and groves. Below lies the artificial and close harbour, appropriated to the use of the kings; and Antirrhodus a small island, facing the artificial harbour, with a palace on it, and a small port. It was called Antirrhodus, a rival as it were of Rhodes.

Above this is the theatre, then the Poseidium, a kind of elbow projecting from the Emporium, as it is called, with a temple of Neptune upon it. To this Antony added a mound, projecting still further into the middle of the harbour, and built at the extremity a royal mansion, which he called Timoneion. This was his last act, when, deserted by his partisans, he retired to Alexandria after his defeat at Actium, and intended, being forsaken by so many friends, to lead the [solitary] life of Timon for the rest of his days.

Next are the Caesarium, the Emporium, and the Apostaseis, or magazines: these are followed by docks, extending to the Heptastadion. This is the description of the great harbour.

Next after the Heptastadion is the harbour of Eunostus, and above this the artificial harbour, called Cibotus (or the Ark), which also has docks. At the bottom of this harbour is a navigable canal, extending to the lake Mareotis. Beyond the canal there still remains a small part of the city. Then follows the suburb Necropolis, in which are numerous gardens, burial-places, and buildings for carrying on the process of embalming the dead.

On this side the canal is the Sarapium and other ancient sacred places, which are now abandoned on account of the erection of the temples at Nicopolis; for [there are situated] an amphitheatre and a stadium, and there are celebrated quinquennial games; but the ancient rites and customs are neglected.

In short, the city of Alexandria abounds with public and sacred buildings. The most beautiful of the former is the Gymnasium, with porticos exceeding a stadium in extent. In the middle of it are the court of justice and groves. Here also is a Paneium, an artificial mound of the shape of a fir-cone, resembling a pile of rock, to the top of which there is an ascent by a spiral path. From the summit may be seen the whole city lying all around and beneath it.[1]

What a splendid city Alexandria must have been when Julius Caesar and Antony came to meet with Cleopatra. This cosmopolitan center at the time was the largest and most beautiful city on earth, far surpassing Rome, which was actually said to be quite a bedraggled city in those days. It is no wonder they fell in love with Alexandria as well as with Cleopatra and the riches she could share with them. A massive walled city overlooking the sea, filled with a bounty of magnificent buildings gleaming in the Mediterranean sunlight, the massive lighthouse of Pharos Island jutting out on the promontory of the harbor, one of the Seven Wonders of the Ancient World, dramatically welcoming ships and their merchants into the cultured metropolis, and, of course, Queen Cleopatra's beloved Caesareum, the grand temple she was building at the time of her death. And, of course, they would spend time at Cleopatra's palace and temples, and these must have been spectacular buildings as well. Although we have little on record as to how these Alexandrian structures looked and were decorated, we can get a bit of an idea from Philo of Alexandria, who spoke of the Caesarium he saw some eighty years after the death of Cleopatra:

> [A] temple to Caesar, patron of sailors, situated on an eminence facing the harbours famed for their excellent moorings, huge and conspicuous, forming a precinct of vast breadth, embellished with porticoes, libraries, men's banqueting halls, groves, propylaea, spacious courts, open-air rooms, in short, everything which lavish expenditure could produce to beautify it.[2]

When I alighted from the train in Alexandria and made my way into the streets, none of this splendor remained. The city is rather drab, the buildings nondescript, and as I walked on toward the harbor it was difficult not to feel rather sad for the residents of the city and for the loss of such former glory. The demise of Alexandria took place in spurts, the buildings and statues and the greenery erased by fire, theft, purposeful removal of the memories by previous rulers, and lack of upkeep likely due to financial distress. During the 1950s, the expropriation of the property of the European businessmen and investors by Gamal Abdel Nasser when he nationalized the country resulted in a mass exodus of foreigners and the closing of the upscale eateries and hotels that lined the Corniche. In later years, Egyptian-born residents struggled to do business under Mubarak's regime and found it very difficult. As one restaurant owner explained to me, "When a tourist points to the picture of Hosni Mubarak on my wall and asks who that is, I tell him that is our President. When he asks who is standing next to him, I tell him that is his son . . . my business partner." The highway-robbery tax imposed by Mubarak went straight into the coffers of his son, which left business owners with a very difficult time running their enterprises, which in turn results in the remaining worn and uninviting restaurants on the harbor. As I walked about the city, I realized that unlike Rome and Athens or even other historic sites in Egypt, pretty much nothing is left of the grand buildings, just a wall here, Pompey's Pillar up on the hill that Strabo speaks of, a couple of Ptolemaic sphinxes, the catacombs and cisterns under the ground, and the Roman odium, a small theatre built in the fourth century CE. The remains of the rest of the Alexandrian Ptolemaic past lie in bits and pieces in museums or down at the bottom of the eastern harbor, where the ancient royal quarters once were situated on the promontory named Silsilah.

During my documentary work with Atlantic Productions, I was to scuba dive down to the bottom of the harbor, where there can be seen a variety of pieces of columns, a giant obelisk, a number of sphinxes and statues, ruins from the palace of Cleopatra discovered by underwater archeologist Franck Goddio.[3] The videographer and I went to make a practice dive the day before we were to film, to make sure I was comfortable with my scuba maneuvers (which I was not since I had failed the mask test). We sank into the water, and after a few moments, I came up and waved at him and asked if he was filming anything.

"Film? I can't see my hand in front of my face in this polluted water."

Apparently, we had hit a bad day, so we gave up and went off for dinner. I spent the rest of the night on the floor of my hotel bathroom, the only time in my travels I ever got horribly ill from either food or water or whatever was in the Mediterranean Sea that day. The next morning, the videographer was late arriving to join the team, and he came practically crawling down the stairs. Whatever I caught, he obviously did as well.

When it came to shooting the scuba segment, there was no way it was safe for me to go underwater in my nauseated state. So I donned the wetsuit, climbed down the ladder, threw water over myself, and came up and excitedly spoke of the wonders I had seen. I felt a bit guilty over the charade, but movie crews take a bit of license with the setup of certain aspects of their programs. The British producer ended up being my body double, and she got the pleasure of viewing the underwater ruins.

Later, when my friends watched the documentary and they commented on my scuba-diving venture in Alexandria, I wryly commented that the backside of the woman they saw in the wetsuit hardly resembled my own.

As I sat in a café on the Corniche drinking my tea, with the vision of Cleopatra's Alexandria in my head, if nowhere in my sight, I could still feel just from my view of the harbor and the buildings lining the semicircular curve of the shore and the colorful fishing boats dotting the waters, that the city she was born into was a fitting place for the last pharaoh of Egypt. It was clear that from the time Alexander the Great envisioned the city he was laying out in 332 BCE to Cleopatra VII's birth in 69 BCE, a dozen and a half Ptolemies before her built the city up to near its zenith before she entered onto the scene. She was born into wealth and power and a world of greatness, and she made herself a star within it.

But exactly who was this Cleopatra, resident of the great city of Alexandria, who has fascinated so many through the years? Was she the emotionally fragile, beautiful siren who selfishly and impulsively lured men to their deaths as so many stories about her portray? Or was she an attractive, brilliant, and clever leader who methodically made political choices to continue her rule and save her kingdom? Was she a pure Egyptian or a pure Macedonian or a mix of the two physically and culturally? Did she resemble the image of the relief of Cleopatra on the backside of the Temple of Hathor in the Dendera temple complex (on the West Bank of the Nile, an hour's drive northeast from Luxor in Upper Egypt), which makes her look like a beautiful, statuesque Egyptian Isis—or did she look more like the hooked-nosed, quite-unattractive profile we see of her on the coins she herself released? Who was she really? What was she capable of? And what line of action would she be most likely to pursue? Understanding the real Cleopatra makes a difference in understanding what behavior she would exhibit over her adult years as queen of Egypt and in the decisions she would make as the months, weeks, and days ticked away toward the end of the Ptolemaic Dynasty.

I placed my Egyptian coins on the table and walked toward the Bibleotheca Alexandrina, a stunning (to my relief) piece of architecture that shines with modernity, a slanted discus of a glass roof on top of eleven floors, the outside wall with the letters of 120 languages, restoring in a sense the ancient library of Alexandria, which some ancient and present historians claim was burned to the ground when Julius Caesar set fire to the fleet in the harbor during the Alexandrian War; however, there is not credible evidence to back such a charge since the distance of the library from the docks and its solid construction would have allowed only its collection of books to burn if half of Alexandria had burned with it, and that never happened. The destruction of the library no doubt occurred over many years, but exactly what happened to it, we will never know.[4]

Now, however, a great library has been resurrected in Alexandria. Some $3.5 million and seventeen years went into building the modern library, which houses an incredible eight million books from many nations, including English-language books on the histories of Egypt and Rome, in which I could review the facts of history that set up Cleopatra's birth, her reign, and her death. I paid my entrance fee and set out in search of Cleopatra's past.

CHAPTER 4

THE MAKING OF THE QUEEN:
PART ONE——THE ANCESTORS

A s I perused the shelves of the library, it was abundantly clear that the history of Cleopatra VII, a queen whose name is known the world over, hardly garners more than a fraction of space among the tomes written of the Egyptian past. Many hundreds of years preceded the queen's few decades in time, and the story of man in Egypt before her arrival is extensive. Who Cleopatra is didn't start with her birth or what she experienced in her childhood. Understanding anyone begins with the person's family history and the culture he or she is part of. Cleopatra was the last ruler in the long line of pharaohs descended from the Macedonian region of Greece and the recipient of generations of Ptolemaic experience and wisdom. Her "modern world" began with Alexander the Great's conquering of Egypt and the placement of her direct relative and Alexander's right-hand man, Ptolemy I, on the throne of Egypt as the first of the Ptolemaic pharaohs. Alexander, the highly aggressive, successful, and gregarious general, gave his name to the great future city of Alexandria, waved his sword above the still-untouched acreage, and envisioned a grand capital, one brought to life by Ptolemy. Sadly, Alexander never again set foot in the future spectacular city that bore his name; only his stolen body was carried back by Ptolemy I to rest temporarily in a marble tomb in Egypt before vanishing forever into oblivion. Alexander, who saw himself as the physical embodiment of the great warrior Achilles, the hero of his beloved *Iliad*, Homer's grand epic poem of the Trojan War, set for himself high standards of bravery, honor, and achievement. These were grandiose aims for a mere mortal, but Alexander can certainly be admired for the level of attainment he achieved as a "good king and a mighty warrior."[1]

A basic understanding of the history of Macedonia is useful since it is out of this milieu that the Ptolemaic Dynasty emerged, along with its history, both cultural and military, that instructed the line of pharaohs down to the very last one. The history of earlier Egypt certainly affected the choices the Ptolemies made to control their vast domain as conquerors. While invaders may be adept at making use of certain aspects of the conquered culture and religion to their advantage (to retain control and to build their wealth), it is quite evident in history that the winner makes the rules and the losers go along with the program if they want to survive.

At the time of the birth of Alexander's father, Philip II, in 382 BCE, the Macedonians were considered backward and uncultured by the elite Greeks of Athens, Sparta, and Thebes. This kingdom to the south of Greece spoke a dialect of Greek considered low and unintelligible by their northern neighbors. They gave little credit to the region or recognized its strength until Philip took the Macedonian throne in 359 BCE. He was a king who had it all. He was brilliant, charming, and aggressive; and he could be both diplomatic and brutal. And he was the ultimate warrior. When such a man rises to the top, it is easy to understand why he was able to conquer his neighbors and seize complete control over vast amounts of land and build himself an empire.

Philip II, however, had one great fault, which was to be his undoing. After he conquered nearly all the Greek kingdoms by 336 BCE and was heading off to take on the Persians, the greatest empire of the time, he managed to get himself assassinated by his own Macedonian enemies (which may have included his wife, Olympias, and their son, Alexander), having neglected to keep himself on their good side. Narcissism has been many a great man's undoing. When he reaches a point where he believes himself to be the epitome of perfection, he often fails to see growing resentment among those he treats as lesser beings. We will later see that this self-centeredness was the undoing of Julius Caesar and Mark Antony as well.

Just as Philip entered the theatre for a grand October celebration of Macedonian might and his own great achievements, one of his seven bodyguards suddenly stabbed the king in the chest. The other bodyguards killed the assassin quickly as he attempted to flee, so it is difficult to judge whether this was one disgruntled underling or if he was the sacrificial lamb for a bigger plot. However, since Alexander simply moved into his father's position, there doesn't seem to be any political incentive to assassinate Philip unless Alexander was becoming impatient to be in charge. There were rumors that his mother, Olympias, instigated the murder, but no one was going to push the issue since Alexander was already on the throne and no good would come of angering the new king. Since Alexander was present at the time of the assassination as well and was a witness the murder, the other possibility was that he was supposed to have been taken down with his father. That would have dramatically changed history. However, it seems a bit odd (to me at least) that the plot would be only half-enacted, unless the assassins were quite pitiful in the execution of the plan. But since father and son were supposed to be seated together and were not, maybe the plan went awry.

One thing is for sure: the young Alexander learned from this incident (even if he was involved in his father's death). Being king was a dangerous job, and he would have to be vigilant over the possibility that he could be next. His father wasn't the only Macedonian leader to be eliminated by domestic rivals, hence the seven bodyguards Philip employed to protect him. But since, as quite often happens, it is one's own men who do one in, Alexander learned that no one was to be entirely trusted—even one's own child. Many a king and queen have been dispatched by their progeny in order for them to assume the throne. Such royal parents, whose own lusting for power brought them to the throne and kept them in power for any time at all, surely are role models for their sons and daughters, and their ruthlessness and narcissism is passed on to the next generation. Some great monarchs even refused to have children to avoid creating equally ambitious versions of themselves. Whether or not Alexander had any part in the demise of his father, the Macedonians were fortunate that this young man was as brilliant and militarily adept as his father when he became king at the age of twenty. In spite of his youth, he was far advanced for his years in wisdom and diplomacy, and he had been trained since childhood for the battlefield. He was just sixteen when he led troops into battle, and within a couple of years, he was the best general in Macedonia. He would develop a devastating Macedonian war strategy: a phalanx equipped with huge wooden spikes that the infantry used to mow down their opponents, which led to many a success on the battlefield.

Philip II also made sure that the son who someday might assume power (Alexander's brothers all died, except for one who was mentally challenged) received the finest education from the best tutors, including the great Aristotle. Alexander's superior intelligence and years of exceptional tutelage led to a grandiosity similar to his father's: he saw himself ruling in the image of Heracles and Achilles, great warriors whom he regarded as his ancestors; in his own mind, they were real—more than mythological half-human, half-Grecian gods. And he made sure many others viewed him the same way, by erecting statutes of himself and visually extolling himself as a handsome warrior descended from the gods. His mother, Olympias, told him from early childhood that she was impregnated by the gods via a thunderbolt on her wedding night (well, it was a dream that her husband hardly found pleasing), and she told Alexander that he was of the lineage of Achilles, which certainly would have made the young Alexander feel quite special. It is, therefore, not too hard to see why it was perfectly comfortable for the Ptolemies to carry on the concept of the earlier pharaohs of ancient Egypt who claimed themselves to be not merely human rulers, but divine ones to be worshipped along with the other gods in the pantheon.

The upside of such narcissistic idealism of one's own character and status is that one has to take on the role of a beneficent god and lift up humankind by devoting oneself to the greater glory of the people, both as a warrior and as a patron of high culture. To this end, Alexander brought along with him in his travels those of the intellectual elite—historians and poets—and encouraged the development and dispersion of knowledge.

The other example Alexander set for future Egyptian Macedonian rulers was that to maintain his image as a supernatural godlike being, he bowed to local traditions and religious practices and deities in the same manner that his father had done during his rule. This practice led to a tolerance in the Hellenistic world to come that the conquerors would allow the conquered to retain some sense of their past and culture, easing the transition to the new rulers and lessening the backlash from the new subjects. Along with a level of peace and unity within conquered territories, Alexander also used the spoils of war to improve the lands he took over, providing them with roads, waterways, and new cities, and expanding trade and bolstering economies. When the Ptolemies took over the governance of Egypt, they followed this concept, which allowed for the citizens to be more accepting of their Macedonian overlords than the ones who had come before or who would come after the Ptolemaic Dynasty.

Alexander fulfilled his father's dream of conquering Persia. He united the ruling classes of Macedonia and Persia, effectively controlling an enormous empire. The very popular Macedonian general was certainly on his way to his next goal of conquering India and Arabia since he had already conquered western Asia Minor, Syria, Palestine, Egypt, and Babylonia, and since cutting a swath through Persia secured a huge fortune (especially from the royal coffers of Babylonia) along the way. He marched his way into India, whereupon his troops finally told him they had had enough and it was time to go home. After a grueling trek back to his new capital, Babylon, he enjoyed only two more years of life. His death at the age of thirty-three is reported to have been due to either malaria, typhoid, West

Nile fever, or cirrhosis of the liver from drinking far too much. There are those, like his mother, who believe he was poisoned, but there is no strong proof of that, and it would have to have been a very slow-acting poison since he lay sick and dying for a period of ten days.

The military might, political prowess, and diplomacy of Alexander and his father, Philip II, were not the only influences coming down to Cleopatra from the Macedonian general. Both Alexander and his father amassed tremendous wealth during the expansion of their territory and were lavish in the spending of it. Certainly, we know from Cleopatra's reign that she, too, had a love of extravagance and made use of the Ptolemaic treasury and taxes to live on a grand scale, so she could easily bedazzle both Julius Caesar and Mark Antony with her lifestyle.

One might point out, of course, that Cleopatra was not from the direct line of Philip and Alexander. She was a Ptolemy descending from Ptolemy I, the first governor of Egypt. This is true, but the Ptolemies still came out of the Macedonian culture. Also, Ptolemy I was Alexander the Great's top general who was always at his side. His lifetime friend, having known him since his birth and being eleven years older than the young ruler, Ptolemy became a big brother and a trusted member of Alexander's inner circle. But, even more than this, it is believed that Philip II was also Ptolemy's father, so Ptolemy and Alexander might actually have been half brothers, even though Ptolemy was considered a member of a lesser branch of Macedonian royalty. Ptolemy also appeared to be highly intelligent, perhaps partly due to the genes of his rumored father (if he were Philip II), but also due to immersion in the environment of Philip and Alexander in which he could take great advantage of what such fortune had to offer.

When Alexander died, the cohesiveness of the various territories of his Greek-Hellenistic empire faltered without his charismatic, autocratic control. Married only four years prior to his death, his wife was carrying his son, but because of his infancy, he would be of no use as a ruler at that point in time. The massive empire simply fell apart. Rome would rise next, with the rule of the First Triumvirate of Julius Caesar, Marcus Licinius Crassus, and Gnaeus Pompey. After the murder of Julius Caesar, the Second Triumvirate of Mark Antony, Octavian, and Marcus Lepidus assumed imperial power. With the deaths of Antony and Lepidus, Octavian would emerge as the great Augustus Caesar, who would reign over the Roman Empire.

Throughout most of these power struggles, Egypt survived as a great nation managed by the Ptolemaic Dynasty. Rule was passed down through the Ptolemies. However, over time, Egypt become weaker and weaker, until it passed to Cleopatra VII, who would find herself fighting to hang onto power with Rome nipping at her country's heels. Since her father rather sold the nation down the river with his excessive bribery of the Roman power brokers, her county would remain dependent on Rome for its survival, as Cleopatra would herself. But, at the time that Alexander died, Egypt was still very powerful, and Ptolemy I saw his opportunity to be a great and autonomous leader. When the fight to divide the Alexandrian-won empire came to an end, Ptolemy had managed to secure for himself the wealthiest and most easily defended land of the sections parceled out.

When Alexander had conquered Egypt (which consisted only of a two-day marginal resistance at the border in Pelusium), he was pretty much welcomed by the Egyptians as the lesser of two evils considering their hatred of being under the Persian thumb, whose domination had gone on for the better part of two centuries. Alexander was feted as pharaoh at Memphis, where he did sacrifice to the gods and was considered a hero to the people for freeing them from their oppressors. During his short four months in Egypt, Alexander set up his plan for moving the capital to his new choice of location at Alexandria. He also took a trip into the desert to Siwa, where he met with priests and went into the temple to worship Amun (the Egyptian form of Zeus, whom he was to be considered the son of), thereby further fulfilling his religious role as a leader of the Egyptian people. It is said that he had an ulterior motive in wanting to consult with the oracle on personal issues and to foretell of his future. For Alexander, who already felt a strong sense of being descended from the gods, it wasn't that big a leap to make. Then he left Egypt, putting a couple of governors in charge, and continued on with his efforts at world domination.

The governor of Egyptian ancestry soon resigned, leaving just the Persian Doloaspis to manage the civil part of the country along with a Greek named Kleomenes, who handled Egyptian finances. But then Doloaspis was pushed aside by Kleomenes, and so the latter ended up as the satrap, the lone governor, which meant he ran the country for the next eight years and pretty much succeeded in moving the country back toward a dictatorship in spite of Alexander's efforts to leave a more democratic government in place.

After Ptolemy I was given the go-ahead to move in and take over as satrap in Egypt, he first made a deal with Kleomenes, then swiftly dispatched him, taking total leadership of Egypt for himself in 323 BCE. Meanwhile, one of Alexander's generals ignored the king's last wish to be buried in Siwa in Egypt, where he had talked to the oracle of Amun, and was instead taking the body back to Macedonia. Ptolemy I stole Alexander's body and had it interred in Memphis (not quite what Alexander wanted). Having brought the great Alexander cum almost Egyptian pharaoh with him, and cleverly appeasing the high priesthood of Egypt, Ptolemy I's transition from satrap to pharaoh was accomplished without much objection from the Egyptians. He became the first true Macedonian-Greek pharaoh and, with a country of his own, he settled in at age forty-four and ruled until his death forty years later.

One could say the Egyptians were fortunate at that time in history to have Ptolemy I and his sons, Ptolemy II and Ptolemy III, as their pharaohs. All of these men were educated, forward thinking, and relatively tolerant of Egyptians handling a good portion of the country's day-to-day business. As J. G. Manning points out in his book *The Last Pharaohs*, "the Ptolemies governed their core territory by exercising power not over society, but rather *through* it."[2] In other words, the Ptolemies hybridized their rule, combining suitable features of both the

Egyptian style of monarchy and priesthoods; allowing for the people to retain their own religion, customs, agricultural systems, and local political structures throughout the country; and having Egyptian law and Egyptian judges rule over their daily lives. The Macedonian-Greeks took over the financial end of things, handling taxation, policing, managing large construction projects, overseeing expansion, and commanding the military, essentially controlling the resources of the country while letting the citizens continue on in their normal fashion.

Ptolemy I put his experience as a Macedonian general to use, but not in the same manner as Alexander. It was not his wish to obtain a huge empire but to secure Egypt and make it a self-sufficient and wealthy kingdom in the eastern Mediterranean. In 313 BCE, he took over Cyprus, then strategic locations in Anatolia and the Aegean and Cyrenaica. He expanded into Palestine and Lower Nubia. In this way, he created a buffer for Egypt on all sides and protected land and sea trade routes. Since Egypt was not involved in fighting wars at home, this allowed for much domestic progress to be made in agriculture and trade.

Vast changes came with the first three Ptolemaic rulers. Ptolemy I developed a coinage that he then required to be the only one used for trade in his region. Road networks throughout Egypt, pursued aggressively by Ptolemy II, allowed for rapid development of trade, especially in gold and ivory. The introduction of wheat made Egypt the breadbasket of the entire region. And, it is said by some early historians, Ptolemy II reopened the canal of the Persian emperor Darius I, which stretched thirty-five miles from present-day Bubastis (a city on the Nile that is thirty-nine miles northeast of Cairo) until it reached the then more southerly Bitter Lakes that led to the Red Sea. This added trade route no doubt greatly helped increase the wealth of Egypt. Sadly, from the fourth Ptolemy on down to Cleopatra's father, Egypt declined due to incompetence and domestic revolts until it had to depend on Roman assistance for survival. The canal that so enhanced the country's economy fell into disrepair, silted over, and could no longer be used by the time of Cleopatra's reign.

However, when Cleopatra was born, in spite of all the country's problems, she grew up in incredible wealth in the most fabulous city in the world. Alexandria was really a separate entity from the rest of Egypt, a polyglot of nationalities that were educated, cultured, and heavily Greek and Jewish. The Ptolemaic pharaoh and the Greek ruling class, the Greek soldiers, and the Greek merchants lived the good life in Alexandria while the native Egyptian peasants tilled the soil like they had done for centuries. Like a gated community, the transplanted Greek-Macedonians lived the high life and used the rest of Egypt as their source of food, wealth, and labor.

I decided to take a break from my examination of the written details of Ptolemaic history and put myself back into the physical world of Alexandria. I left the library and took a long walk over to the hill to where Pompey's Pillar (which Pompey didn't build and really has nothing to do with him) remains intact, an elevated historical site where Alexandria's ancient acropolis used to stand. Entering the site, I stood beside the pillar and looked down over the city. I mentally superimposed the Alexandria of the last century before the Common Era over what I saw in front of me; it must have been an incredible sight. I could only imagine the extraordinary luxury that surrounded Cleopatra, even for royalty. Not only were the palace and its grounds stunning, so was the rest of the city, with amenities far beyond what the world had seen anywhere until that day.

The year was 69 BCE and it was now time for Cleopatra to enter the scene.

CHAPTER 5

THE MAKING OF THE QUEEN: PART TWO— THE MACEDONIAN LINEAGE

L et me quickly address the parentage of Cleopatra VII and put an end to the theory that has been bandied about in the recent decades that Cleopatra was not a full Macedonian-Greek but a half-Greek and half-Nubian-Egyptian, that she was not the daughter of her father, Auletes, and his wife, but of her father and a black handmaiden whose company he enjoyed on some randy Alexandrian evening. Clearly the desire of some to add the brilliant queen to the history of people of color who lived in or descended from Africa is evident. I think this is perfectly understandable; with so much history focused on the achievements of Europeans and Caucasians, it would be inspiring that such an illustrious ruler could be claimed as non-white and add a dash of black pride to this time in history. But there is no particular evidence to support the claim that Cleopatra was half-black and not a Mediterranean Greek, in spite of certain arguments that this is what we should believe.

The most often used "evidence" that Cleopatra was at least partially black would be the artistic relief made of her at Dendera, a temple in Upper Egypt. Her profile shows African features, a wider nose than one would see on a Greek, and a generally non-European appearance.

Yet those reliefs were never intended to portray the true appearances of the kings and queens of Egypt but were representations of the history of the ruling pharaohs and their supernatural connection to the gods. The relief of Cleopatra on the Temple of Hathor at Dendera shows her as Isis, which the other Cleopatras, I through VI, also had their "likenesses" sculpted as. No one has questioned the heredity of the other Cleopatras as being any lineage other than Macedonian, so there is no reason to suddenly assign African genes to the last Cleopatra simply because the relief said to represent her displays some African features. Even Plutarch, who wrote of Cleopatra's features, did not attempt to portray her as a member of a black or brown race, nor did he infer that she was not a true Ptolemy and not a fully Macedonian-descended queen. He could have used her mixed race in either a positive or a negative way—to downplay her acceptability to Romans and Greeks or to paint her as an exotic, sexually promiscuous siren, a woman from one of those supposed "races with looser morals."

> For her beauty, as we are told, was in itself not altogether incomparable, nor such as to strike those who saw her.[1]

In fact, we can see from this simple statement of Plutarch's that Cleopatra was quite normal to look at; there was nothing particularly unusual to be noted about her appearance. She was not a great beauty and had no unusual skin color, nothing to make her stand out from other Macedonian women, from the other Ptolemaic queens, and certainly not to men seeking sexually exciting experiences. Cleopatra was just average in appearance to those who met her. It was *how* she enhanced that appearance—her very alluring personality, her exceptional mind and palaver—that raised her above other women of her time, that entranced the men who spent time in her company.

Plutarch goes on to explain what was special about Cleopatra:

> For her beauty, as we are told, was in itself not altogether incomparable, nor such as to strike those who saw her; but converse with her had an irresistible charm, and her presence, combined with

the persuasiveness of her discourse and the character which was somehow diffused about her behaviour towards others, had something stimulating about it. There was sweetness also in the tones of her voice; and her tongue, like an instrument of many strings, she could readily turn to whatever language she pleased.[2]

Some will point out that Plutarch stresses her beauty at another point in his writing of the *Life of Antony* with this quote:

Judging by the proofs which she had had before this of the effect of her beauty upon Caius Caesar and Gnaeus the son of Pompey, she had hopes that she would more easily bring Antony to her feet. For Caesar and Pompey had known her when she was still a girl and inexperienced in affairs, but she was going to visit Antony at the very time when women have the most brilliant beauty and are at the acme of intellectual power.[3]

Interestingly, Cassius Dio also speaks of Cleopatra's beauty:

For she was a woman of surpassing beauty, and at that time, when she was in the prime of her youth, she was most striking; she also possessed a most charming voice and a knowledge of how to make herself agreeable to every one. Being brilliant to look upon and to listen to, with the power to subjugate every one, even a love-sated man already past his prime, she thought that it would be in keeping with her rôle to meet Caesar, and she reposed in her beauty all her claims to the throne.[4]

However, it is important to recognize that young women with incredible access to the most beautiful of gowns and jewels, and endowed with an artistic skill in the use of makeup as Cleopatra was known to possess, could be made to look quite lovely with all those accoutrements. In fact, all one needs to do now to understand this is to watch a makeover show on television; a good wardrobe and a top hair stylist and makeup artist can make a not-so-beautiful woman quite stunning. Cassius Dio points out that Caesar was past his prime at age fifty-four, and a girl as young as Cleopatra—age twenty-one when she met him—was bound to look pretty ripe and pleasing to the eye. By the time she met Mark Antony, Plutarch points out, Cleopatra would certainly have been mature enough to know how to work her wiles and make herself extremely attractive to her prey. So, likely not a true beauty, but not unattractive either, and with youth, intelligence, charm, and money, there is no doubt that Cleopatra was quite an alluring woman of her time.

It is worth mentioning that of the statues of Cleopatra made after her death and found in the museums of Rome and Berlin, not one of them shows her as an "African" queen; they all show her to be Mediterranean and looking quite similar to the other men and women sculpted from the same period. She may well have had somewhat of an olive-skinned complexion, but then so would many Macedonians. This could hardly be construed as evidence that she was the child of a mixed-race couple. And if she were, wouldn't Octavian, who was her biggest detractor and enemy and who put out many an insult concerning the queen in an attempt to degrade her in the eyes of the Romans, jump on the opportunity to claim she was less than white and ridicule her as the offspring of the lowly peasant class, the "natives" of Egypt, the illegitimate child of a slave woman? In this profiler's opinion, absolutely.

Most of these statues do not show Cleopatra to be a great beauty, but range from depicting her as tolerably decent-looking to lovely-enough. It wasn't until later in history when artists whitened her skin to resemble marble, exposed her breasts, draped her in diaphanous finery, and positioned her in sensual poses that Cleopatra became the foxy lady we envisage today. In none of these early renderings is she ever shown as being of Nubian descent. These portrayals of Cleopatra as black have cropped up only in the most recent decades and, like that of the black Jesus, serve more as a philosophical and cultural icon than a historic one.

The only real clue to what Cleopatra looked like, tangible evidence as opposed to mere rumor or stories passed down over the years, would come from the coins she issued during her years as pharaoh. There is nothing in the profile of her face on the money that would suggest she was a woman of color; in fact, she has a hooked nose, which is more common to Mediterranean people than those of sub-Sahara Africa. The Ptolemy line appeared to be endowed with a long, hooking nose, but it is hard to say whether the coinage represented Cleopatra's exact facial features. After all, coins were a method of advertising the person in power, and the profile of the queen was intended to show omnipotence, not necessarily her true appearance or her beauty. It is interesting to note that none of the coinage bearing Cleopatra's name and likeness show her as an Egyptian pharaoh/goddess/Isis, as she is represented on the walls of the temple in Dendera, but always as a Greek with a Macedonian-Greek appearance and a Greek hairstyle. Clearly, these diametrically opposed portrayals of Cleopatra serve as propaganda to their respective audiences, and neither is overly concerned with a literal representation of her appearance.

Some argue that had Cleopatra not been a beauty, Julius Caesar and Mark Antony would not have been so taken with her and history might have turned out differently. I disagree. Cleopatra, the great city of Alexandria, and the Ptolemaic treasury were a package deal, and if Cleopatra weren't quite as charismatic or tolerable to look upon, both men might still have attached themselves to her due to the other benefits that came along with her person. That Cleopatra was actually attractive enough, witty, and beguiling certainly made things a bit easier for her and, perhaps, her influence on the men was improved due to these advantages. The more arrows one has in one's quiver, the more one has to work with, so it is hard to believe that Cleopatra's attractiveness, of whatever type or extent, didn't play some part in her success with the two men with whom she partnered.

There is another piece of "evidence" often brought up to support a Nubian-Egyptian background, namely that Cleopatra VII was purportedly the first pharaoh to speak the Egyptian language, a rarity that questions the purpose of her doing so. On this, Plutarch writes:

She could readily turn to whatever language she pleased, so that in her interviews with Barbarians she very seldom had need of an interpreter, but made her replies to most of them herself and unassisted, whether they were Ethiopians, Troglodytes, Hebrews, Arabians, Syrians, Medes or Parthians. Nay, it is said that she knew the speech of many other peoples also, although the kings of Egypt before her had not even made an effort to learn the native language, and some actually gave up their Macedonian dialect.[5]

I find this passage from Plutarch humorous due to its incredible exaggeration. He clearly states that all the previous Ptolemies spoke Greek, not the educated dialect but the Macedonian bastardization of the language, and none of them bothered learning the language of their subjects. Yet, along comes Cleopatra, taught by the finest of tutors in the culturally cosmopolitan Mediterranean capital of Alexandria, and she learns to speak a half dozen languages or more and is fluent in the language of the commoners. If the previous pharaohs did not feel the need to lower themselves to the level of the populace to gain their favor, why would Cleopatra? After all, the Egyptian rulers were gods and goddesses, and they would hardly be expected to speak the language of mere mortals, especially that of the common people. Some try to claim that Cleopatra was different from the other Cleopatras, more involved with the Egyptian-speaking population, and that speaking the language is proof she is half-Nubian and most likely learned the language from her mother. I can follow the logic here, but there really is no proof that Cleopatra spent more time with the regular folk or had any particular caring for them than the other pharaohs. I think circular logic is actually employed here: Cleopatra spoke an Egyptian language because of her mother and, therefore, cared about the people because she was one of them; and we have proof she was one of them because she spoke their language, which she must have learned from her mother! This is most likely wishful thinking, since the historical record shows Cleopatra to be as disinterested in the lives of the common people as her predecessors.

If it were true that Cleopatra had mixed blood and was so exotic,

whether those at the time viewed this as a positive or a negative, such a deviation from the Macedonian-Greek lineage would surely have been the talk of the town. Such unusual features would likely be exaggerated in those sculptures of her and in writings about her, and yet such gossip about Cleopatra being a dark-skinned anomaly of a Ptolemy is nonexistent. And, to reiterate the most important proof of Cleopatra's Macedonian appearance is Octavian himself, Cleopatra's archenemy, who spent much time slandering Cleopatra, claiming to the Roman people that she was a loose-living vixen, a witch who destroyed good Roman men with her clever wiles. Surely he would have worked overtime on his insults had she actually been an illegitimate child born of a Nubian servant and not of royal lineage at all. Yet, in spite of all the attacks Octavian made on Cleopatra's character, he never claimed she wasn't a Macedonian Ptolemy; he understood quite well that imperialists who conquer countries don't just "go native." Ruling classes remain ruling classes and Cleopatra was clearly from that stratus of society.

To a profiler, the importance of Cleopatra's appearance has nothing to do with supporting claims that this or that race has made specific contributions to history. This is irrelevant in profiling Cleopatra's life and death. What *is* important is how she viewed herself, whom she viewed herself as, and how others viewed her. She was comfortable with the Greek and Roman world to her north, and travelers from these places were quite content to spend time in her country as well. They were Mediterraneans, all of them, not Nubians, and Octavian's propaganda campaign against Cleopatra was really about her massive wealth, which he didn't want Antony to get his hands on, so he excoriated her lascivious and lavish lifestyle, which quite frankly he was not wrong about; but while the Ptolemies were big spenders, they were far less promiscuous than the Roman ruling class were noted to have been. Regardless of the truth of these matters, Octavian purported that he feared Cleopatra would steal the Roman general away, and with him, pull the Roman people into an indolent, immoral lifestyle. The most difficult pill Cleopatra had to swallow

was that for centuries Egypt was bigger and better than any another country in the known world but, due to the rising military strength of Rome and the foolishness of her father's rule, Cleopatra had to kowtow to more powerful but less cultured regimes. However, it is because Cleopatra considered herself a Greek Ptolemaic ruler *of* Egypt and not *for* Egypt that she felt comfortable putting herself and her children's future before the Egyptian populace's well-being, to make choices that made it possible for her to keep her riches, maintain her rule, and increase her status, whether it be combining forces with Rome or fleeing it. She certainly wasn't worried about going down with the ship (i.e., dying in a tomb on behalf of her people). I believe the manner in which Cleopatra represented herself as a purely Macedonian pharaoh is key to Cleopatra's character and the charting of her final destiny.

CHAPTER 6

THE MAKING OF THE QUEEN: PART THREE—THE FAMILY

C leopatra became queen at age eighteen. Her father and mother were dead, and her siblings wanted her dead. Ah, to be a Ptolemy in the year 51 BCE. It was anything but fortuitous to ascend the throne of a dynasty that was in its decline, and to stop its demise would take a great deal of strategy, iron will, moxie, and a great deal of luck, given that Rome was breathing down her neck. Not nearly enough credit is given to the last pharaoh of Egypt, who lasted far longer than she should have under such conditions and who almost pulled off a coup of melding her country with a would-be conqueror that, had she been suc-cessful, might well have caused many in the highest classes of both countries to spin around and ask those beside them, "What on earth just happened?"

What Cleopatra was made of, the core of her being that would allow her to take on this mighty challenge and almost cross the finish line, was her ability to combine the strengths of each of the Ptolemies before her, thereby making herself a formidable foe whom Octavian would eventually have to face.

As I pointed out concerning her bloodline and heritage, Cleopatra would see herself as the next Macedonian in line for the throne when her father died. She did not see any other Ptolemy of her family who deserved the honor, and she worked to make sure that the crown passed to her, the one to whom she believed it was owed.

The early pharaohs, Ptolemy I, Ptolemy II, and Ptolemy III, were the leaders Cleopatra saw as her mentors, the ones who built and made Egypt great, who vaulted the Macedonian Ptolemies to the height of their power. Having been thoroughly educated, which was encouraged for both male and female Ptolemies, Cleopatra would no doubt have been quite aware of the history of her brilliant and capable early forebears. She would also be quite cognizant of the later Ptolemies, including her father and her older sister, Berenike, who systematically depleted the strength of Egypt until Rome, desiring the wealth the country still had and especially its immense amount of wheat, added Egypt to its list of countries to be conquered rather than bartered with.

In spite of the fact that women did not receive education of any significance in the Macedonian culture due to a solidly entrenched patriarchy—it was only the boys who were sent to the gymnasium to receive education—the Ptolemies loved learning and clearly provided excellent tutors for their daughters as well as their sons. Since the Cleopatra of this work is the seventh, there were a number of prior Cleopatras who ruled or coruled Egypt for number of years, as well as queens with the names of Arsinoe and Berenice, who also held power during the Ptolemaic Dynasty. All of these women no doubt had intelligence and ability in the skills of governance adequate to hold onto their positions of power even if they were overlooked by many historians because Cleopatra VII was the last one to rule and her intense relationships with Caesar and Antony as well as her death dramatically described by Plutarch caused her to remain more firmly in our memory. By the time our Cleopatra was growing up in the Alexandrian Lagide household (Lagide is another name for the Ptolemaic family descended from Ptolemy I, who also was titled Ptolemy Lagide because he was legally the son of Arsinoe and Lagus of Macedon), she had access to the museum on the grounds of the royal palace, the meeting place of world-renowned mathematicians, poets, historians, and artists. Clearly, with Plutarch and others singing the praises of her intelligence, wit, and ability with languages (even if this is highly exaggerated), she excelled as a student and her lessons prepared her well to take over as pharaoh and rule the country for almost two decades.

Cleopatra learned many valuable lessons from her unusual ancestors. For example, a good leader doesn't waste the family genes and encourage unnecessary strife and dissent by partnering and spawning children with leaders of lesser dominions; in fact, so concerned were the Ptolemies that their line be pure and the future royals be Egyptian Ptolemies that they introduced incestuous relationships that had not been part of Macedonian history: Ptolemy II married his own sister Arsinoe II in 274 BCE and established a precedent for future pharaohs, guaranteeing no outsiders on the throne and enhancing the claim of divinity for the royals. Early non-Macedonian pharaohs were incestuous on and off during their dynasties; it would seem that the Ptolemies embraced the concept quite avidly, and this would continue into Cleopatra's reign. She married each of her two brothers (and most likely killed them off in order to be sure she retained the throne), and then found more suitable husbands in her pseudomarriages to Julius Caesar and Mark Antony—a brilliant and unique political strategy for a Ptolemy to marry "out" and "up"—to produce children with a dual claim to both the Egyptian throne and the Roman emperor (or emperor-to-be) who would undoubtedly co-opt Egypt in the future. Cleopatra's unusual choice of fathers for her children was her best effort to ensure she and her Ptolemaic offspring would continue to rule in Egypt and the Mediterranean world. The Ptolemies were hardly a peaceful lot, and Cleopatra had many fine examples of using murder as a method of eliminating one's rivals and making sure to be the first to do the family downsizing. Cleopatra's father, Auletes, had her older sister, Berenike, murdered. Berenike had taken over the throne when her father fled Alexandria during a revolt by his people in 58 BCE. He had her killed when he returned to reclaim his position as pharaoh. Cleopatra's other older sister, Cleopatra VI, mysteriously vanished around the same time, and nothing much has been noted about her in history. Cleopatra's younger sister, Arsinoe IV, the remaining one whom Cleopatra always saw as a threat, was eventually killed off by Antony at Cleopatra's behest.

Auletes wasn't the first pharaoh or Ptolemy to kill off his family or rivals to the throne in order to succeed to power. Here is a condensed history of Ptolemy intra-family annihilation that may be a bit overwhelming with the many similar names and titles and intrigues. I present this compilation not to detail each specific event or to present an analysis of these goings on, but to acquaint you with the vicious past activities of the Ptolemies that would educate Cleopatra on methods of dealing with threats to her continuation as a ruler. Do not worry about who did what and when, but rather allow the violence of the years leading up to Cleopatra's rule to set the tone for her entrance into Ptolemaic history.

Let us begin with the sister of Ptolemy II, Arsinoe II. She eventually ended up marrying her brother, the then king of Egypt, but she first married the elderly king Lysimachos, who controlled all of Macedonia in 285 BCE. Wanting one of her own three sons with the king to be successor to the throne, she got the king to poison his own very capable eldest son from his first wife on trumped up treason charges. After King Lysimachos was killed in battle, Arsinoe II married her half brother, Ptolemy Keraunos, son of Ptolemy I, who then killed Arsinoe's two younger sons after she and her sons conspired against him. Arsinoe's eldest son went into hiding. Never one to give up, Arsinoe II then went to her other brother, Ptolemy II, in Alexandria; encouraged him to exile his wife (Arsinoe I); and promptly married him. She became quite an influential queen. This incestuous marriage in the Ptolemaic Dynasty of Arsinoe II to her brother Ptolemy II was a fine example to the young Cleopatra that ruthlessness and determination are necessary if one wants to be an important part of the ruling family.

Ptolemy III, son of Ptolemy II and Arsinoe I, took over the throne in 246 BCE and promptly married his sister, Berenice II. When he died, his twenty-year-old son, Ptolemy IV, took over and immediately married his sister, Arsinoe III. The most powerful man in his court, Sosibios, who quite frankly was dictating what the young pharaoh would do, quickly murdered the top three members of the ruling family, including the pharaoh's mother, to ensure his continued control of the king. It is at this point that the downfall of the Ptolemies began. Ptolemy IV wasn't terribly good at his administrative duties, and he preferred partying to handling more important matters. When he died at age forty, he left a son, Ptolemy V, as the new king at age six.

Unfortunately for Egypt, Sosibios also died soon thereafter, leaving an even nastier man in his stead, an Alexandrian by the name of Agathoklos, to watch over the new little king as regent. He swiftly eliminated Arsinoe III, the pharaoh's mother, capturing the place of power for himself. But apparently his bad behavior wasn't appreciated by the Alexandrian mob that, in 203 BCE, executed him in the stadium along with his family. Cleopatra would learn from this that the Alexandrians could turn on their leaders and the results could be extremely unpleasant. Thereafter the "mob" was to be considered a serious threat. Even after Octavian came to Egypt and defeated Antony and Cleopatra at the battle of Actium, he was very well aware of the power the Egyptian people held, and he made good use of his time winning their favor. As we will see later in this story of Cleopatra's death, there was good reason for him to want to appease this group and not incur their wrath over his mistreatment of their beloved queen.

Ptolemy V, who succeeded his father, Ptolemy IV, actually didn't marry his sister. At sixteen years of age, he married a Syrian named Cleopatra I, who was just ten years old. His rule was an unmitigated disaster during which he managed to lose most of Egypt's foreign possessions in Europe and in Asia. When he died, *his* six-year-old son, Ptolemy VI, was placed on the throne and ruled jointly with his mother, Cleopatra I. After his mother died and he was all of eleven years old, Ptolemy VI married his little sister, Cleopatra II. It was during the administration of Ptolemy VI that Rome gained a foothold in Egyptian fortunes and would continue to be both a thorn in Egypt's side as well as a necessary partner.

The power struggles continued when Ptolemy VIII, younger brother of Ptolemy VI, also became a coruler in a triumvirate of the two brothers and their sister, Cleopatra II. In a struggle for power between the two brothers, Ptolemy VI found himself ruling Cyprus with his sister-wife Cleopatra II, and Ptolemy VIII became sole ruler of Egypt. The lone pharaoh wasn't well liked; he was a tyrannical king and was hated for it. The Alexandrians wanted the older brother back. They drove Ptolemy VIII out and had Ptolemy VI as their pharaoh for a year, but then Ptolemy VIII made a play for the position of pharaoh again with an assassination attempt on his brother and won back the spot. Meanwhile, in an attempt to regain Syria, Ptolemy VI fell from his horse and died. Ptolemy VIII then married his widow-sister, Cleopatra II. Ever the loving brother, he had his nephew murdered in his mother's arms during the wedding celebration. He let his wife-sister live. Then he married his niece, Cleopatra III, setting the stage for massive bitterness and hatred between mother and daughter as he now had them both as wives.

After a nasty bit of time as a ruling threesome, a fire was set to the palace and Ptolemy VIII fled with his second wife, Cleopatra III, to Cyprus. Cleopatra II, his first wife, became the sole ruler. This quite displeased Ptolemy VIII, so he had his own son with Cleopatra II brutally murdered right in front of him and sent the body parts back to Alexandria to his first wife as a birthday present. When Ptolemy VIII died, the throne went to Cleopatra III. The murders continued. Cleopatra III and her son Ptolemy X had a falling out, and after ousting him, she relented and allowed him to return to Egypt, after which he had her murdered. Ptolemy X was eventually driven out of Egypt and killed. His elder brother, Ptolemy IX, came back from Cyprus (where he had been forced to flee). He actually died of natural causes in his bed, and his daughter Cleopatra Berenike III became pharaoh. She ruled for one year, then married her stepson, Ptolemy

XI. Ptolemy XI ruled with her for fifteen days before he murdered her. He was then dragged out by the mob to the gymnasium and killed.

If you are now exhausted by reading these machinations of the Ptolemies, we are thankfully nearing Cleopatra VII's time. With their rulers both dead, the Alexandrian elite put Cleopatra's father, Ptolemy XII (also known as Auletes the flute player), in power, after which he married his sister, Cleopatra V (some say Cleopatra VI). Berenike IV was born to them, then Cleopatra VI (some call her Cleopatra Tryphaena), then Cleopatra VII and her other three siblings—Arsinoe IV, Ptolemy XIII, and Ptolemy XIV. By the time she reached adulthood, Cleopatra VII fully represented the Ptolemy mind-set: their high level of intelligence, their incredible lust for power, and their desire to keep Egypt as a separate country or at least not completely under the thumb of another country. When Cleopatra VII arrived on the scene, in spite of the decline of the country, she still saw herself assuming a seat of great power and wealth, and she would put all her Ptolemaic abilities to work. It was in her nature and, quite frankly, it is not clear that she had much of a choice; it was rule or be destroyed, kill or be killed. She would either step up and take control of the reins of power or be eliminated; and once she assumed the role of pharaoh, there would always be efforts afoot to unseat her. She wasn't likely to come out like a fighter in the early rounds and then go out with a whimper. Cleopatra VII was a Ptolemy through and through.

CHAPTER 7

CLEOPATRA VII BECOMES QUEEN

Cleopatra inherited quite an array of problems when she was born into the Ptolemaic Dynasty in 69 BCE. She had a reported fool for a father, not one of the more accomplished or acclaimed Ptolemies in the long line of rulers; a country on the verge of being gobbled up by Rome; and far too many siblings in a fight for the throne to have a good chance of winning it (she had two older sisters who could claim it first, two brothers who no doubt would be preferred as rulers due to their gender, and one younger but very aggressive sister who couldn't be discounted as a threat). That she won out is a testament to her aggressiveness and astuteness—neither of which she seemed to have inherited from her father, so the earlier Cleopatras must have been running solidly in her blood.

Her father, Auletes, was not chosen by his father to ascend the throne. He was rather a desperation choice by the Alexandrians since the recently killed couple left no children. Auletes was the elder son of one of the Ptolemies who had been in hiding in Syria, and his mother was not of royal lineage (*that* Ptolemy was not expecting to be pharaoh), but Alexandrian elites had to pick someone, some Ptolemy, and he was the best they thought they could do. All they could hope was that he wouldn't be a total failure in the role. It is important to remember that although the pharaohs held great power, they did not actually rule entirely alone; they had the Alexandrian elite, the high priests, and a great many administrators who kept the country afloat when they were flagging in their duties, off fighting wars, or hiding from familial attempts to assassinate them. Even Cleopatra had times when she left the management of Egypt in the hands of others when she spent time in Rome with Julius Caesar or was off in battle with Mark Antony. Her father, Auletes, Ptolemy XII, would not have lasted any time at all on the throne if there were not others around to mind the store for him.

Cleopatra's father was well aware—he wasn't totally ignorant of the facts—that the Alexandrian mob put him in his place of power and they could just as easily remove him. Since that mob was always quite fickle and contentious, he needed some strong backing to keep him on the throne, and the only place he could get it from was Rome. He could be a temporary patsy, one to be totally used by the Romans without any say or sway, or he could be a puppet, meaning he could at least levy some favors to his and Egypt's benefit. He chose to be a puppet.

It all worked rather well for Ptolemy XII, bribing the Roman officials on a regular basis; that Lagide treasury and taxes kept him going for quite a while since his ascension to the throne in 80 BCE. In fact, rather than having Egypt become a mere province of Rome, he managed to bribe his way to having the Romans title him "King," so he was able to continue as pharaoh and keep Egypt a sovereign country. To be fair to him, considering that all the other countries in the Mediterranean were fully under Roman dominance even if they were nominally independent, Egypt was still solidly under its own rule and Alexandria was still their own city and the one port the Romans didn't control. But, as always seems to occur when one has to keep forking over money to virtual loan sharks, the price keeps increasing over time. In 58 BCE, Ptolemy XII ceded Cyprus to Rome, and the Ptolemy family member ruling there at the time took poison rather than endure the insult. Cyprus remained in Roman hands until Caesar returned it to Cleopatra ten years later.

Giving away Cyprus was Ptolemy XII's undoing, at least temporarily, and it was a massive loss to Egypt because this move permitted Rome to assert its military power over Egyptian territory. The Alexandrians did not take kindly to the pharaoh's decision, and they revolted. The king had to flee the country, leaving the mob to put Egypt in the hands of his firstborn daughter, Berenike IV (there is no clear record of whether her mother was already dead or died soon after leaving Berenike IV at the top of the succession). The Alexandrians presented Berenike IV with a husband so she would not be ruling as a female alone on the throne. She clearly didn't like their choice, since she had him strangled.

Berenike IV lasted three years as queen. One advantage her father had was that he was liked by the Romans, so he had their support. With the Roman army behind him, he reentered Egypt, wreaked major violence and destruction, killed off Berenike IV, and regained the throne. Admittedly, now that he was so indebted to the Romans, he was rather more a governor than a king, but he still had the title and he was satisfied with that. Now he had no coregent since his wife was dead, so he appointed Cleopatra VII, who was his next-oldest child (the elder Cleopatra disappeared from history and we do not know why). Cleopatra was quite a bit older than her younger siblings. Auletes died just four years later, and Cleopatra, at age eighteen, was at the pinnacle of power.

In spite of the requirement of having the eldest of the brothers, Ptolemy XIII, appointed to rule with her (he was her husband), she was eight years older than the boy and fully able to rule on her own. She didn't take kindly to having him tag along, so she ousted him from the position and ruled alone for the next eighteen months. One thing she knew, she could not beat the Romans at their military game at this point, so she had to take up where her father left off and do damage control by working with the Roman oppressors in the hope that they would give up Egypt entirely. Like her father, she chose survival, but she had one advantage over him. Cleopatra was quite clever, and she knew how to play the cards she was dealt to her best advantage. She would continue to do so throughout her reign, up until the very end; she wasn't about to fold her hand if she could see any way to play to the best of her ability, and she would bluff if necessary. She would eliminate every other foe in the game and keep a few aces up her sleeves by winning key Alexandrians, Romans, and the priests over to her side. She was a brilliant strategist, even at the young age at which she became coregent.

Of course, this was Egypt, and given the tempestuous history of Alexandria and the Ptolemies, nothing was going to come that easy to a new ruler. Her little brother had his supporters, or should I say, his controllers, and they wanted to have the power in their hands, not Cleopatra's. When I say "they" wanted power, I am speaking of Gnaeus Pompey, who at the time was the supreme controller of Rome, the man who gave her father the title of king, and the person to whom was given the right to possess Cyprus. It is highly possible that Pompey, like Octavian, would see Cleopatra as too smart to be simply mollified like her father. She would be hard to control and a constant threat to Roman dominance over Egypt. Her little brother needed some assistance and this he was given in the form of Roman support: Pompey would show up occasionally to formally recognize the little brother over the big sister as ruler of Egypt. With Pompey's backing, Ptolemy XIII went to war with his big sister, driving her from power. In 49 BCE she fled to Syria.

Cleopatra was not long gone. She returned with an army of her own, perhaps staffed with mercenaries, and made her way to Pelusium, the border garrison that all armies attacking Egypt must pass through. There she confronted the army of her brother. Things might have gone badly for Cleopatra had the two sides actually skirmished, but here Cleopatra's brother and his handlers proved Cleopatra was the wiser of the lot, and luck fell upon her at just the right moment.

❖

We need to stop here and catch up with the struggles of Rome in which Egypt became entangled. General Julius Caesar, in his own battle with General Pompey for power and control of Rome, was conducting a bloody civil war that raged on and on. Pompey arrived in Pelusium, hoping to get money, food, men, and ships because he was running low on what he needed to defeat Caesar. He went to Egypt to get these needs met, from Ptolemy XIII, who he figured owed him. Until that point in time, Ptolemy XIII, just thirteen years of age, had been on the receiving end of much support from Rome due to the relationship established between Cleopatra's father and Pompey before Caesar rose up to challenge the Roman general. And now Pompey had just lost badly to Caesar in Pharsalos, he needed Egypt's help.

Meanwhile, Caesar was in pursuit and also looking for aid for his military needs; he arrived in Alexandria with what wasn't a huge contingent. However, it seemed to Ptolemy and his advisors that Caesar was going to be the eventual victor; they had to pick one side or the other because, well, what else could they do? Ptolemy XIII was forced into a bad situation. If he continued supplying Pompey and giving him enough strength to continue the battles against Caesar on Egyptian soil, the campaigns could devastate Egypt; and if Pompey lost after helping him, Ptolemy XIII's support for Pompey would infuriate Caesar. Ptolemy and his advisors evaluated whom the winner of a civil war would be and how quickly that winner would finish the job and vacate Egypt; they concluded that it would be Caesar. Not wanting to bet with the odds against him, Ptolemy switched sides.

Positioned between a rock and a hard place, as soon as Pompey landed with his troops at Pelusium, Ptolemy XIII had Pompey ambushed and killed. He delivered Pompey's head to Caesar. However, Ptolemy XIII miscalculated how happy Caesar would be to see his enemy's head presented to him by the Egyptian king. Pompey may have been his rival, but it was up to Caesar to decide Pompey's fate, not have the upstart Egyptian king usurp the right. Caesar was galled. Maybe Ptolemy XIII should have simply done away with Pompey quietly and not forced Caesar to confront the head of his dead adversary and the embarrassment that came with it.

Ptolemy XIII did not make a new friend with such a brash move. Meanwhile, Cleopatra knew she would be unlikely to beat her brother militarily, so she worked out a more subtle plan by out-witting him. She slipped past Ptolemy's general Achillas, who was blocking Pelusium, and sailed along the coastline to Alexandria (or by way of the Nile). Then she went to see Caesar at the palace.

Here we have one of Plutarch's most fanciful stories that certainly has been depicted in film after film of Cleopatra's life. Cassias Dio wrote of the episode in simple terms in his *Roman History*.

> Therefore, she requested permission to go before Caesar and, when she received it, she put on her finery so as to appear to him stately and pitiable at the same time. Once she had devised the perfect look, she entered the city (for she had been outside it) and approached the palace at night, keeping her arrival a secret from Ptolemy.[1]

Plutarch, always one to embellish and add a grand entrance, writes of this scene:

> She took a small boat and one only of her confidants, Apollodorus, the Sicilian, along with her, and in the dusk of the evening landed near the palace. She was at a loss how to get in undiscovered, till she thought of putting herself in a coverlet of a bed and lying at length, whilst Apollodorus tied up the bedding and carried it on his back through the gates to Caesar's apartment. Caesar was first captivated by Cleopatra's bold wit, and was afterwards so overcome by the charm of her society that he made a reconciliation between her and her brother.[2]

Ah, such a terribly "cute" and utterly degrading way for a queen to meet a renowned Roman general, demeaning to the utmost, to be rolled out of a carpet as is oft repeated, or in a bit of a better container, a bedroll, onto the floor groveling at his feet, sweaty, hair a mess, clothing askew, a true rug rat to an experienced, very mature man.

Cleopatra was no longer a teenager at that moment. She was twenty-one years old, a very mature twenty-one if you count her upbringing and what she had experienced during her royal childhood. She had observed years of political wrangling, experienced the murder of her sister, the death of her father, war, expulsion, being a fugitive, and most important of all, the young woman had ruled alone as pharaoh for almost two years. She was not a naïve waif, chuckling over her "cool" style of arrival in a carpet, thinking she was going to so amuse the lauded general Caesar of Rome. She was a queen, temporarily separated from her kingdom, who desired to meet and impress the general, not with her coquetry, but with her ability to govern better than her brother, to manage Egypt in an intelligent manner, which would be to Caesar's benefit. Caesar was not overly impressed with Ptolemy, so she already had an advantage.

There is evidence in the literature, and this can be backed up by logic, that she did not need to go to quite so covert lengths to get an audience with Caesar in Alexandria. She had been communicating with him from her post over the border at Pelusium. Surely, before sneaking past Achillas and heading toward Alexandria, she had sent word to Caesar that she was coming or he had sent word to her telling her to come; either way, it likely was no surprise that Cleopatra was arriving in the harbor that night.

While Cleopatra was taking a risk, she had to be concerned that some of her brother's supporters might get wind that she was coming, see her arrival, and take violent action against her. She also had to worry about those volatile Alexandrians who might not wish her well. However, Caesar was installed in Alexandria with two legions, which was not necessarily a lot for going into a huge battle, but those legions numbered over three thousand men and they reported to Caesar. He also had eight hundred cavalry that served as his bodyguard. Now, the palace is on the harbor, a relatively short walk from the docks. She would not even actually need to get from the bigger ship to a smaller boat (as written) because the large ships could pull right up to the wall since the harbor was so deep. However, she might have taken a small boat to the dock and been brought to the palace. Regardless of how she exactly came on shore, I find it hard to believe that Caesar would not have made arrangements for her to arrive in one piece. No doubt she was met and escorted, possibly with a solid flanking of men about her and a shawl over her head, but, when she entered the palace and stood before Caesar, I am quite confident she was ravishing to look at and she looked him directly in the eye, proud and defiant and strong. This would be the queen the general had heard of and this would be the queen Cleopatra would want him to meet and choose to support.

Cassius Dio, ever more sensible and less dramatic than Plutarch in examining history, elaborates on the event and Cleopatra's reasoning:

> It seems that Cleopatra was pleading her case against her brother with Caesar through intermediaries, but as soon as she learned of his nature (for he had a propensity for affairs and had been with many women every time the opportunity presented itself) she sent word to him saying that her friends were betraying her and requesting that he let her speak for herself. She was a particularly beautiful woman and, at the time, being in her prime, she knew how to use her charms to be attractive to everyone. Thus, she thought it appropriate for her to meet with Caesar and she rested all her hopes of a successful outcome on her beauty. It worked, and Caesar gave her the throne back.[3]

Naturally, when Ptolemy XIII arrived in Alexandria to find Cleopatra in the palace reinstalled as coregent, he was not at all pleased and he threw a royal fit. As impressed as Caesar was with the queen, he wisely took into consideration the support Ptolemy XIII had among many of the upper-crust Alexandrians and handled the delicate situation quite astutely. Caesar wisely read to Cleopatra and Ptolemy XIII the will of the Ptolemaic siblings' father, which stated that he wanted them to rule together. Never mind that Cleopatra had blithely ignored her father's wishes and pushed her brother off the throne. Never mind, water under the bridge. Well, perhaps for Cleopatra. Ptolemy XIII was not so willing to forgive and forget, because clearly Caesar was leaning toward Cleopatra as his long-term associate; he promised to return Cyprus. Now, some think that Caesar was simply smitten with Cleopatra, that they had spent a hot night together, and he made a poor choice of Cleopatra over Ptolemy XIII considering the male ruler had more military might and Alexandrian support. I see his choice to be far more rational in the scheme of long-term thinking. Ptolemy XIII may have had more Egyptians in his corner at the time, but he was emotionally unstable and easily swayed. Cleopatra would provide the tenacity, vigor, and continued support for his goals of being sole leader of Rome and for stabilizing Egypt. He also knew that she needed him as well. A petulant, annoying boy or a confident, attractive, available goddess; whom would you choose? Caesar was known to be a womanizer, and he liked smart, ambitious women. Cleopatra fit his type perfectly.

Julius Caesar may have rid himself of Pompey, but the Egyptian army was still out at Pelusium, and General Achillas and the minister Pothinos felt this would be a good time to attack Caesar since he was low on forces. They conducted a siege of Alexandria (the Alexandrian War) against him, but Caesar held up surprisingly well in spite of Achillas's and then Ganymede's tactics. Ganymede, Cleopatra's younger sister Arsinoe's tutor, assassinated Achillas during the battle; Arsinoe had joined up with her brother Ptolemy XIII, but had a falling out with Achillas. She had Ganymede kill General Achillas, and then she promoted Ganymede to lead the Egyptian army. He did his job well and came up with the clever idea of rerouting seawater into the drinking water and trying to dehydrate Caesar's men. Caesar struck back by setting fire to the Egyptian fleet in the harbor.

Meanwhile, over these four months, Cleopatra was cooped up with her brother, Ptolemy XIII, in the palace. She could watch the battle from the roof, but her new lover was gone all day long. I bring this up to make a point about the paternity of Cleopatra's son, Caesarion.

There is much argument over whether the son Cleopatra named

Caesarion was truly the son of Julius Caesar. Some think it is silly to question the paternity of Caesarion; after all Caesar did have at least four months to connect with Cleopatra while the Alexandrian war raged on. Cleopatra was in the palace the whole time, and why wouldn't Caesar enjoy a bit of sexual healing at the end of a long day of battle? Whether Caesar actually took that long Nile boat ride with Cleopatra when the war ended is fairly irrelevant; she supposedly had gotten pregnant with the child within the approximate time frame of the Alexandrian War when Caesar was available to provide the DNA. So why wouldn't he be the father of Caesarion? Wouldn't word get out if Cleopatra was having trysts with soldiers, or the help, or some other important person? One would think—but then again, if the pharaoh told you never to mention the moment, it would be terribly foolish to spread that information around. For that matter, even if she didn't tell you to keep your mouth shut, it still might mean your death to say that you slept with the queen. So I wouldn't discount the possibility that Cleopatra slept with someone besides Julius Caesar, someone who could also have impregnated her.

Clearly no DNA tests existed in those days to prove or disprove paternity. And I think it matters little that some Greek writers claim that the boy looked like Caesar and even walked like Caesar. It is true that sometimes children look incredibly like their parents and have mannerisms that mimic them, but little Caesarion never grew up around his supposed father, so I doubt his gait would in any way resemble Julius Caesar's, except by luck.

There is also an interesting human trait of making public statements about how much a boy looks like his father. Oddly, one hears much less often how much a child looks like his mother. This is especially true with babies, who, for the most part, look like any other baby. Why does this happen? This peculiar human behavior may harken back to the days when there were no paternity tests, when questions of whom the father of that baby might be were unable to be proven and were very questionable, especially if papa was a traveling man or there was any rumor that the mother ordered far more milk from the milkman than her family could drink. Saying the baby looked like the father was a way of making him feel more comfortable, to give him a slap on the back and assure him that his wife hadn't cheated on him. We have no way to compare the looks of Caesarion to Caesar, so we really don't know much about whether they looked alike. And if Cleopatra wanted to pass off a child as the son of Caesar, she needed only to not get pregnant by a man who looked terribly different from him, like a Nubian.

So we can't know if the child was Caesar's through physical appearance. Is there any reason to believe, since it is hardly believable that Caesar and Cleopatra did not sleep together, that he could have a problem fathering her child? Let's see. Caesar was fifty-two years old at the time Cleopatra got pregnant. This is certainly not too old to be able to sire a child, as long as he was capable of doing so, which is something quite frankly not known. Caesar may be "every woman's man and every man's woman,"[4] as one of his detractors (Curio) publicly stated, but we don't know how and when he might have been these things. He could have slowed down in the years before Cleopatra, or he could have resorted to other methods of sexual pleasure than intercourse. He may have had prostate problems and been unable to perform. Or he may have been a stallion in bed. We have no idea. The only bit of evidence that raises eyebrows is that he was only ever known to have fathered one child, Julia, some thirty-six years earlier, with his first wife. He had no children with his second or third wives, nor were any known to have been issued by way of his countless adulterous affairs. Since he never had a son, it would be odd for a man not to want to advertise the ones he did have (even if they were illegitimate, since this was not such a huge matter for the Romans as it was for the Macedonians); and in nearly four decades, Caesar does not link himself to one male heir.

But when Cleopatra has "his" child, he "allows" her to use the name Caesarion but does not brag about "his" son, nor does he put the child in his will. One would think he would be quite thrilled to admit the child was his. It would seem that his lack of acknowledgment speaks volumes, although some might say he didn't want to admit he had a son with some foreign queen, especially an Egyptian one. But, since Caesar was known to have numerous affairs and he openly spent time with Cleopatra and had her stay in Rome with the child, I hardly think that argument is very strong.

Let's assume Julius Caesar knew full well or at least had a pretty good clue that he couldn't get a woman pregnant or at least suspected he couldn't. I don't know of any man who was told that he absolutely could not father a child and yet is not willing to believe he actually could, even if it was just once in fifty years. This might well be the best argument for why Caesar could possibly have known a child might not be his but might not openly deny it. He would quietly allow Cleopatra to make her claims as to paternity. Impregnating the young Cleopatra makes him look virile, and that in itself is quite an ego boost. He can brag, at least privately, about how he got her pregnant and how he finally has a son. He can also tell friends that he has to keep it to a dull roar due to politics. Not claiming the child in his will, though, is rather a big clue to the likelihood of the child not being his.

"Fathering a son" with Cleopatra has some benefits for Caesar. Along with male bragging rights, having a son born to Cleopatra means that the child will one day become pharaoh. This also means Cleopatra doesn't have to marry and start another contentious and possibly lethal Ptolemaic battle for the throne. Having a son as coruler with Cleopatra, especially a very young son, allows a better possibility for peace in Egypt and a controlled handling of the country by Cleopatra for a long time. Having a son in name as pharaoh in Egypt connects Egypt to Rome in a familial way, ensuring Egypt and its rulers continue to support Rome.

What of Cleopatra? What is in it for her? Well, certainly the protection of Rome would be secured, at least in a relative way. Also, as I stated earlier, Cleopatra wouldn't have to find a husband if she didn't want one (especially another Ptolemy with whom a "till death do us part" marriage usually came sooner than later). She would follow in her father's footsteps in a strong relationship with Rome, and what better way than to be a consort to Caesar and the mother of his child as well as being the best pharaoh for the job? Cleopatra proved over and over she did not leave things to chance, and she always had a Plan B and C just in case the first one wasn't panning out. She stacked the deck in her favor as often as she could.

If you were Cleopatra and you had only a short time with a man who had fathered a child only once in his four decades of sexual escapades, what would you do? What would you do if you wanted to ensure you were pregnant before he left, that you would have a baby by him, if you had no way of knowing whether or not he was sterile? The only way to make sure you became pregnant would be to add another male to the mix, one who was virile and close enough in looks to either Caesar or oneself for any potential child to not have his or her paternity in question.

There is clearly a top candidate a female Ptolemy would choose under those circumstances: one's brother. Ptolemy XIII must have been a hormone-infested young teen at the time, so what better man or boy to seduce than him? Her brother was available at the palace, and incest wasn't looked down upon by the Ptolemies, so even if Cleopatra changed her mind on naming Caesar as father, the real father was more than acceptable. Ptolemy XIII would look like Cleopatra and was available while Caesar was off being general. In fact, her brother was likely stir crazy from staying in the palace and, in spite of the enmity between Cleopatra and the older of her two brothers, I am sure Cleopatra could easily find a way to entice him into a little sex. And it didn't hurt that Ptolemy XIII then disappeared in the river during the final battle of the Alexandrian War! He certainly couldn't claim paternity from beyond the grave.

The elder Ptolemy brother decided to join his troops when Caesar's backups from Asia (under the leadership of Mithraidates, along with reinforcements from the Nabataeans and the Jews) arrived in Egypt. They came up behind Ptolemy's forces on the Nile, and he supposedly drowned. His body was never found, just his armor, which for some reason didn't have his body in it, so excuse me for being a bit skeptical. One wonders if Cleopatra had any hand in his death. She eliminated a rival and, possibly, the real father of her son, which left a much more manageable situation for the future.

Since Cleopatra never liked leaving anything to chance if she had any method of controlling or influencing the turn of events, I would bet she added a male Ptolemy to the trysting to be very sure she was pregnant before Caesar went on his way. We will see again and again that she could have simply let events play out, but she did not leave anything to the Fates; she took specific action in an attempt to determine the desired outcome. The Ptolemies married their own siblings to limit any outside influences and incursions on their families; they killed anyone, even their own, if they were a threat. Cleopatra tossed her coregent brother aside as soon as she reached the throne. She ruled with him temporarily again only because Caesar had to appease the Alexandrians. Then by luck or "made" luck, Ptolemy XIII was out of the picture again when he "drowned" in the Nile. Caesar immediately appointed the younger brother, Ptolemy XIV, to rule with Cleopatra (as her second husband). Ptolemy XIV, what a surprise, died (of disease—or was he poisoned?) just two years later, while "she was away on business." This left Cleopatra and Caesarion as corulers until the end.

CHAPTER 8

JULIUS CAESAR

I arose early in the Egyptian morning and gazed out of my hotel-room window at the Mediterranean Sea that lay between me and Italy, where I was headed in a few hours. As I packed my bags at the hotel, I thought about how closely connected Alexandria and Rome were for so many years, even though they were on different continents with over a thousand of miles of water between them. No matter how hard Cleopatra worked to hold onto the sovereignty of her country and to extinguish the male threats in her life, she had little choice but to deal with the Roman men who kept coming at her. She handled them all as well as she could, but clearly the Roman general Julius Caesar was her most fortunate encounter; their individual political needs complemented each other, and neither had a problem with (i.e., was threatened by) the existence of the other or their behavior. Caesar was generous and Cleopatra was cooperative. As long as Caesar was in power, Cleopatra was doing well, as was Egypt. She could last for years in relative peace with him as her beneficent dictator. Too bad he was assassinated. Cleopatra was left with the choice of Antony or Octavian; like her brother's dilemma with Pompey and Caesar, she had to pick one of them to woo, bribe, and gain the favor of if she wanted to survive.

At noon, I caught my flight to Rome. I realized halfway there that my hijab was feeling a bit strange in the company of my fellow female passengers, of whom very few had head coverings. I made a quick run to the airline toilet and pulled it off. Then I ran a brush though my hair and went back to my seat. Even though I now matched more of the ladies on the plane, I felt a bit naked after having my head covered for so long. It took a ride into the center of Rome and seeing all the women in short skirts and blond, red, and black hair before I started feeling comfortable again. Once I checked into my hotel, I changed out of my long skirt, slipped into some jeans and (oh my!) a sleeveless shirt, and went out to tour the city.

Rome is a vibrant, busy, and fascinating mix of old and new, with churches built centuries ago, *Trevi Fountain*, and bridges that are hundreds of years old, but I found it hard to really imagine the world in which the three Roman leaders—Caesar, Antony, and Octavian— occupied, developed their unique perspectives, fought for dominance in the Mediterranean world, and came to blows over the politics of the day in the Senate. As I walked through the city, what I saw left from ancient Rome were some columns and a remaining wall here and there. In one area, my favorite, were the ruins of the Temples of Concord and Saturn, which stood along the side of the road, modern buildings behind them. In spite of the mixture of ancient and modern scenery, following the road, one can imagine walking through Rome in those bygone days. But, unlike Egypt where entire structures exist—like Dendera with its roof intact and fully painted rooms inside or the pyramids that have stood solid for eons, missing only their veneer; or Luxor, which covers a substantial area and still has many soaring walls with reliefs and intact massive statues—what is left of the Rome of Caesar and Antony are mere bits and pieces. To get a real picture of the city as the inhabitants of the time might have seen it, I had to stop and purchase a book with overlays that show what the buildings may have looked like at the time. Only the Coliseum stands as a nearly complete structure in which you can see its magnificence and grand size from inside and out.

From what remains of the city, I understand that Rome was quite a metropolis with its fine architecture, but I couldn't help feeling that Egypt rather outdid the Roman homeland in its heyday, and this could well be why the Romans were so enamored by Cleopatra's Alexandria. Simply put, Alexandria was richer and grander.

But certainly you can find in Rome a great many statues and busts of all the famous characters of Italian history. While this is pretty much nonexistent in Egypt—there are no public statues of Cleopatra or her father or any of the other Ptolemies—in Rome I could "see" Julius Caesar, Mark Antony, and Octavian. During my last trip to Rome when I was working with Atlantic Productions, we stopped in front of a statue of Octavian, and I was asked to profile the man based on his facial features in marble. I had to laugh. I told them it was not really possible to extract a personality from a simple physical reproduction of someone's face; likewise, in our modern world, one cannot make detailed commentary on a still photo of an individual, decide if he is evil or cruel, capable of a violent crime or not. It is not all that rare to come across a photo of a smiling man posing with his seemingly adoring wife and happy children, only to learn he shot his family to death in their beds a few days after the picture was taken. However, there is something that can be learned from a reproduction of a person if it is verified to relatively accurately depict the person's features. In a wax museum, we can see the height and weight of a person, note their level of attractiveness. What we do see from the statues of our three Roman men is that Mark Antony is a bit of a hunk, strapping and handsome; Julius Caesar appears to be good-looking and rather patrician in appearance; and Octavian is quite effeminate, unimposing, shall I say, a bit wimpy and boyish. Their outward demeanors would indeed affect how they would have seen themselves, how others would have seen them, and how Cleopatra would have seen them. Interestingly, I find the statues to be quite representative of the men after reviewing their behavioral histories.

Just as it was important to examine the history and culture into which Cleopatra was born, our Romans also came into a place and time that influenced their characters and choices and helped shape the men they became. They were all born into a republic; the monarchy of the past had been dismantled by Brutus, who encouraged the Roman people to depose the king and then establish a democratic system with elected representatives. Although the Roman citizens were members of different social strata and the levels of status these represented, they were expected to recognize their duty as members of the republic. From what I could discern, duty was the most important measuring stick with which they evaluated themselves and against which other Romans judged them. Duty would be a major influencing factor in the success or failure of these men.

The republic did quite well, and along with that achievement, Rome had defeated the Greek kingdoms following the demise of Alexander the Great, and by 146 BCE, Rome was the major power in the region. Then something went amiss. Many wonder, if Rome was so successful in its governing method and it had conquered vast territory ruled by many nations and, in so doing, could easily supply its citizens with a high quality of life, why did dictatorship raise its ugly head again, and why did the empire devolve into civil war?

A rather flippant answer would be that nothing lasts forever. For example, if a church is running well, into the calm someone introduces tension, dissatisfaction with the status quo, or a viewpoint that doesn't jibe with the majority; factions develop, and over time the church splits, with the dissenting group forming a new church with the word *reformed* added to it. There is also an innate desire many people have to be led, to believe that there is a greater future in front of them, and if a charismatic leader happens to appear in their midst, his ability to change the course of events can be astounding. We have seen this often in history with figures such as Abraham Lincoln, Winston Churchill, Adolf Hitler, and Nelson Mandela. Leaders usually vault to prominence when there is either a feeling of inferiority, desperation, or malaise within the population. I believe that the rise of Julius Caesar and what followed was due to a time in Roman history where there was not enough positive leadership and the citizens wanted something more, something exciting, something new.

Gaius Julius Caesar was a striking figure. As a man from the ruling class, he had royal bearing and, interestingly, a claim to be descended from the gods, much like the claims of Philip and Alexander and the Egyptian pharaohs. It would be easy for the populace to be in awe of him, to look up to him as quite a superior man. Of course, it was to his advantage that the reign of a man named Sulla, a military leader who had stormed Rome, crushed his political opponents, and established himself as a dictator who terrorized everyone, had been in power just before Caesar's appearance on the scene. Not long before his death, Sulla resigned. Compared to his brutal dictatorship, Julius Caesar was viewed as a much more pleasant option. Sulla not only failed in his duty to be a good "king," he was cruel and vicious. Caesar, on the other hand, was a much more magnanimous ruler, and he aimed to please his people in a variety of ways. He was even kind to his slaves and to gladiators, who won him a lot of points with the masses. He had more problems with the Senate and his peers because they viewed him as a bit of a dandy with his elaborate clothing, his love for the ladies, and his extravagance.

Pompey, the other Roman general whose army Caesar would defeat in Egypt during Rome's civil strife (and whom Ptolemy XIII killed in his mistaken attempt to please Caesar), was one of his foes. Not one to let bad feelings stand in the way of a good political move, Caesar married his only daughter, Julia, to Pompey. Then Caesar surprised everyone by turning out to be an extremely good military leader as well as a great political strategist. Caesar simply was very intelligent in the political sphere and on the battlefield—a genius of his generation. One more military leader, Crassus, made up the third man of the triumvirate, the three men who were supposed to be managing Rome but instead ended up fighting each other for it, causing the civil wars that tore the country apart for years. Crassus fell first, killed in battle, leaving just Caesar and Pompey to determine the fate of the empire.

After Julia's death and Pompey's demise in Egypt, Caesar gained virtual control of Rome, and he managed to do a fine job of eventually suppressing the rest of the civil uprisings and came back to Rome the conquering hero. Then, over time, he made the same mistake as

King Philip. He began to believe his own inflated public image and allowed himself to be honored with the title "Dictator for Life," which annoyed and aggravated the ruling class. They saw their power being diminished; they were made to feel small in Caesar's presence and forced to remain too much in his shadow to feel kindly toward him. Julius Caesar forgot one of his required duties. When you crush the egos of those who think they are entitled to share the spotlight (unlike the populace who is just thrilled not to be mistreated and to get a few more crumbs than they expect), you create enemies. It is always important to remember that those closest to you and who have some power can be a dangerous lot. This Caesar found out when he was murdered on the Ides of March in 44 BCE.

Caesar's biggest problem was that once he obtained nearly complete political authority, he became increasingly autocratic, as is common when a ruler possesses too much power. He used this power to overrule, control, and eliminate those he found to be troublesome or threatening. Narcissism, which is pretty much a common trait among all great leaders, can render a head of state oblivious to how others view their ruler and thereby breed a great deal of enmity and discontent. Caesar's enemies quite clearly understood that he was already a dictator and, if he managed to crush Parthia, the only major threat left against Rome, he would become emperor.

How much damage control Caesar attempted to do is a bit unclear. He brought Mark Antony back to be his consul, possibly to appear as though he was still sharing some power and was in tune with his military. During one public ceremony, it is reported that Antony attempted to crown him with a laurel wreath to signify his position as king but Caesar twice declined the honor. Plutarch writes about this peculiar event:

And it was Antony who also unwittingly supplied the conspirators with their most specious pretext. For at the festival of the Lycaea, which the Romans call Lupercalia, Caesar, arrayed in a triumphal robe and seated in the forum upon the rostra, was viewing the runners to and fro. Now, the runners to and fro are many noble youths and many of the magistrates, anointed with oil, and with leathern thongs they strike in sport those whom they meet. Antony was one of these runners, but he gave the ancient usages the go-by, and twining a wreath of laurel round a diadem, he ran with it to the rostra, where he was lifted on high by his fellow runners and put it on the head of Caesar, thus intimating that he ought to be king. When Caesar with affected modesty declined the diadem, the people were delighted and clapped their hands. Again Antony tried to put the diadem on Caesar's head, and again Caesar pushed it away. This contest went on for some time, a few of Antony's friends applauding his efforts to force the diadem upon Caesar, but all the people applauding with loud cries when Caesar refused it. And this was strange, too, that while the people were willing to conduct themselves like the subjects of a king, they shunned the name of king as though it meant the abolition of their freedom. At last Caesar rose from the rostra in displeasure, and pulling back the toga from his throat cried out that anyone who pleased might smite him there. The wreath, which had been hung upon one of his statues, certain tribunes of the people tore down. These men the people greeted with favouring cries and clapping of hands; but Caesar deprived them of their office.[1]

As my readers are now well aware, I do not take Plutarch's stories as necessarily facts of history. It is difficult to know from his words what exactly happened and what is just his way of telling a good tale. My analysis of this account is that Plutarch details some behavior on the part of Caesar that doesn't quite make sense. I think Plutarch is embellishing in an attempt to explain why future events unfolded, why rising anger of those around Caesar erupted after this celebration, and led to the decision to murder him. I think Plutarch is also attempting to show Antony as an unwitting participant, that he just did things without thinking that allowed others to use his foolish behavior to justify their own violent actions.

In analyzing this particular story, I find the event itself to be believable. Why? Caesar had brought Antony back to be his mouthpiece in what I believe to be an attempt to downplay publicly what he and the Senate already knew, that his position as head of state was virtually unassailable. This was a rather poor attempt to show he was not hogging all the power for himself. Antony had not been in his good graces since Caesar returned from his sojourn with Cleopatra only to discover that Antony had completely mismanaged the finances of the "republic" while he was gone. He summarily dismissed Antony from his position, but now, with the Parthian campaign about to go forth, he needed to express some goodwill toward his general and other "leaders." He may have felt Antony would be grateful to him for being brought back to Rome and honored in such a way and, therefore, would be a relatively safe choice as one of his inner circle. Caesar may even have thought Antony would bring him a level of protection from those who wished to unseat their dictator from his pedestal. And he no doubt wanted to keep an eye on Mark Antony.

This ceremonial gesture of having Antony come up from the crowd and attempt to crown Caesar king would serve two purposes. First, it would show Antony's support for him and, second, it would show the people and his detractors that he did not consider himself to be so grandiose a figure as to think himself a king at all. It would be a staged piece of propaganda, not unlike other such shows put on in the past. But that Caesar stood up and bared his throat, challenging his enemies to kill him, makes no sense whatsoever. Such a gesture would only serve to anger his enemies and it would gain him nothing to have the citizens of Rome view such a challenge, especially at that time, since it is diametrically opposed to his earlier humble refusal of the crown. I believe the first event most likely occurred, but Plutarch tossed in Caesar's brazen action to give an excuse for Caesar's future murderers to take great offense and reach a tipping point where they must then act on their resentments.

Before we discuss that crime scene in which Caesar was brutally eliminated from the Roman tableau, let's stop to review why Cleopatra smartly tied her future to him. He was a great general who had proved he could provide military support and safety for Egypt.

He provided an heir and coregent for Cleopatra (at least he didn't dispute the paternity), which allowed her to rule without keeping her dangerous brothers around to constantly threaten her life and position. He was willing to leave Egypt in the hands of Cleopatra, which was her fervent wish—to continue as pharaoh for life. He was her best opportunity and the perfect distant partner she could have hoped for.

Sadly, her perfect situation would come to a quick and unpleasant end.

CHAPTER 9

MARK ANTONY

The next two important players in the game of power would end up being Mark Antony, Caesar's consul and top general, and Octavian, Caesar's nephew. At the time of Caesar's assassination on March 15, 44 BCE, Mark Antony was thirty-nine years old and the long-time protégé of Caesar. He had been a popular general, a fine orator, and a consul to Caesar for a short time prior to the assassination. But Caesar was not always enamored with Antony. He wasn't too pleased with a number of Antony's traits. Plutarch writes this of Antony:

[He] was completely ignorant of much that was done in his name, not merely because he was of an easygoing disposition, but because he was simple enough to trust his subordinates. His character was, in fact, essentially simple and he was slow to perceive the truth. Once he recognized that he was at fault, he was full of repentance and ready to admit his errors to those he had wronged. Whenever he had to punish an offence or right an injustice, he acted on the grand scale, and it was generally considered that he overstepped the bounds far more often in the rewards he bestowed than in the punishments he inflicted. As for the kind of course and insolent banter which he liked to exchange, this carried its own remedy with it, for anyone could return his ribaldry with interest, and he enjoyed being laughed at quite as much as laughing at others. And in fact it was this quality which often did him harm, for he found it impossible to believe that the real purpose of those who took liberties and cracked jokes with him was to flatter him. He never understood that some men go out of their way to adopt a frank and outspoken manner and use it like a piquant sauce to disguise the cloying taste of flattery. Such men deliberately indulge in bold repartee and an aggressive flow of talk when they are in their cups, so that the obsequious compliance which they show in matters of business does not suggest that they associate with a man merely to please him, but seems to spring from a genuine conviction of his superior wisdom.[1]

Basically, Plutarch was calling Antony a fool. But he also points out some good qualities:

But, indeed the traits that seemed vulgar to some—his boastfulness and his jesting, his open indulgence in drink, his habit of sitting with his soldiers when they ate or eating standing at the common table—gave the troops an amazing amount of goodwill and even love for him. He was lustful but charming as well: he captivated many people, as he often helped those in love and could make light of his own love life. Also the liberal generosity and unthrifty indulgence he showed his soldiers and friends afforded him an auspicious beginning to his quest for power and, once he became prominent, these tendencies increased his power manifold despite the hindrances posed by his many flaws.[2]

So Plutarch may say Antony is not that bright and has some bad habits, but he was popular with his men, knew how to have a good time, and could make people feel good.

Caesar and Antony had a long period of separation that finally ended when Caesar let him back into his good graces as co-consul. Antony continued in that position for seven years until Caesar's murder in 44 BCE, so he likely served quite a useful purpose for Caesar in maintaining control of Rome. However, when Antony was given that position, he was thirty-two years old, still relatively young in comparison to Caesar and most likely at a time in life when being second to the great man was a good spot to be. Fast-forward to Antony nearing forty and still in that position, and we can see that midlife crisis and ambition may well have melded together and led to a lust for power that would never be achieved if Caesar remained dictator.

There is no question that Antony was ambitious; we can certainly see with his future partnering with Cleopatra, he was not willing to take a back seat to Octavian. Even immediately after Caesar's death, we see that he happily stepped into the power vacuum and didn't attempt to return Rome to a republic. For this reason, I don't agree with Plutarch that Antony was just a passive, impotent bystander to the assassination. This is what Plutarch claims to have happened:

These events encouraged Brutus and Cassius: enlisting those of their friends who were trustworthy in the plot, they inquired about Antony. Everyone was eager to admit him but Trebonious opposed it: he said that, at the time when many went to meet Caesar as he returned from Spain, he and Antony had traveled together and shared a tent and that he had gently and discreetly inquired about Antony's opinion, but that, while Antony understood him he did not approve of the plot, but he said nothing to Caesar, instead faithfully keeping the secret. After this, they thought of murdering Antony after they had killed Caesar; Brutus stopped them on the grounds that a deed undertaken in the name of the law and justice should be pure and uncorrupted by injustice. Some, afraid of Antony's strength and political reputation assigned several of the conspirators to watch him, so that when Caesar entered the Senate and the deed was about to be done, they might restrain him by engaging him in some urgent conversation.[3]

Antony may not have had quite the intellect of Caesar or Octavian, but I find it hard to believe that he was quite as oblivious as Plutarch makes him out to be. He would not have been so successful as a general for so many years, nor would he have done so well in politics for nearly a decade, if he didn't have a fairly calculating mind. His main downfall was likely that he was quite a drinker, and it was this failing that the fairly alcohol-abstaining Caesar did not like about him, in addition to the fact that Caesar was insulted by Antony's power-grabbing move of stealing the spoils of Pompey's estate out from under him. Antony also had a massive ego, which clashed with Caesar's own impressive image of himself—two men with strong narcissistic personalities often find it difficult to tolerate each other's presence. However, in the long run, Caesar may have decided that keeping his friends close and his enemies closer might be the wiser move, and this is why he brought Antony back to Rome as his consul; by having him returned to Rome, essentially as his lieutenant, Caesar quashed Antony's independent upward rise. This was a clever move, but, as with many a good plan, time and other events can eventually turn the tide, and as the Ides of March neared, there was considerable dissent in the ranks and Antony would know it would be time to make his move or forever lose the opportunity.

Caesar was planning to head off on his Parthian campaign on March 18, and if he won, he would remove in one stroke all remaining threats to the empire and any opposition to his assumption of the role of emperor. His enemies, and in my opinion that included Antony, had to strike quickly to prevent him from achieving that goal. More than sixty senators were involved in the conspiracy, so it is hard to believe that Mark Antony had no clue as to what was about to happen and, more likely, as Plutarch did point out, he knew exactly when and where it was to happen. Had he really been in Caesar's corner and satisfied with his lot in political life, he would have run to Caesar and told him of the plan. In fact, had any of the conspirators believed that Antony might have any misgivings about the assassination, it hardly makes sense that they would have been foolish to even bring up the subject in his company. They absolutely knew he was on their side, and whether he was the actual ringleader, as I believe, or just a willing co-conspirator, Antony knew full well what the Ides of March would bring to Caesar. He liked power quite well himself, so no great empathy for Julius Caesar would stand in his way.

Plutarch writes that Antony was detained from entering the Senate, which indicates that Antony did not know exactly what was going to happen inside. As I have just pointed out, this is ridiculous. If Antony did not go inside, he himself did the lingering, purposefully staying outside the building until the deed was done. Furthermore, if Antony was not leading this band of murderers, it would have been to their advantage to have him inside next to Caesar and "accidentally" stabbed along with the dictator. Antony could be viewed as collateral damage, and it would make sense to kill these two powerful birds with one stone.

But, no, he was outside, "unaware," and spared. This allowed him to be innocent of any wrongdoing in the eyes of the citizens of Rome and the Senate and, then, in this position, he could even arouse the support of the Senate to give amnesty to the supposed two main conspirators, Lepidus and Brutus. All of this was, in my analysis, a show to allow the large number of guilty parties to be civilized in the handling of the aftermath.

> The plot was carried out as it had been devised and, when Caesar fell in the Senate, Antony immediately went into hiding dressed as a slave. When he was certain the men were not harming anyone else but were assembled on the Capitoline, he persuaded them to come down, taking his son as a hostage he even dined with Cassius and Lepidus with Brutus. Calling a meeting of the Senate, he recommended amnesty and the assignment of provinces to the supporters of Brutus and Cassius; the Senate ratified these measures and voted that none of the motions brought by Caesar should be changed. Antony left the Senate a most illustrious man: he was credited with averting civil war and demonstrating great discretion and diplomacy in matters that carried unusual difficulties and disturbances.[4]

Interesting, isn't it, how Plutarch suddenly raises Antony's level of astuteness after the crime; he was the easily-led stooge before the murder and now suddenly he was incredibly shrewd in handling matters afterward? Would this man who had been in Caesar's shadow for so many years, who was highly ambitious, just allow events to take their course without ensuring that he came out on top? I hardly think so.

And it gets even more interesting. His subsequent behavior leads me to believe that Mark Antony was behind the assassination attempt and had strategically planned it out just as he would a military campaign. Look what Plutarch says Antony did next:

> The mood of the public, however, quickly shook Antony from these reasoned considerations and he steadfastly hoped that, with Brutus out of the picture he might be the most powerful man. It happened that, when Caesar's body was carried out as was the custom, Antony delivered the eulogy in the Forum. When he noticed that the crowd was incredibly moved and enthralled he added to his praises pity and outrage at what Caesar had suffered. As he ended his speech he held aloft the slain man's tunic, bloodied and torn by the blades, and called the men responsible for these things murderers polluted by blood-guilt. The extent of his anger incited the crowd to cremate Caesar's body in the Forum after gathering up benches and tables and then, lighting torches from the pyre, to take them to the homes of the assassins and attack them.[5]

I would say nothing just "happened." Mark Antony, an excellent orator and a man who understood the people, knew exactly what their response would be, and once he settled things in the Senate, he moved on to eliminating his rivals. He was not the dupe in this; in fact, he more likely duped Brutus and Cassius, who supposedly believed they were reestablishing Rome as a republic, and then got them driven into exile once they served their purpose. In so doing, Antony now had a chance to make his mark without Julius Caesar barring his way and pushing him around. Eventually, he would be included in the New Triumvirate with Octavian and Lepidus, and it only remained a matter of time before one would win out over the others. Antony, of course, assumed he would become a member of the triumvirate, since he was the successor to Caesar in many citizens' eyes. Lepidus was not as aggressive and strong a personality as Antony, and he didn't have nearly the support. At the time of Caesar's death, Lepidus posed little challenge to Antony becoming the one-and-only leader of Rome, and I am sure Antony felt he could eliminate Lepidus with relative ease at the appropriate moment in the future. As to Octavian, he was just nineteen years old at the time of Caesar's assassination, and he probably had not impressed Antony with having enough power to be of any threat to him. Even though he was the nephew of Caesar and had spent time alongside his uncle in Rome, Octavian was unassuming in his looks, was only a minor player in recent political history, and was a known coward in battle (he would become indisposed at the very times he needed to don his armor and head out to the front line). Antony must have laughed at the thought of this wimpy excuse of a man ever challenging him for the role of dictator and, one day, emperor. Even I, as a profiler, can't fault Antony for believing he had nothing to worry about with respect to Octavian; the boy was truly an anomaly, a surprise that suddenly appeared out of nowhere to somehow outsmart and outlast everyone.

While all this turmoil was occurring, where was Cleopatra? She had been there in Rome, ensconced in a nice villa with her son, when Caesar was assassinated. She made the wise move of getting out of town and returning to Egypt. She had no idea where the chips were going to fall, and her whole future was now in limbo, her plans turned upside down. She would wait out events in Alexandria and hope that the Romans kept busy with yet more civil war while staying far away from her country. Due to distance and disturbances in the ancient world, years could pass and fortunes could radically turn depending on who was killed, who was in power, and whom those in power were kept busy dealing with. Egypt had some hope that Rome would decline, and with that, power would be more evenly distributed in the region, perhaps even affording time for the Ptolemaic Dynasty to increase its strength. Had events been different, we could have read in our history books that Cleopatra lived to a ripe old age, presiding over a wealthy country free of its oppressors. Maybe she even thought that while the loss of Julius Caesar's support was a serious blow, it might be a blessing in disguise if all the major players in Roman politics would eliminate each other in a prolonged civil war, leaving her and her beloved Egypt on their own.

CHAPTER 10

OCTAVIAN

U nfortunately for Cleopatra, and for Mark Antony, Octavian moved his pieces onto the political chessboard.

Who was this unexpected adversary? Let's take a look at Octavian (later called Augustus), the man who would become emperor of Rome, to everyone's surprise.

Octavian was only four years old when his father died. He was raised by his rather overbearing mother, his grandmother, and a manslave. He received an excellent and stern education, albeit one devoid of physical training or sports. He excelled early in public speaking. When he was fifteen, Octavian was small for his age and sickly, but a very pretty boy. He finally met his uncle, Julius Caesar. Obedient, smart, and already quite politically motivated, Octavian was very appealing to Caesar and eventually was taken under his uncle's wing. He would become Caesar's adopted son and inherit enough money upon Caesar's death to enter into politics and begin to make his mark in the governing of Rome.

Clearly, Octavian was a great politician and, in the end, the ruler of the Roman Empire. But, when Cleopatra came into conflict with him, just who was Octavian? What kind of man did she encounter, and what was it about Octavian that was to be such a problem for her?

The ancient historian Suetonius describes Octavian's interesting characteristics in his book *Lives of the Caesars*, traits which should be interpreted neither in positive light nor in a negative one but with an eye to how these characteristics contributed to Octavian's view of the world he wanted to rule, how he might view others, and how he might use his traits to control and manipulate people and events to his advantage.

For example, Suetonius observes that Octavian personally lived a very controlled life, avoiding excess in his surroundings and preferring a simple and nonflamboyant lifestyle. As Octavian was a very shrewd and calculating man, I view his pious and rather fastidious manner as a combination of motives: (1) to not be distracted from his one desire—to win and rule; (2) to present himself to others as a serious man, one to be respected; and (3) to suggest that he was a man who could be trusted by the people, as one who is not after riches, but rather an opportunity to serve the citizens. I also believe Octavian's spare lifestyle gave him a feeling of superiority over those who had less controlled lives—Julius Caesar, Mark Antony, and, certainly, Cleopatra.

In other aspects of life, it is well known that he valued moderation and was without suspicion of any vice. At first, he lived next to the Roman Forum just above the Ringmakers' Stairs in a house formerly owned by the orator Calvus. Later he lived on the Palatine but in a modest dwelling that had been Hortensius's and that stood out neither for its spaciousness nor for its refinement: the porticoes had squat columns of Alban stone and the rooms had no marble or mosaic flooring. For more than forty years, he slept in the same bedroom, winter or summer, even though he did not find the city conducive to good health in the winter and he always wintered in the city. If he ever needed to do anything in private or without interruption he had a secluded place on the top floor, which he called "Syracuse" or "little studio": he would retreat to this place or to the suburban estate of one of his freedmen.

Roomy and elaborate country houses annoyed him. He even razed to the ground a house his granddaughter Julia had lavishly built. His own estates were modest.

The economy of his décor and furnishings is evident from the couches and tables still in existence, of which most are scarcely of a quality suitable for a private citizen. They say he would only sleep on a bed if it were low and modestly made up. He scarcely ever wore clothing that was not homemade by his sister and wife and daughter and granddaughters; his toga was neither fitted or loose, the stripe neither wide nor narrow, his shoes were somewhat high-soled, so that he would appear taller than he was. He always kept in his room a set of business clothes and shoes in case of sudden and unexpected occasions.[1]

Octavian was moderate to severe with regard to life pleasures, but he was a pretty good host at dinners and celebrations. Although he himself ate sparingly, he provided elegant food for his guests, good entertainment, and, on those special occasions and holidays, he put on spectacular and fun events and gave excellent presents. He had the gift of making his guests feel welcome and excelled at stimulating conversation and encouraging others, especially those who were uncomfortable in expressing themselves, to speak up and enjoy a pleasant interaction. One might believe that Octavian was, therefore, a very warm individual with much empathy for his guests. However, as Octavian's actions throughout his entire life indicate he was always intently focused on being the leader of Rome, I would believe any entertaining he did would have been motivated by political goals, not emotional or physical needs or desires. For example, Octavian spent a great deal of time preparing and practicing speeches and preferred to read them aloud to his audience so as not to make errors. His voice was pleasing, and the calculated discourse he offered usually achieved its objective; his motive was not to bond with others but to convince them of whatever it was he wanted them to do or to believe in order to serve his political goals.

From his earliest youth, he studied rhetoric and the liberal arts with great enthusiasm and diligence. It is said that, even in the hectic conditions of the Battle of Mutina, he read, wrote, and declaimed daily.

From then on, he never spoke before the Senate, the people, or the soldiers without a planned and prepared address, even though he was not without talent in speaking extemporaneously. He adopted the practice of reading from a prepared text so as not to be betrayed by his memory or waste time in memorization. He did not even make statements to individuals, or even to his wife Livia except by writing them down and reading them aloud, lest he say too much or too little by speaking causally.[2]

We see a man who does not allow emotions or the moment to dictate his speech or actions but rather speaks exactly to ensure a specific outcome to be reached successfully and not left to chance or accident. Octavian's very regimented and controlled behavior indicate that he is a man who does not allow uncontrolled desires to get the better of him, whose ego cannot allow itself to be bruised; he can allow no man, and certainly no woman, to get the better of him. Octavian was a calculating, purposeful man who knew exactly what direction he wanted Rome to move in and who the person was to make sure it happened. The fatherless boy controlled by women, delicate, and prone to illness would prove to all that he was not the weakling they once thought he was. He strove to outlast and outmaneuver them all. And he did.

However, when he came onto the political playing field, he was not a very great general and certainly not a man's man, not the kind of fellow whom either Caesar or Antony would find ideal as a potential leader. Antony probably couldn't stand him, and Caesar no doubt found him quite acceptable as an intelligent underling and subservient enough in the presence of his mighty uncle to be tolerated, even as amusing company, but not a tough guy to worry about or one you could count on to have your back in a major conflict. In the later propaganda wars between Antony and Octavian (when they were vying for Roman support in the civil war against each other), Antony spread rumors that Caesar didn't mind having the young man around for other reasons. Suetonius said of Octavian:

For relaxation he would sometimes go fishing with a rod, and sometimes play at dice, or marbles or nuts with little boys. Boys whose
looks and manners were endearing he would seek out from all over
the place, but particularly Moors and Syrians.[3]

In his early youth he was accused of many kinds of vice. Sextus
Pompeius attacked him for being effeminate. Mark Antony alleged
he had brought his adoption by his uncle with sexual favors.[4]

In other words, Mark Antony was claiming that Octavian was
gay, something he himself was not, and that Octavian should be
looked down upon. As for Caesar—we must remember the taunts
that he was "every woman's man and every man's woman"[5]—it is
possible that Julius Caesar *did* enjoy the company of his nephew and
adopted son in more than a paternal way. Although homosexual
activity was certainly not unknown at the time, Antony's comments
clearly show that homosexuality was still something one could use as
a slur against another man. What is most important about this issue
is how Caesar might have viewed Octavian, why Octavian might
have gotten extra attention from his uncle and may have used this
to his own benefit. There is no question that Octavian had a slight
and feminine body, and he did not seem to display overtly masculine
traits in his mannerisms or his lifestyle. He did marry, but there were
political reasons to do this, and it was claimed that he slept with
important men's wives; but Suetonius explained his dalliances in this
way:

> Even his friends do not deny that he was guilty of adultery, but they
> justify it by claiming that he acted not out of lust but rather as a
> calculated strategy: he could more easily learn the strategies of his
> enemies through their wives.[6]

I would have to side with Antony and those friends in their
assessment of Octavian's sexual preferences that he likely preferred
men to women in the bedroom. I find the likelihood of Caesar being

bisexual in behavior not too unbelievable, either (fun is fun, especially when one has no females about to make use of). Antony, however, appeared to be heterosexual to the core and saw himself as the height of masculinity in battle, with his comrades, and with his women.

Now, some might object to this discussion of the sexual appetites of these Romans; after all, this is a private affair, so what is the point of discussing it here? Actually, in profiling personalities and behaviors, all the interests and proclivities of those being analyzed are important to the whole makeup of the person. For Cleopatra, this issue was of extreme importance. Her liaison with Julius Caesar fed his ego; she had his "son" and heir to the Egyptian throne, and she served as an attractive partner in handling his interests in Egypt. Later, after Caesar's death, she hooked up with Antony to conquer Octavian and rule an empire, to be a royal couple, produce a couple of children, and live the good life. As for Octavian, there was no chance to liaise with him in any way, and Cleopatra knew it.

What could she offer him? Clearly not sex, since Octavian was not much of a womanizer (at least not in the long-term sense of a relationship), and not even a tryst would lead him to gaining information from her husband, as she might have heard was his reason for bedding connected women on rare occasion . . . the buck stopped with her. Octavian had no interest in attaining the grand and lavish lifestyle of Alexandria; he did not appreciate her cleverness and cunning; and given his temperament it is likely he wouldn't trust her. When it came down to choosing between partnering with a Roman after Caesar's death, Antony was simply the only choice Cleopatra had. Thankfully, he would end up needing her support to continue his fight against Octavian, and he enjoyed the other amenities of Alexandria and the royal lady. So Antony and Cleopatra it would be, but, right now, let's backtrack to what happened after the Ides of March.

Julius Caesar is dead; Brutus and Cassius are banished, leaving Mark Antony temporarily the only man of the hour in Rome. I am sure he was feeling pretty good about how the assassination turned out, until that blasted will of Julius Caesar was made public. It seems

Caesar wrote a new will during 45 BCE, and when his father-in-law read the contents of the will to Antony, he was not pleased. It stated that his nephew, Octavian, would be one of his heirs (the others were his grandchildren, whose inheritance would be relatively insignificant). Caesar gave Octavian three-quarters of his estate, which made him an extremely rich man.

That, Antony could have dealt with. It was the provision making Octavian his son, which was rather unusual but legally allowable, that was the insult. What came along with that adoption was Caesar's name, his soldiers, and the citizens who loved him. Octavian was now set up to enter politics at the top, which was something he would want to do in the shortest amount of time possible.

The will was a major blow to Antony and a very great and unexpected gift for Octavian. It wasn't, however, smooth sailing for Octavian to work his way into the triumvirate. He had many political hurdles to clear, and he and Antony would clash numerous times. Octavian had to command his new troops and massage the distraught Caesarians who were struggling to maintain control of Rome. He inherited a lot of money to work with, which he put to good use. Finally, as Caesar's son got the chance to rule Rome, and with this unexpected and very powerful newcomer into politics, Antony realized he had a major adversary to contend with—one who would do everything he could to be the person to gain Caesar's throne, including annihilating his political adversaries. Octavian may not have been much to look at, and Antony may have mistakenly presumed that being a weak man physically meant being a weak man mentally. There he would have erred in his judgment. Octavian was to prove himself to be the brightest of any man to rule Rome.

For Cleopatra, Octavian was her worst nightmare. He was a man she couldn't partner with due to his physical issues and personality, but he was also a man whose intellect meant he would meet her head-on when it came to playing for the ultimate prize. I believe Cleopatra was fully aware of what she was dealing with; the only snake that would do her in would be one with the head of a Roman.

CHAPTER 11

THE ROAD TO ACTIUM:
PART ONE—THE CONFLICT

S o much is made of Cleopatra's love affairs with Julius Caesar and Mark Antony, her passionate love and lust for them and their lust and love for her. In reality, it is likely that neither love nor lust were motivators in the hearts of these three great leaders of history. Instead, another dyad of needs, namely, intense desire for power and control, would be the major factors. The desire for power and control is the major trait of narcissists and psychopaths, along with being extremely self-centered, ruthless, grandiose, coldblooded, manipulative, and not a bit remorseful when it comes to the woes they heap on others in their quest for glory. Narcissism and psychopathy are very closely related; assigning one label or the other to certain individuals is difficult when all we can do is read about them from ancient historians. It is also only a matter of degree when we are not dealing with two completely different sets of personality disorders but when the two are intertwined. I believe psychopaths are simply farther down the narcissism scale to the degree that they do not even recognize the need to have anyone else's approval or admiration; others become the psychopath's pawns, nothing but total objects to be used, abused, or removed. Some psychologists prefer to differentiate between a psychopath and a sociopath, claiming that the former is somehow biologically determined while the latter is created by the society he lives in. These professionals assign lower-functioning individuals the term of *psychopath* and higher-functioning ones the label *sociopath*. In reality, there is no scientific difference between the two; in my opinion, there are simply less-educated and socialized psychopaths and more highly educated and socialized psychopaths. The lower strata of psychopaths fill a large number of prison cells; the higher strata may find spots open for them on Wall Street and high political offices. Oftentimes, many of us don't even realize that those we work with, hang with, are married to, or raise to adulthood, are psychopaths or pathological narcissists. We just wonder why we always feel as though we have no power with these individuals, that something is not quite right about them. But many of us chalk it up to some previous difficult life issue or culture or "just being him" or "just being her." At some point, we end up on the losing end of the relationship and we aren't quite sure why.

It can get very interesting during those times when psychopathic or highly narcissistic personalities have to deal with each other, when they have to get along for the benefit of both parties, or wind up dueling to the death. One thing is for certain: I doubt Julius Caesar, Mark Antony, Octavian, or Cleopatra trusted each other. They each recognized that just as they considered certain individuals useful to them until they were not, their counterparts saw them in exactly the same light. It was always a cat-and-mouse game, even with those they bedded, married, or confronted in battle. If two psychopaths or narcissists end up together, they often can't get along and so quickly go their separate ways; at other times, they become a dangerous team that goes out with a bang like Bonnie and Clyde; or one of them eventually out-psychopaths the other.

Pompey lost out to Caesar, Caesar to Antony, and, now, the stage was set for the final throw down. With a "republic" that had not really been one since before Lucius Cornelius Sulla (138–78 BCE) and clearly was not going to return to a democratic state with such strong personalities and such a massive amount of power and money to be controlled by anyone who could rise to the top, the Roman

Senate knew all too well that the best it could do was attempt to divide the power among three dictators, a triumvirate, in a somewhat-poor attempt to avoid being ruled by a king. In fact, all the Senate did was delay the inevitable and encourage civil war between those who had their eye on total power. I do believe, though, that the Senate, having chosen Octavian as one of the triumvirate, might have considered this choice to be their last hope of regaining the republic. At that time (about 45 BCE), Octavian was playing a very good game of appealing to the Roman senators with intelligent discourse, words rather than war, and he appeared to support the idea of a true republic; and, being a man of diminutive physical stature, maybe the Senate thought Octavian preferred to use his brain rather than brawn to rule, to share power, and to delegate without damning those around him. Octavian, I am sure, made them believe this; he was a very patient and careful tactician. They wouldn't know what had happened until it was too late. Somehow he convinced them that he would restore the republic, yet all the while he was chipping away at their liberties and rights. Eventually he had them convinced that only an emperor could possibly govern a massive Roman empire—and they agreed. Octavian was truly the heir to Julius Caesar's rule, the only one with the incredibly high level of intelligence, ruthlessness, dispassionate decision making, and political savvy to overcome the other contenders—and, lucky for him, no one realized that one of the most brilliant psychopaths ever to rise in the political world was one of their own, until it was too late.

Cleopatra no doubt knew just how dangerous Octavian was by the time she and Antony teamed up against their common enemy. She knew she would need more than Antony's military skills and Egypt's wealth to prevail or even survive. She would have to outsmart the man at some point in the game.

Octavian grew up without a father, rarely seeing him when he was a tot and losing him to illness when he was just a boy of four. Octavian was raised by his grandmother and then by his mother, a seeming combination of overbearance and overindulgence. However, his father and stepfather were both politicians, and he didn't lack a good education during his youth. He learned to compensate for his lack of physical stature with a quick mind and the ability to size up situations and people to his advantage. By the time he came into Caesar's life as a teenager, he had great skill at sliding into a role that pleased Caesar; obviously he did a pretty good job in a short time, considering how Caesar made him heir so soon after. Manipulation is a key trait of psychopathy, and a smart and educated psychopath can essentially con everyone with whom he comes in contact. Considering Octavian's meteoric rise, he likely was a master at it.

After Caesar's murder, Octavian really milked his connection, roused the emotions of Caesar's supporters both in the political sphere and among the populace, and he waged a propaganda campaign, his first major one, due to Antony's own poor behavior. Antony managed to get control of Caesar's finances by convincing his widow, Calpernia, that he should handle them. Not long thereafter, a large sum of money went missing. Antony suddenly was doing quite well in the financial department. Octavian took this opportunity to spread rumors about Antony to everyone who would listen. Of course, Octavian was a thief himself, somehow getting hold of the Parthian campaign money and then using it to pay the citizens what Caesar had promised them before his death, showing up Antony quite effectively.

Antony struck back with his own slander campaign, accusing Octavian of trying to assassinate him. Back and forth it went, each man trying to turn the populace or the army or the Senate against the other and win their affections. In other words, it was politics as usual in ancient Rome. Then Octavian learned to lead an army, and in spite of the stories that he was never around when the action started, there at least was a claim in circulation that he actually appeared in the middle of a foray he led against Antony. Now the Senate established the New Triumvirate and for a period of time, they were civil to each other, even though Octavian got the short stick of the distributed territories and Lepidus was just a yes-man for Antony. Antony ended up with the greatest power of the three, including the best part of the Roman territory to govern. But Antony and Octavian did join forces in a reign of terror on their adversaries in Rome by executing more than three thousand of the upper class; so neither one of them could be called a nice guy. Then they joined militarily to attack the ousted Cassius and Brutus, who were mounting a campaign against the duo. Their eventual defeat of these killers of Caesar eliminated that political annoyance. This occurred in 42 BCE. Then Pompey's son, Sextus, attacked Antony and Octavian, and this part of the civil war lasted for the next six years. There were other outbreaks of unrest and other civil wars, so this was no time of peace for the Romans. Cleopatra, however, was likely quite pleased that the Romans were busy trying to kill each other off, leaving Egypt out of the fray for the time being.

Antony and Octavian continued to tolerate each other, and in 40 BCE, Antony married Octavian's sister, Octavia. For three years, Antony and Octavian managed to continue to get along, and when they both were finding themselves on the losing end of battles, Octavian against Sextus, and Antony in his failing Parthian campaign, they renewed the triumvirate. This political move lasted one year until Octavian defeated Sextus and got rid of Lepidus behind Antony's back.

Now there were just the two, Octavian and Antony, pitted against each other. And this time there would be no reconciliation; one would emerge victorious to win the title of emperor. At this point, Cleopatra and Egypt found themselves in trouble. When, not if, one of the Roman generals became solo dictator, Egypt would be under his thumb, in some fashion. Cleopatra's only hope would be to attempt a repeat of the type of relationship she had with Caesar, one in which her new partner would see the reasonableness of her continued rule in Egypt with her son as long as she gave Rome what it needed. She saw that linking herself to Antony, offering him her vast wealth, troops, and ships to defeat Octavian, was her best option; she would get on his good side early and hope that he would win the day, and she could continue to be of use to him in her own Ptolemaic way.

She knew there was no point in trying to partner with Octavian, and it didn't matter if he hated her for hooking up with Antony and supporting Antony's offense against him. Being fully aware of the kind of man Octavian was, Cleopatra knew he would not tolerate her continuing as pharaoh, nor would he even desire her to remain alive after aligning herself with his adversary. So it seemed to Cleopatra that the only prudent thing to do was throw all her weight behind Antony and hope that he would win. I agree; she made the wisest decision, indeed the only decision she could under the circumstances.

For Cleopatra it wasn't about increasing the Ptolemaic Empire; the Ptolemies never worried much about extending their territory; they preferred to annex nearby nations in order to protect their country, their ports, and their trade routes. Unlike Philip, Alexander, the Persians, the Parthians, and the Romans, the Egyptians were content to control their own lands since they were terribly wealthy already, in wheat and in gold and in their control of valuable trade routes; so other than timber that they obtained from a few locations outside Egypt, they were quite happy to stay within their own borders. History has been quite unfair to Cleopatra in this matter, often claiming she was terribly greedy and used Antony to further her own imperialistic desires, but I see little truth in this. She appeared to be content being the Egyptian pharaoh, as had the entire Ptolemaic line for centuries. She didn't need expansion; she needed protection, and Antony was her only hope.

CHAPTER 12

THE ROAD TO ACTIUM: PART TWO—THE PARTNERS

Some historians fault Cleopatra for teaming up with Antony, claiming that she was poison for him, that she caused him to lose the battle of Actium and then deserted him in the midst of fighting to save her own skin, at least for the moment. They believe that Antony was so enamored with Cleopatra that he was blind to her foolish choices that ended up depleting his manpower and causing him the loss to Octavian; and that then, so shackled by his love for her, he left his men to their doom as he chased after Cleopatra, following her to Egypt and committing suicide with her when there was no escape left. In other words, Cleopatra ruined Antony and took him down with her. According to this view, Octavian won by taking advantage of their mistakes and, had it not been for Cleopatra, maybe Antony would have been the victor and eventually become emperor of the Roman Empire.

That is quite a bit of anti-Cleopatra spin, courtesy of Octavian, Plutarch, and a host of future detractors. In reality, neither Cleopatra nor Antony made particularly bad choices, and Octavian was one lucky guy at Actium. Well, at least luck played a part in his success, and it is hard to determine how much was strictly unexpected good fortune and how much of the "luck" was actually of his own doing.

Luck is a funny thing; some people seem to have great things come to them, and it appears those fortuitous events "just happened." Yet much of what passes for luck is actually a combination of hard work, risk taking, networking, and clever strategy. When the "lucky" thing happens, people are unaware of what the individual did to get to the point where he was in the position to be the beneficiary of something good, or they have forgotten the past entirely. For example, Antony wouldn't have had the "luck" of having Caesar bring him back to Rome as consul if he hadn't first made himself useful or needed. Likewise, Octavian wouldn't have received his windfall in Caesar's will if he hadn't impressed Caesar through his behavior or, perhaps, sex. And Cleopatra wouldn't have become partner with Caesar or Antony if she hadn't polished her political and social skills and maneuvered herself into a position to pitch her usefulness to each of them.

Sometimes bad luck is not accidental, either. Ptolemy XIII had bad "luck" when Caesar chose Cleopatra over him, but then he beheaded Pompey and acted foolishly around Caesar, which didn't exactly inspire confidence in his ability to rule Egypt or work well with the Romans. Cleopatra's and Antony's less-than-stellar treatment of King Herod and the Nabataeans (Anthony had given their balsam groves to Cleopatra, and then Cleopatra had incited war between Herod and the Nabataeans, causing both parties to have negative feelings toward them) probably created the bad "luck" Cleopatra encountered when she needed their help or at least needed them not to turn on her (like when the Nabataeans burned her ships when she first attempted to flee Egypt after the Actium debacle).

Then again, certain things truly are just luck, like weather and outside players popping up out of nowhere and creating havoc, or the unexpected murder of Caesar. These events are quite often just bad luck and unfortunate timing. While Caesar may have made his own misfortunes because of his attitude and dictatorship style, the impact on Cleopatra was collateral damage. As we follow the history of the intersection of Cleopatra, Antony, and Octavian, I will attempt to separate the events caused by the behaviors of each player from those that were truly beyond their control, whether for good or ill.

Octavian certainly worked hard to raise his status and level of power after he benefited tremendously from the assassination of Caesar, courtesy, in my opinion, of his nemesis, Antony. On the one hand, he could have been raised up politically by Caesar had the latter not been murdered, but who knows how patient the ambitious Octavian would have been and how long he could have stood being in Caesar's shadow. He may have eventually been forced into making some "luck" of his own by eliminating Caesar in the same manner as Antony. Of course, he may have been Antony's target of assassination if Antony didn't take kindly to being displaced by the nephew of Caesar. We will never know how history would have played out if the Ides of March had gone by peacefully.

A very fascinating facet of Octavian's life and luck centers around his health. He was considered a weakling and a frail child, and this image carried into adulthood and stayed with him all his life until his death at seventy-seven years of age! I am sure countless enemies held out hope that he would keel over at some opportune time, but this never happened. Which leads me to question how physically challenged he really was. Did Octavian actually fall victim to as many illnesses as have been reported, or was he "incapacitated" at convenient times? Was Octavian feigning illness and playing people at the same time? Certainly, he was a master manipulator, so it could very well be that his precarious health was nothing but a ploy to get out of certain situations he felt he would benefit from avoiding. Did he play his role as fragile and frail to fool people into overlooking the crafty mastermind behind the near "invalid" who would soon deal a fatal blow to them?

I think we may be looking at a combination of reality and spin. Early on Octavian may have learned from some real event how useful it could be to play sick and unable to rise to physical activities like going to battle. How convenient! Mocking aside, although skipping the fight doesn't do much for one's image as a general, sometimes it makes more sense to stay alive and be the man behind the scenes, delegating the job of general to someone like the brilliant Agrippa, Octavian's finest general, rather than get oneself killed trying to impress people. I believe Octavian realized he would never rise to the level of as beloved a general as his uncle, Julius Caesar, or his adversary, Mark Antony; so, being a thinking man, he chose to pull the strings behind the curtain instead of risking misfortune on the battlefield.

It is claimed that he had headaches and epileptic seizures that grew worse as he grew older. Yet it is also stated that he ate a simple diet and was an excellent horseman who could ride bareback at full gallop, which meant he had strong leg muscles and he was capable of withstanding long journeys. But he was also quite often reported to be ill, unable to fight or travel, or indisposed at certain times. Let's look at the reported incidents of illness and see if we can detect a pattern that might indicate Octavian was dissembling about his health or if such times really inconvenienced him and were true debilitating sicknesses.

One of the first reported incidences of Octavian falling ill at a very important moment occurred during the combined efforts of Antony and Octavian to attack Philippi and take down Brutus and Cassius. It was said that he had dropsy, a fluid accumulation in his body. I am not sure why he should have suffered this malady since there is no particular cause for such a response in the body that is mentioned. Some think it was psychosomatic, that he freaked out when it came to having to go to battle and risk his life. I think he held back with this excuse in order to let Antony take the risk alone since the outcome of the battle was very much in doubt. It would be a win-win situation for Octavian. If Brutus and Cassius were vanquished, these two enemies would be taken care of and Octavian would still be around to take advantage of fewer opposing factions. If Antony was killed in battle, then Octavian would be ahead of the game. I think it may have been a strategic decision and as a new player, so young and frail-looking, he probably reasoned that he could get away with not leading his men into battle.

As it turned out, Antony got himself into a bad situation, not one that ended in his death but one that meant a lack of success for the

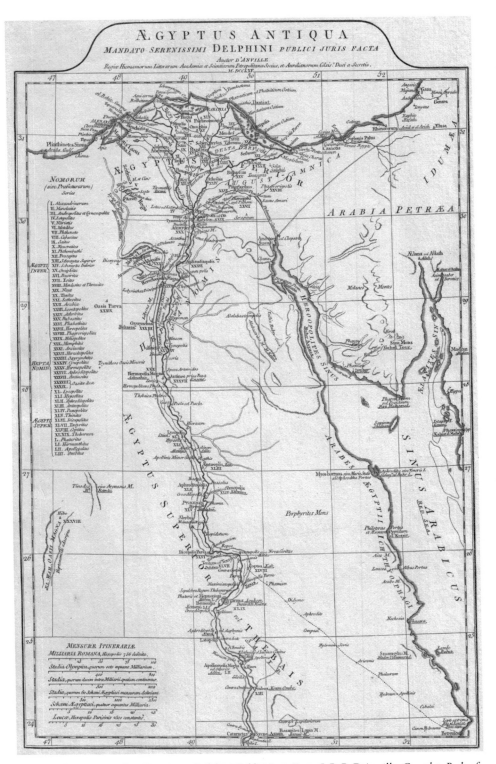

Aegyptus Antiqua Mandato Serenissimi Delphini Publici Juris Facta. J. B. B. D'Anville, *Complete Body of Ancient Geography* (London: Laurie and Whittle, 1795).

The Nile at sunset in Cairo. *Photo by Pat Brown.*

Cairo from the Citadel. *Photo by Jennifer Walker.*

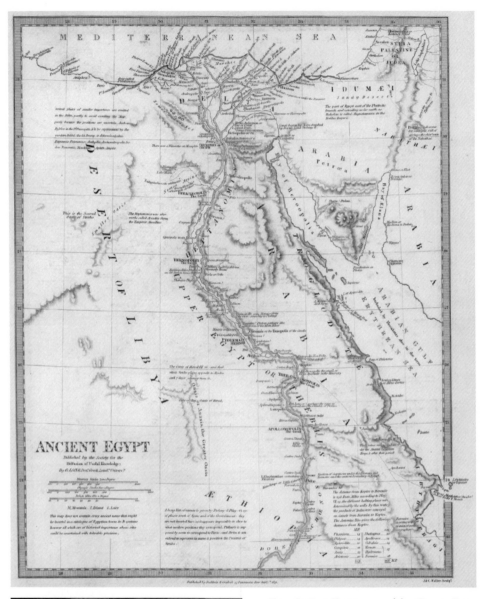

Top: Ancient Egypt, created by George Long and the Society for the Diffusion of Useful Knowledge in 1831 and published in *Maps of the Society for the Diffusion of Useful Knowledge*, vol. 1 (London: Chapman and Hall, 1844). *Image courtesy of the David Rumsey Map Collection, www.davidrumsey.com.*

Left: A cobra of the sort that Cleopatra supposedly smuggled into her tomb. © *Atlantic Productions Ltd.*

The immense desert across which Cleopatra would attempt to drag her ships on rollers. *Photo by Pat Brown.*

Pat at the Step Pyramid. *Photo by Jennifer Walker.*

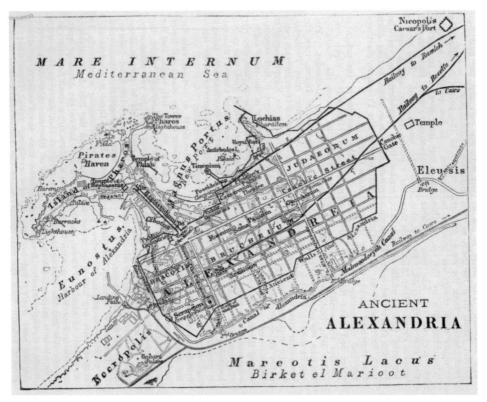

Unknown author, *Ancient Alexandria* (1888), from Travelers in the Middle East Archive (TIMEA), http://hdl.handle.net/1911/9433.

The Step Pyramid of Djoser at Saqqara. *Photo by Jennifer Walker.*

The Great Pyramid through the window of the nearby Pizza Hut. *Photo by Jennifer Walker.*

The Bent Pyramid of Sneferu at Dashur. *Photo by Jennifer Walker.*

The Red Pyramid at Dashur. *Photo by Jennifer Walker.*

At the Red Pyramid, the Great Pyramid, and many tombs in the Valley of the Kings, one often walks up to the tomb and then down into the tomb via a long passageway. There are no windows and there is no roof one can ascend to and stand on. *Photo by Pat Brown.*

Descending into a tomb in the Valley of the Kings. *Photo by Pat Brown.*

More than two thousand years later, the architecture of the Temple of Isis at Dendera shows solid construction, which I found to be consistent in all the temple structures and tombs I visited; there are no gaps in the walls or where the floors meet the walls that would permit a snake to slither its way out of any sealed room. *Photo by Jennifer Walker.*

Even this passageway down into a tomb in the Valley of the Kings, which is far older than the temples and tombs of Cleopatra's time, shows how solid the construction was and how there are no holes or gaps anywhere for asps to escape from the interior of a burial vault. *Photo by Pat Brown.*

Face-to-face with a marble head of a Ptolemaic queen from the first century BCE at the Musei Capitolini, Rome. © *Atlantic Productions Ltd.*

Underwater archeologist Jean-Yves Empereur helps prepare Pat to dive in Alexandria Harbor to see the ruins of the alleged Cleopatra's palace. © *Atlantic Productions Ltd.*

The amphitheater in Ephesus where Cleopatra and Antony sojourned with their fleet while making their way to the Battle of Actium. Ephesus, once a Greek and Roman city, is six miles from the Aegean Sea in present-day Turkey. *Photo by Pat Brown.*

Ruins of ancient temples mix in with the modern buildings of today's Rome. *Photo by Pat Brown.*

Pharoah Cheops's funerary boat at the Solar Boat Museum in Giza. *Photo by Pat Brown.*

Depiction of the making of Cheops's boat in the Solar Boat Museum. *Artist unknown.*

The Temple of Karnak gives us an idea of the height of the windows and the roof in an ancient Egyptian temple. Plutarch claims Cleopatra and her handmaidens hauled the dying Antony up by a rope into a window or onto the roof of the building into which she had locked herself. *Photo by Jennifer Walker.*

The hypostyle hall at Luxor (without its roof). *Photo by Pat Brown.*

The magnificent columns of the hypostyle hall in the Temple of Isis at Dendera. *Photo by Pat Brown.*

Egyptologist Dr. Said Gohary explains to Pat the meanings of the reliefs on the walls of the Temple of Isis at Dendera. © *Atlantic Productions Ltd.*

Reliefs of Cleopatra (as Isis) with her son Caesarion. © *Atlantic Productions Ltd.*

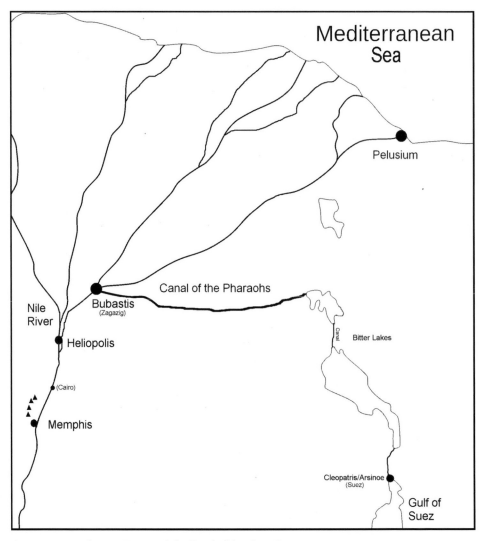

Approximation of Lower Egypt and the Canal of the Pharaohs.

mission; he needed reinforcements, so Octavian, still ill, somehow managed to crawl out of bed and take his men in. However, when Cassius later attacked Octavian's camp and speared all his men, Octavian's body was not on the ground with them. Yes, he had removed himself in his "illness" to a safer location and survived the rout. He was called a coward, but somehow I think his decision served him well. Being the lesser of two evils, an image of weakness could be used as a ruse to attract opponents to a fight that they would find was more in Octavian's favor than they thought. Octavian also made up for his wimpy image by having his henchmen brutally kill selected victims and watching with ice in his veins. He may not have shown himself to be courageous in battle, but he was a rather scary, sadistic guy to be feared in many other ways.

In his book *Augustus*, Anthony Everitt writes of Octavian's return to Rome after he and Antony shared the victory over Brutus and Casius, and, apparently, I am not the only one to question Octavian's use of sickness as a ruse:

> Octavian was carried back to Italy, where his arrival was awaited with fear and loathing. His illness flared up again dangerously on the journey, and he stayed for a while at Brundisium. He was thought unlikely to survive and at one point a rumor circulated that he was actually dead. Some thought his sickness was a charade, that he was delaying his return because he was planning some devilish new scheme for fleecing the citizenry. Despite his reassurances to the contrary, people hid their property or left town.[1]

Being sick or dying or dead is a great way to buy time, toy with people's emotions, and get sympathy. With Octavian being a master manipulator, I tend to lean toward his use of his health as a foil.

When Octavian went off on another joint venture with Antony at Brundisium with far more troops, his illness, yet again, forced him to let Antony take the lead, alone. Even during his victorious final battle against Sextus, Octavian was flat on his back while Agrippa won the day.

It is no wonder Antony did not like the man.

As the showdown with Antony and Cleopatra was yet to come, I am sure both Cleopatra and Antony were hoping Octavian wasn't faking all his illnesses and would do them a favor and die during one of them. Although that never did happen (and, as it turned out, Octavian lived a long, long life), neither of them could be absolutely sure he was totally faking these incidents. The hope that illness might slow him down or do him in always must have been in the back of their minds as one possibility that could change the course of events. Even putting him in physically or emotionally stressful situations could be a tactic to try to force a change of outcome. Outlasting Octavian, I believe was always something Cleopatra kept in mind to the bitter end, that one more day before any showdown was one more day that might mean Octavian's health would decide the fate of all involved.

As an amusing side note, here is but another example of why Cleopatra chose to partner with Antony and not Octavian. When Lepidus was eliminated from the triumvirate (sent into exile) and the uprising of Sextus was ended (Sextus escaped but was found and executed), it was just Antony or Octavian who held the future of the Roman people in their hands. The remaining republicans, who still held onto some hope that Rome would escape the rule of an emperor, were willing to accept a dictator who they felt would rule in a less autocratic way or would at least be a bit flexible. Whom did they choose to throw their weight behind? Antony, the lesser of two evils, for many of the same reasons Cleopatra preferred him to Octavian: he was more amenable to others and a hell of a lot more fun.

CHAPTER 13

THE ROAD TO ACTIUM: PART THREE — THE PREPARATIONS

One thing that is rather deceptive and causes us not to quite understand why things happened the way they did in the ancient world is that time is often "condensed" in the books we read. From one page to the next, years may pass, but there is a tendency not to realize exactly how much time actually went by. Also, with what are sometimes long distances being covered by foot, horse, camel, and ship during the days of Cleopatra, the time that may pass from the moment one decides to invade a country or embark on a visit to when that invasion or visit actually takes place may be months or even years. Travel was extraordinarily slow, relative to today's standard, and because of this, there was always a big problem with carrying enough provisions to make the trek. One had to bring them, purchase them along the way at outposts or major centers of trade, or confiscate them from the local people—essentially force the locals to turn over whatever is needed for the survival of one's men. Even obtaining drinking water could be a major problem.

Here is the way some people think of the history of Cleopatra: Cleopatra becomes queen and soon Julius Caesar shows up. She beds him, has a baby, and soon thereafter Caesar is murdered. So, a few months later, she hooks up with Mark Antony and soon she has twins; and then a few more months later, they go off to fight Octavian at Actium. They lose and run back to Egypt. A few weeks pass, Octavian shows up, and both Cleopatra and Antony die. If you ask a number of people how long it was between the time Cleopatra became queen and date of her death, they would say two hours—the length of a film! Yes, I am joking; but, seriously, some would say, "Maybe, five or six years. . . . Maybe seven."

In reality, nearly twenty years passed. To get a good feel of the time frame of all the events, let me lay them out.

Cleopatra's birth—69 BCE
Cleopatra becomes queen—51 BCE (age 18)
Cleopatra hooks up with Caesar—48 BCE (age 21)
Caesar is murdered—44 BCE (age 25)
Cleopatra hooks up with Antony—41 BCE (age 28)
Battle of Actium—31 BCE (age 38)
Cleopatra dies in Alexandria—30 BCE (age 39)

From this time line, one can see that Cleopatra was with Caesar for four years and with Antony for eleven years; the struggle between Octavian and Antony carried on for fourteen years; and it took Octavian nearly a year to arrive and deliver the final blow to Cleopatra and Antony in Alexandria after their loss at Actium. With such large blocks of time, anything can happen in the interim, and this is important to keep in mind when we try to get inside the heads of Cleopatra, Antony, and Octavian. Life had a different pace in ancient Egypt and Rome (and decisions were made on the way things worked back then—how fast one could accomplish one's goals and what might slow one down or completely disrupt one's plan).

Two other issues are extremely important to keep in mind when it comes to how Cleopatra and her Roman counterparts would make decisions: the prevailing weather conditions and the current status of ongoing wars and military actions. The entire region was a war zone for the whole of their lives, and one always had to take into account who might attack, who might keep your enemy busy and at bay, or the chances that your land would get caught up in the power struggles of someone else's war. The other major factor was weather, which had a massive influence on how things often turned out. I believe the biggest "luck" factor was indeed the weather, which is the most difficult factor to predict and one that could completely upend one's plans and lead to disaster. Invasions could be stalled or entire fleets run aground in a storm.

❖❖❖

After Caesar's murder, Cleopatra escaped to Egypt and waited things out. I have no doubt that she hoped the Roman civil wars would end with the empire crumbling and Egypt being left alone or, even better, her native land would rise up and become a stronger player again among the Mediterranean nation-states.

She enjoyed three years of peace while the Romans were at war with each other. Then Antony came calling or, shall I say, called for her. It was an invitation she had little choice but to accept, even though Plutarch writes that she played coy for a while before agreeing to visit him. One has to give her credit for arriving with such outrageous style. She made it appear as though she were honoring Antony with a seat at her parade rather than arriving to answer a call from the future occupier. Although Plutarch may be exaggerating Cleopatra's arrival in Tarsus (a quite cultural Turkish city of the time, just a few miles inland from the Mediterranean Sea), one can get a feel from his prose that Cleopatra was working to impress Antony with her wealth and lifestyle, two things Antony would be interested in. He needed her funding for his military plans, especially the Parthia campaign, and, besides, he was a sucker for a good time. Just as Cleopatra was wise in how she approached Caesar, she was also bright enough to tailor her meeting with this new Roman man to his unique needs and desires so that she could ensure herself a secure place in his future and make her own future as bright as possible. As Plutarch wrote:

> She had received many letters from Antony and his friends summoning her but she disdained and mocked the man by sailing up the River Cydnus in a ship with its stern covered in gold, with purple sails fluttering, with rowers pulling with silver oars as flutes played accompanied by pipes and lyres. Cleopatra reclined beneath a canopy embroidered with gold, decked out to resemble a painting of Aphrodite, and boys, made to look like the Erotes we see in art, stood on either side and fanned her. Likewise, her most beautiful maids, dressed as Nereids and Graces, stood, some by the rudders and some by the ropes. The marvelous scent of copious incense fills the riverbanks. Some of the men escort her from either side, directly from the river, while others come down from the city to see the sight. As the crowd thinned in the marketplace finally Antony was left alone sitting on the speaker's platform. The news went around that Aphrodite had come to revel with Dionysus for the good of Asia. Then he sent word inviting her to dinner; instead she suggested he come to her. He, wishing to display his courtesy and kindness, accepted and went. He found the preparations beyond words and was struck most of all by the multitude of lights. Indeed it is said that so many were suspended and displayed everywhere at once and were ordered and positioned at such intricate angles to one another and in such patterns, like squares and circles, that it was a sight of beauty and delight for the viewer.[1]

This show was probably just some frosting for the cake, since both Antony and Cleopatra already knew that they needed each other, but they also needed to maintain a level of diplomatic dignity. This showy pretext allowed the necessary partnership to be sugarcoated and spiced up, thereby making the whole concept of cooperation much more palatable.

Why, then, at that particular time, did Antony send for Cleopatra? He certainly knew that Octavian would go to any extreme to attack his character and stir up as much animosity as he possibly could with the Roman people, the ruling class, and the Senate. Octavian did not disappoint him. He went all out, trashing Cleopatra and Antony's liaison with her.

Cassius Dio writes his interpretation of how Octavian viewed his two enemies and how he might have presented them to the Roman people:

> Who would not be dismayed to see the queen of the Egyptians with Roman bodyguards? Who would not lament to hear that Roman knights and Senators fawn over her like eunuchs? Who would not moan to hear and see Antony himself, twice a consul, many times a commander, to whom, along with me, leadership was entrusted and so many cities, so many legions—who would not weep to see that he has now left behind his ancestral customs, that he has imitated foreign and barbaric ones that he does not respect the laws or gods of his ancestors but bows before that woman like Isis or Selene, names her children Helios and Selene and finally calls himself Osiris and Dionysus, and, after all these things, he gives as gifts whole islands and parts of continents, as if he were the lord of the whole earth and sea? These things seem unbelievable and amazing to you soldiers, I know; and because of that, you should be even more outraged. Indeed, if what you do not believe when you hear it turns out to be true, and if that man commits crimes of luxury at which anyone would shudder to learn, then how is it not appropriate for your anger to know no bounds?
>
> And yet, at first, I was so enthusiastic about him that I shared with him my command, married my sister to him, and gave him legions. After this, I was so sympathetic and kind to him that I did not wish to go to war with him because he insulted my sister, or because he did not care for the children he had with her, or because he honored an Egyptian woman instead of her, or because he gave that woman almost all the things that are rightfully yours, or because of anything else. I considered the first reason to be that the same approach should not be taken with both Cleopatra and Antony, for she was clearly an enemy because of what she did and also because she was a foreigner, but he as a citizen, might possibly

be reasoned with. Secondly, I hoped that, even if he did not want to, he might, under duress, change his mind because of the decrees passed against Cleopatra. Because of this, I did not declare war on him. But he, since he despises and disparages these favors he will not receive pardon even if we wish to grant it, and will not receive pity, even if we feel it. He is either irrational or insane (for I have heard this and believe that he is under that abominable woman's spell) and has no respect for our magnanimity and kindness, but, since he is enslaved to that woman he brings war and its dangers which he voluntarily incurs on her behalf, against us and against his fatherland. Therefore, what choice do we have but to defend ourselves against him and Cleopatra.

Therefore, let no one consider him a Roman but rather an Egyptian; let no one call him Antony but rather Serapion; let no one believe that he was one time a consul or commander but rather a gymnasiarch. He himself has chosen willingly the latter rather than the former titles; casting off all the respectable titles of his homeland, he has become a cymbal player of Canopus. Let no one fear that he will turn the tide of war, for previously he was nothing outstanding, as those of you who beat him at Mutina know well. But even if at one time he had some success in an expedition when he was on our side, be confident that now he has destroyed his abilities through his change in lifestyle: it is not possible for someone living in royal luxury and being treated like a woman to think or act like a man, because it is always true that one's behavior reflects one's way of life. As evidence I submit that he, having fought one battle in all this time and having engaged in one campaign, lost many citizens in the battle, shamefully retreated from Praaspa, and lost many more in the flight. As a result, if this were a contest of dancing ridiculously or comic buffoonery and one of us had to compete against him, our man would surely lose, for Antony is the expert at these skills; since, however, the contest is one of weapons and battle, what could anyone fear from him? The fitness of his body? He is over the hill and thoroughly effeminate. His mental powers? He has the mind of a woman and the physical desires of one too. His respect for our gods? He fights against them as he does against his homeland. His loyalty to his allies? Who does not know that he deceived the

Armenian and put him in chains? His fairness to his friends? Who has not seen those whom he has wickedly destroyed? His reputation among the soldiers? Who among them has not condemned him? This is evident because the crowds of them desert to our side on a daily basis. Indeed, I think that all of our citizens will follow suit, just as has happened previously, when he went from Brundisium to Gaul. As long as the men expected to enrich themselves without risk, some were very happy to be among his troops, but they will not wish to fight against us, their fellow citizens, on behalf of things that are not theirs, especially if it is possible for them to be safe and to get rich without danger if they join us.[2]

I think Dio probably did a fine job channeling Octavian through his writing; was Octavian's harsh propaganda campaign denigrating Antony's character, his military prowess, and his commitment as a Roman leader to his people, even as a Roman citizen and husband and father, unfair and totally without merit? Actually, I tend to think someone is a good profiler, either Dio or Octavian; I think the description of Antony was rather spot-on at this the point in his life, right before he and Octavian butted heads at Actium.

The three players left in the game for Mediterranean dominance took their places. At Tarsus, Antony and Cleopatra would solidify their partnership and begin their relationship. Octavian, the odd man out, would ready himself to do battle against the couple. And why exactly did Cleopatra decide to hook up with Antony? Well, from the time of Julius Caesar's assassination until this point in time, Cleopatra had had her freedom and had ruled her kingdom with little interference. But all good things come to an end, and Cleopatra always knew that unless Antony and Octavian canceled each other out, one of them was going to show up in Alexandria someday as friend or foe. Thus when Antony sent word to Cleopatra that he wanted to meet with her, she had no choice but to go and become his best friend.

And what spurred Antony to partner with Cleopatra? Simply put, he wanted to look better than Octavian to the Romans. Italy in general, and Rome in particular, were suffering from a variety of ills: starvation, homelessness, and rioting. Once Brutus and Cassius had been eliminated, fourteen thousand soldiers returned to Rome, and all of them needed to be paid and housed. Overtaxation and the stealing of freeholders' lands in Rome and other cities by both Octavian and Antony did not make the citizens very happy; nor were these men very popular in the eyes of the veterans who felt they weren't getting their due quickly enough. Meanwhile, Sextus (before his defeat and execution at the hands of Octavian) decided to blockade the city, starve everyone, and cripple the Roman army until he was given control of Sicily, Corsica, and Sardinia).

Octavian was struggling to keep things under control in Rome, but Antony, out in the east, came up with a better plan to deal with the mess: Cleopatra. The Lagide treasury of the Ptolemy Dynasty could afford to give up a bit of its riches to make Antony the savior of Rome for the moment and also fund his invasion of Parthia. In return, along with promises of future Roman goodwill, Antony was willing to kill off Cleopatra's sister Arsinoe IV (who was the only family threat left), and a few other problematic folk.

Antony went on to enjoy some time with Cleopatra (although in their near decade-long relationship, the actual number of hours they spent with one another was quite limited), and apparently he really appreciated the charms of Alexandria as well as the charms of the queen. Octavian naturally made much of this liaison, claiming Antony's desire for what Egypt had to offer was akin to being a traitor. On a personal level, Octavian was being rather a pill, insisting others adhere to a stricter, austere life simply because he felt this was what exemplified the proper Roman. Antony should not have had to ignore music, art, culture, fine food, festivities, and other activities that gave him pleasure, just because Octavian was such a repressed fellow. On the other hand, Octavian did point out a trait that may have been detrimental to Antony in the long run. Octavian was an extremely hardworking, forward-thinking leader, while Antony did what he thought was necessary at various times but preferred a bit more of a laid-back lifestyle. Antony would go for the gusto when certain opportunities presented themselves but not necessarily spend every day running Rome with the obsessive management style of Octavian. While some in Rome liked Antony's less organized approach to life and leadership, feeling comfortable that this meant he was not going to become another Julius Caesar and end any semblance of Italy being a republic, others felt Octavian's methods were more appropriate: on the ball, attentive, and astute at taking care of business. Remember, Caesar banished Antony for failing to handle the economy of Rome properly while Caesar was off in battle. This was not likely to be a problem with the ever-working, micromanaging Octavian. It seems that Octavian might have had a bit of a chip on his shoulder, perhaps due to a long-held inferiority complex that would have developed in childhood, caused by being fatherless, being raised by controlling women, and having a less-than-gladiator body—and because of any number of other traits that damaged his ego and made being the next Caesar the one and only purpose in Octavian's life. He not only wanted to be emperor, but he wanted to be regarded as the *greatest* emperor. He did not have time to spend playing around, wasting his energies on lesser goals. Octavian probably resented Antony's more carefree attitude and found it to be a bad trait, one he thought should cost him the prize; how unfair it would be for Antony to charm his way to the top while Octavian was spending every waking hour planning strategies and putting them into action.

Octavian also promoted the idea that by enjoying life with Cleopatra in Alexandria, Antony had belittled the Romans and their culture. He labeled Antony a traitor over it. In a way, Octavian had a point. Immersion in a new location, in a different culture, and spending a great deal of time with a person from that culture can indeed cause a dramatic shift in perspective. "Out of sight, out of mind" can encourage a lessening of concern and association for the place and people one no longer experiences on a daily basis.

Conversely, by spending a great deal of time with someone from another culture, one's choices could be influenced; it is possible that Cleopatra would have had ideas and attitudes that could sway

138 THE MURDER OF CLEOPATRA

Antony's actions. To some extent, one could say it is not impossible that Antony was "under Cleopatra's spell"—but then, she could have been "under Antony's spell" as well. However, the behaviors of both Cleopatra and Antony show that while they appreciated each other's worth and personalities, they still liked who they were and they were not intending on vacating their positions of power. Each would try to add to their own, but not trade them. It is possible that together, they became a dangerous and daring duo, living larger together than either would have on their own. Indeed, this seemed to be a possible explanation of Cleopatra's and Antony's behaviors with what has been called the Donations of Alexandria.

Plutarch describes this unprecedented event of 34 BCE as a major spectacle staged in Egypt by Cleopatra and Antony, in which Antony sat on a tall throne next to Cleopatra with all four children on lesser thrones, presenting a unified front to the Egyptians and proclaiming themselves the future rulers of a Roman/Egyptian empire, with their children sharing in the control of the world for decades to come.

> He was hated, too, for the distribution which he made to his children in Alexandria; it was seen to be theatrical and arrogant, and to evince hatred of Rome. For after filling the gymnasium with a throng and placing on a tribunal of silver two thrones of gold, one for himself and the other for Cleopatra, and other lower thrones for his sons, in the first place he declared Cleopatra Queen of Egypt, Cyprus, Libya, and Coele Syria, and she was to share her throne with Caesarion. Caesarion was believed to be a son of the former Caesar, by whom Cleopatra was left pregnant. In the second place, he proclaimed his own sons by Cleopatra Kings of Kings, and to Alexander he allotted Armenia, Media and Parthia (when he should have subdued it), to Ptolemy, Phoenicia, Syria, and Cilicia. At the same time he also produced his sons, Alexander arrayed in Median garb, which included a tiara and upright head-dress, Ptolemy in boots, short cloak, and broad-brimmed hat surmounted by a diadem. For the latter was the dress of the kings who followed Alexander, the former that of Medes and Armenians. And when

the boys had embraced their parents, one was given a bodyguard of Armenians, the other of Macedonians. Cleopatra, indeed, both then and at other times when she appeared in public, assumed a robe sacred to Isis, and was addressed as the New Isis.

By reporting these things to the senate and by frequent denunciations before the people [Octavian] tried to inflame the multitude against Antony.[3]

Essentially, Plutarch claimed that Antony through this spectacle honored the deceased Julius Caesar and then recognized Caesarion as his true son and heir, effectively saying Octavian, and Italy, should be cast aside. Cleopatra was officially titled, "Queen of Kings and Her Sons Who Are Kings," and Caesarion was given the title of pharaoh of Egypt, and as son of Caesar, a pharaoh approved of by Rome. Cleopatra and Caesarion would rule Egypt together (and Libya and Cyprus and part of Syria), and the two sons and daughter she had with Antony would eventually rule Persia, Macedonia, Armenia, Parthia, Cyrenaica, Crete, and parts of Syria and Cilicia (even if neither Rome nor Egypt had control of all of them yet)—effectively, all the Roman lands. Antony would be ruler of the world over all of them; Cleopatra would be his queen and continue to rule Egypt; their children would rule with them; and, finally, the lands would be united in peace. It would be an eastern empire, Roman/Egyptian but with the Roman part of the empire diminished due to the addition of the Egyptian queen to the equation.

This description of such a bold display of royalty in Alexandria would not appeal to the Roman people. Neither would the will that Plutarch claimed Antony had written while in Alexandria, stating that he wanted to be buried in Egypt (a will that supposedly was hand-delivered to Octavian by one of Antony's men who supposedly had defected at Actium). That either of these stories has much truth in them is of little import. If Octavian convinced the Roman populace that Antony was indulging in grandiose thoughts concerning his life with Cleopatra and that he was indeed forsaking Rome in favor of Egypt and its dangerous queen, Octavian would have little choice in declaring war on Egypt.

But is there any merit to this story of Antony being overtaken by ego to embrace Cleopatra and Egypt? I think the answer is yes, but not because of the story Plutarch tells us. If we look back at the assassination of Julius Caesar, and if we believe that Mark Antony was not an innocent bystander, we can see that he did have some ambitions of being as big as or bigger than Caesar. Then, he divorced his wife, Octavia, which certainly makes it seem as though he was working toward having Cleopatra as his wife and partner, especially after having three children with her, spending time in Alexandria with her, and using her wealth to fund his military campaigns (most significantly the final one against Octavian). He sought the prize that was Parthia just as Caesar had, and if Antony had been successful, he would have eliminated the last major enemy of Rome and would have made himself the new Alexander, something that Julius Caesar had hoped to become but failed to accomplish.

However, it is one thing to see your future with the Egyptian queen and to be content to leave her in her place as you become the dictator of Rome (much in the same manner as Julius Caesar), and it is quite another to be so foolish as to announce your plans to take over the Mediterranean world with a non-Roman ruler when you need the Roman people behind you to strike against Octavian. The Donations of Alexandria were no doubt an extreme exaggeration of a holiday celebration in Alexandria spun by an astute propagandist (and there was none better than Octavian) for the purpose of justifying his attack on Antony. Octavian was a master at fabricating outrageous behaviors on the part of Antony and Cleopatra that would work to his political favor. He no doubt saw their partnership as a catalyst for Antony to increase his power, which would in time crush all opposition. Octavian knew he had to strike quickly, toss the dice while he might still come up with a winning roll rather than to allow time to stack the deck against him.

It is hard to say, if Octavian had not been such an aggressive player, whether Antony would have tolerated having him around as a lesser partner in a regime of shared power. Then again, Antony might well have shared Octavian's view that two Caesars is one Caesar too many. Both men may have recognized that when you leave a very adept enemy alive, you have to watch your back twenty-four hours a day, and it might not be long before one of you takes the other down. On the other hand, Cleopatra knew she had to have a Roman in her corner if she wanted to keep her country. She needed Antony to keep Egypt.

Back in Rome, Octavian was making his case that Antony was showing too much interest in another country and scheming with that Egyptian vixen to sell out Rome, while he, Octavian, was keeping his feet firmly grounded in Rome and spending all of his time in its service. And for many Romans his argument would have been quite convincing. On top of the vicious propaganda campaign against Antony and Cleopatra, Octavian also had won against Sextus while Antony lost badly in Parthia (no thanks to Octavian, who failed to send him proper troop support). The commentary from Octavian that Antony was a washed up, over-the-hill, traitorous has-been who was losing the love of his men and was planning to become dictator with an Egyptian queen as part of the package may have had just enough truth in it to be disturbing to both Cleopatra and Antony. Antony needed the support of his men and of as many of the Roman people as possible if he was going to beat Octavian, reassert his power, and redeem his reputation.

Octavian wasn't spreading such propaganda for his personal amusement. To start his campaign against Antony, he needed to turn enough Romans against his foe so that they became enraged and would supply him with what he needed—ships, men, and provisions—as soon as possible. He needed to take out Mark Antony quickly. He declared war on Egypt and Cleopatra, but not against his fellow Roman, Antony. Octavian promoted himself as saving Italy from foreign control, not turning on his fellow Roman coruler and trying to take over Italy and the Roman Empire for himself. It was a smart political move—risky, but smart. The final showdown between Antony and Octavian was about to begin.

CHAPTER 14

ACTIUM

I took a train from Rome to the docks where the ships came in, and I boarded a ship that would take me to Ephesus, Turkey, where Antony and Cleopatra wintered on the way toward Greece, gathering their fleet and relaxing before moving their ships into their final positions in Greece that autumn (31 BCE). Ephesus is quite a beautiful spot where the ruins of the city include a fabulous main street that rises up to the top of a gentle hill overlooking the Mediterranean Sea for miles in both a southerly and westerly direction. One can envision the charm of the city in ancient times, the fine architecture and the still quite intact coliseum that attests to the beauty of the city during Antony and Cleopatra's sojourn there. As they viewed from the hill the panorama of their might and wealth, their ships coming from all directions and pulling into the port, they no doubt could sense victory in the wind. How everything went wrong from that point on has been extensively argued by historians.

Most of our information comes from Plutarch, who we know was biased in favor of Octavian and against Cleopatra. Yet, it is worth reading his complete description of the battle and how he claims it played out. Then we can dissect it for a more probable rendering of what actually occurred. Although anyone who tries to make sense of the events cannot help but do so in hindsight, such a final and drastic turn of events for the Egyptian queen is an extraordinarily important event that we must take a look at it carefully if we are to understand the choices she made during that time and the following nine months until she met her death at the hands of her nemesis, Octavian. Plutarch writes a very detailed account of the Battle of Actium, I have selected the most important parts from Plutarch's *Life of Antony* to highlight and analyze so we can get the clearest idea of what happened in 32/31 BCE:

> Antony heard of this [how Octavian was turning the Romans against him and keeping all the spoils of war for himself and his soldiers] while he was tarrying in Armenia; and at once he ordered Canidius to take sixteen legions and go down to the sea. But he himself took Cleopatra with him and came to Ephesus. It was there that his naval force was coming together from all quarters, eight hundred ships of war with merchant vessels, of which Cleopatra furnished two hundred, besides twenty thousand talents, and supplies for the whole army during the war.[1]

Once Cleopatra had provided these ships, manpower, money, and supplies, Octavian claims Antony tried to send Cleopatra back to Egypt on the advice of others, but she wanted to stay because, after all, she was his partner and a queen, and she had the right to do so. He relented.

Meanwhile, Octavian wanted to declare war on Antony, but first he had to stem discontent from the citizens over tax issue and get the people behind him.

> Wherefore, among the greatest mistakes of Antony men reckon his postponement of the war. For it gave [Octavian] time to make preparations and put an end to the disturbances among the people.[2]

Plutarch says that this delay of attack by Antony and Cleopatra gave Octavian time to convince the Roman people that they should back him in declaration of war against the duo. Also, Plutarch claims that during this period of time Octavian got his hands on Antony's will, which further showed Antony to be a traitor and a pawn of Cleopatra.

[Octavian] laid most stress on the clause in the will relating to Antony's burial. For it directed that Antony's body, even if he should die in Rome, should be borne in state through the forum and then sent away to Cleopatra in Egypt. . . .[3]

When [Octavian] had made sufficient preparations, a vote was passed to wage war against Cleopatra, and to take away from Antony the authority which he had surrendered to a woman. And Caesar said in addition that Antony had been drugged and was not even master of himself, and that the Romans were carrying on war with Mardion the eunuch, and Potheinus, and Iras, and the tire-woman of Cleopatra, and Charmion, by whom the principal affairs of the government were managed.[4]

Now the die was cast.

When the forces came together for the war, Antony had no fewer than five hundred fighting ships, among which were many vessels of eight and ten banks of oars, arrayed in pompous and festal fashion; he also had one hundred thousand infantry soldiers and twelve thousand horsemen. [Octavian] had two hundred and fifty ships of war, eighty thousand infantry, and about as many horsemen as his enemies.[5]

While it seems that Antony clearly had more ships and men, Plutarch points out that Antony had a great many mercenaries in his army who were getting disgruntled and men who were not the best at sea either. Octavian, while he had less to work with, had far higher quality in his men and equipment.

This fleet [Octavian's] kept assembled at Tarentum and Brundisium, and he sent to Antony a demand to waste no time, but to come with his forces.[6]

But Antony refused to bring the fight to Italian waters, wanting Octavian to fight him over in Greece, in neutral territory.

[Octavian] got the start of him by crossing the Ionian Sea and occu-
pying a place in Epirus called Toruné (that is, ladle); and when
Antony and his friends were disturbed by this, since their infantry
forces were belated, Cleopatra, jesting, said: "What is there dreadful
in Caesar's [Octavian's] sitting at a ladle?"[7]

What was dreadful was that Caesar nailed Cleopatra and Antony
with a surprise attack.

The enemy sailed against him at daybreak[8]

It didn't go well for Antony and Cleopatra.

Since his navy was unlucky in everything and always too late to be
of assistance, Antony was again compelled to turn his attention to
his land forces.[9]

But Plutarch says:

Cleopatra prevailed with her opinion that the war should be decided
by the ships, although she was already contemplating flight, and
was disposing her own forces, not where they would be helpful in
winning the victory, but where they could most easily get away if
the cause was lost. . . .[10]
    When it had been decided to deliver a sea battle, Antony burned
all the Egyptian ships except sixty; but the largest and best, from
those having three to those having ten banks of oars, he manned,
putting on board twenty thousand heavy-armed soldiers and two
thousand archers.[11]

While Antony was heading into battle, Plutarch also admits
Antony put sails on some of his ships, which indicates he and
Cleopatra had a plan to flee.

He had no good hopes himself, since, when the masters of his ships
wished to leave their sails behind, he compelled them to put them

on board and carry them, saying that not one fugitive of the enemy should be allowed to make his escape. . . .[12]

During that day, then, and the three following days the sea was tossed up by a strong wind and prevented the battle; but on the fifth, the weather becoming fine and the sea calm, they came to an engagement. Antony had the right wing, with Publicola, Coelius the left, and in the centre were Marcus Octavius and Marcus Insteius. [Octavian] posted Agrippa on the left, and reserved the right wing for himself.[13]

The battle is slow to begin, but Antony finally had no choice but to move forward:

After surveying the rest of his line of battle, he was carried in a small boat to his right wing, and there was astonished to see the enemy lying motionless in the narrows; indeed, their ships had the appearance of riding at anchor. For a long time he was convinced that this was really the case, and kept his own ships at a distance of about eight furlongs from the enemy. But it was now the sixth hour, and since a wind was rising from the sea, the soldiers of Antony became impatient at the delay, and, relying on the height and size of their own ships as making them unassailable, they put their left wing in motion. When [Octavian] saw this he was delighted, and ordered his right wing to row backwards, wishing to draw the enemy still farther out from the gulf and the narrows, and then to surround them with his own agile vessels and come to close quarters with ships which, owing to their great size and the smallness of their crews, were slow and ineffective. . . .[14]

Though the struggle was beginning to be at close range, the ships did not ram or crush one another at all, since Antony's, owing to their weight, had no impetus, which chiefly gives effect to the blows of the beaks, while [Octavian]'s not only avoided dashing front to front against rough and hard bronze armour, but did not even venture to ram the enemy's ships in the side. For their beaks would easily have been broken off by impact against vessels constructed of huge square timbers fastened together with iron. The struggle was therefore like a land battle; or, to speak more truly, like the storming of a walled town. For three or four of [Octavian]'s vessels were engaged at the same time about one of Antony's, and the crews fought with wicker shields and spears and punting-poles and fiery missiles; the soldiers of Antony also shot with catapults from wooden towers. . . .[15]

And now, as Agrippa was extending the left wing with a view to encircling the enemy, Publicola was forced to advance against him, and so was separated from the centre. The centre falling into confusion and engaging with Arruntius, although the sea-fight was still undecided and equally favourable to both sides, suddenly the sixty ships of Cleopatra were seen hoisting their sails for flight and making off through the midst of the combatants; for they had been posted in the rear of the large vessels, and threw them into confusion as they plunged through. The enemy looked on with amazement, seeing that they took advantage of the wind and made for Peloponnesus.[16]

It is clear to Octavian that Cleopatra and Antony are going to make a run for it.

Cleopatra recognized him and raised a signal on her ship; so Antony came up and was taken on board. . . .[17]

At this point, Liburnian ships were seen pursuing them from [Octavian]'s fleet; but Antony ordered the ship's prow turned to face them, and so kept them off.[18]

Plutarch speaks of Antony being depressed and ashamed of leaving his men and escaping with Cleopatra.

He spent three days by himself at the prow, either because he was angry with Cleopatra, or ashamed to see her, and then put in at Taenarum. Here the women in Cleopatra's company at first brought them into a parley, and then persuaded them to eat and sleep together.[19]

And, finally, Plutarch writes of the effect of Antony's decision to bolt with Cleopatra on his men, which had detrimental and long-term ramifications.

> This, then, was the situation of Antony. But at Actium his fleet held out for a long time against [Octavian], and only after it had been most severely damaged by the high sea which rose against it did it reluctantly, and at the tenth hour, give up the struggle. There were not more than five thousand dead, but three hundred ships were captured, as [Octavian] himself has written. Only a few were aware that Antony had fled, and to those who heard of it the story was at first an incredible one, that he had gone off and left nineteen legions of undefeated men-at-arms and twelve thousand horsemen, as if he had not many times experienced both kinds of fortune and were not exercised by the reverses of countless wars and fightings. His soldiers, too, had a great longing for him, and expected that he would presently make his appearance from some quarter or other; and they displayed so much fidelity and bravery that even after his flight had become evident they held together for seven days, paying no heed to the messages which [Octavian] sent them. But at last, after Canidius their general had run away by night and forsaken the camp, being now destitute of all things and betrayed by their commanders, they went over to the conqueror.[20]

Now you have read what happened before, during, and after Actium from Plutarch's point of view (well, Plutarch's version on whatever story was passed on to him by the victor, Octavian, and those who wanted to portray Antony, and especially Cleopatra, in a less than favorable light). Sometimes it takes only a slightly different framing of a situation to cause people to come away confident they have a "true" understanding of what happened and, if enough people agree over time, it seems like it must be the proper view of history.

But let's view this account with a bit more of a jaundiced eye and look for possible alternate explanations for events, especially in light of what Cleopatra and Antony were attempting to accomplish under the circumstances.

It is said that Octavian was quite worried when he saw that Antony had linked himself with Cleopatra and together they were amassing ships and soldiers to take him on. He rather broke into a sweat in the spring of 33 BCE when it became clear that, at some point, the twosome planned to bring the fight to him and stage an all-out fight for Italy and the Roman Empire. Yet, it is also said that Antony then became lazy, perhaps avoiding battle by not pushing the offensive until the fall of 32, when he finally gathered his fleet in Patras; and by winter, nineteen of his legions had arrived on the coast.

So why did Antony wait so long to go after Octavian if Octavian was gaining political power and momentum by the week? It is quite possible that it was just this fact that made Cleopatra and Antony very aware that this battle was going to be extremely decisive. Antony was on the ropes, and he had to come back with a massive barrage to overcome Octavian; otherwise, Octavian would grow so powerful politically and militarily that it would be unlikely Antony could pick himself off the mat, even with Cleopatra in his corner, and come back for a win. Actium was going to be the proving ground, winner takes all; and Cleopatra and Antony, with everything riding on this fight, no doubt wanted to go in with the most massive force possible. Indeed, this they did accomplish, and Plutarch admits it.

Antony had six squadrons, five hundred ships in all (but the number is in question and it is possible he had even more, or if one believes Plutarch, just half that), and he had spent that time during 33/32 not twiddling his thumbs, but building the biggest ships he could. He constructed ships that would outweigh Octavian's and have strong reinforcement to interfere with ramming, tough bows that do ramming quite nicely themselves, and sound catapults on the decks of the ships. Cleopatra's wealth and logistics were in place to fund and feed this large military force, and no doubt Octavian had a number of sleepless nights considering what he was up against, even if Plutarch downplayed his concerns. There was also the weather to consider as autumn and winter could be treacherous times to attempt battle on either sea or land. It would seem Cleopatra and Antony decided it was far wiser to spend the time of tricky weather increasing their fleet and then going to war later, at a better time of the year and with the strongest military possible.

No, Antony did not come to Italy to fight his enemy nor did he attack at sea when he had the chance of confronting Octavian as the latter was forced out into the waters while making his way around the peninsula toward Antony's encampments. Instead, Antony preferred to meet his adversary on land (where he was most comfortable) and in Greece (which would make it a civil war between two Roman factions and not an invasion by an Eastern enemy—Egypt) with a Roman as its leader. Also, by forcing Octavian out of Italy to make his way to Greece served two additional purposes: (1) it would take him time and effort to reach the location of battle, during which time Antony hoped Octavian's resources would dwindle along the way; and (2) fighting at Actium would leave open an escape route back to Egypt, which clearly would make Cleopatra a lot more comfortable. Even though losing the battle at Actium would be a disaster, an escape to Egypt at least would allow some hope of survival for the duo. I think this Plan B escape route was hardly a foolish addition to their military strategy.

Was allowing Cleopatra to accompany him at the battle a highly damaging move for Antony? I do not see this. It was not unusual to be accompanied by leaders of countries that provided military support, and with so many of the troops not being Antony's but Cleopatra's, if she were not with him, he would likely have had difficulties controlling these men; and if the battle turned against them in any way, would these Egyptian warriors support a Roman general? Perhaps not, but with Cleopatra in command of the men, their willingness to fight would be much stronger.

Octavian's propoganda took what was the norm for such massive military campaigns and twisted it into something perverted: Antony being handled by a woman, a wicked Egyptian queen, an eastern poison that was about to spread into Italy. Emotions would run wild among the Roman population, and this could set the entire country against Antony. Hence, Antony decided not to invade Italy but to force the fight in neutral territory *with* Cleopatra at his side, a perfectly reasonable strategy.

Of Antony's two-pronged strategy, one can say that the first did not work out but the latter did. It turned out not to be Octavian who ran out of resources, but Antony, which then caused the rout that did indeed send Cleopatra and Antony scurrying back to Alexandria. What went wrong? I believe an analysis will show there was actually nothing terribly wrong with Cleopatra and Antony's plan; in fact it was really a pretty good one, and, if Octavian hadn't ended up the victor, we might easily believe today that it was brilliant (because if Cleopatra and Antony had won, they would be the victors and would have written history to favor themselves). Antony and Cleopatra amassed greater forces, had the stronger support system, and were to have fought on neutral ground on both land and sea. They should have won. Only they didn't.

Let's break it down further.

It was in the winter of 33/32 BCE that Cleopatra and Antony made their preparations for battle by assembling their fleet and forces in Ephesus. The fleet was quite impressive—huge, in fact—and Antony may well have felt the spirit of Alexander the Great with him (Macedonian though he was) since he now controlled the entire sea power of the east. Three hundred transport ships were at Antony's disposal, ships that were to bring food from Egypt and also carry the troops from Ephesus over to Actium across the Aegean Sea (preparations which took place in the spring and summer of 32).

There is another important issue to understand concerning Cleopatra and Antony's decision not to invade Italy. This action would not be a winner-take-all battle but would require a number of assaults to win the war. While each of these assaults was occurring, the weather could switch up, the convoys could be attacked, and then everything could fall apart. And, again, we must remember that with

Cleopatra by his side during an invasion, the Roman citizenry may well have come out en mass to support Octavian and thereby increase his military force.

So the decision was made to have the showdown in Greece. In May of 32, Cleopatra and Antony were stationed in Athens with their troops. By September, they had moved the base of operations to Patras, and their fleet was moored in more than a dozen locatons along the western Grecian coast, from Actium in the north to Methone in the south. The plan was to force the encounter at Actium, at which Antony and Cleopatra had built two towers with artillery covering the mouth that connected the Ionian Sea and the Gulf of Ambracia, where Antony had the ships waiting in protected waters. There Cleopatra and Antony waited comfortably enough through the winter, until Octavian made his move.

But when Octavian did make his move, just as winter ended in 31 BCE, it was not at all what Antony had expected. He had thought, quite reasonably, that Octavian would push off Italy, straight over to Greece in relatively protected coastal waters, and then work his way down to Actium. But Octavian, with his brilliant General Agrippa, made a very daring move. Agrippa took his fleet straight across open water, away from the coast and the prying eyes of enemy messengers who would carry word of their progress down the coast. They risked dangerous storms at sea; took the long route down the Italian peninsula and over to the southernmost outpost of Antony's land force, Methone; surprised their adversaries; overran the isolated garrison; burned all the ships stationed there; established Octavian's forces in Greece; and cut off Antony's supply route to Egypt all in one fell swoop.

Brilliant and risky, Octavian's move paid off. Again, had the weather not cooperated, the maneuver might have spelled the end of Octavian's campaign. But he got lucky, and if you are both smart and lucky, you will find yourself in a fine position to win a war. By the time Cleopatra and Antony knew what had hit them, Octavian had moved his forces northward and brought them to Actium.

All was not lost yet, however. Even though Octavian and Agrippa were inflicting a good bit of damage, Antony and Cleopatra could still continue the fight at sea and on land, and there was still a plausable chance of victory. In truth, they had the larger number of men and so they may well have felt that once Octavian attacked, they could win the battle.

But then more things went wrong. Octavian perched his camp up on a very defensible hill overlooking the bay while Antony's camp was on a low-lying mosquito-infested sandy bit of land, an acceptable location for a few days, but not the place to be positioned for a protracted period of time. As Antony waited for Octavian to make a move, his men became sick from malaria and dysentery and mental fatigue, and since so many of them were mercenaries and not all that dedicated to the mission, desertions dramatically increased.

There Antony's troops remained trapped into the summer. He tried to block the water supply to Octavian's camp but failed. Desertions continued along with deaths in his own camp, and then Agrippa captured the island of Leucas to the south of Actium, which is where Egyptian ships had been bringing in supplies and reinforcements. Then he went on to capture Patras and Corinth, wiping out more supply routes in addition to barricading the harbor. Antony and Cleopatra found themselves in a pretty dire position. By August, I believe Antony and Cleopatra knew that they were, to put it bluntly, in a hopeless situation.

Antony did not have enough warriors to man the ships, to row, or to fight on land and at sea effectively. One possibility was to simply abandon the fleet and take all the men, still a large force, and fight on land or retreat and come back to fight another day. There is much dissension over why Antony did not choose either of these options. The most negative viewpoint is that Cleopatra wouldn't let him and he gave in to her wishes. A slightly less jaded view is that Antony recognized that if he abandoned the fleet and Cleopatra, he would lose her support and her treasure, and he would have to take a disgruntled bunch of men off through difficult terrain, through high mountain passes, with dwindling supplies and morale, and survive through the coming winter. This was not a very attractive prospect.

In my opinion, Antony had to choose the lesser of two evils. If he escaped with his army, he might just as well sign his own death warrant or at least accept that his military and political career was over. He would spend the remaining years of his life in some back-water, hiding from Octavian. But if he left with Cleopatra, he would still have a fleet and a lot of money, and he could rejoin the rest of his dozen legions that had remained behind in Egypt. As I have often said, if he and Cleopatra escaped, anything could happen over the course of the next year that could hold out the hope of (1) putting them back in contention to take over the empire (especially if Octavian happened to die of one of his many alleged illnesses); (2) allowing them to hold onto Egypt (if Octavian's power dwindled); or (3) giving them the opportunity to reestablish themselves elsewhere (if they needed to flee). I think a number of historians, ancient and modern, have been overly harsh with respect to Cleopatra and Antony's decision to bolt from Actium with whatever they could take with them. And this is clearly the plan of action they decided to take and successfully enacted.

I think it is odd that Plutarch and future tellers of the tale of Cleopatra and Antony's escape from Actium try so hard to portray Antony as oblivious to Cleopatra's plan to hightail it with her fleet at the height of the battle. Even Octavian knew they were planning to break out and flee; what choice did they have? And Octavian had two choices. One was to simply allow them to go through his blockade and then pick off as many ships from their fleet as he could while they sailed away, but that would be seen as a sign of weakness. The more ships and men remained in their fleet, the more he would have to deal with later. On the other hand, he could reduce their numbers as much as possible by forcing them to fight but make sure the Lagide trea-sury did not sink to the bottom of the sea during the battle. Octavian would actually want Cleopatra to sail away safely at that point, and later he would go to Egypt, conquer her, and retrieve the treasure.

I think the battle actually went as planned on both sides. Cleopatra loaded sails onto her ships, and her fleet stayed safely behind the battle lines. Antony loaded sails onto some of his ships as well. Octavian knew they had done this and that sails meant a plan to hurry off, not stay and fight, since added sails reduced the maneuverabilty of the ships, which is obviously not a great idea if you are planning to use the ships in battle. Octavian moved his ships out into the harbor so that Antony would be forced into the open with his warships. Then, the battle would begin but this time with Octavian in possession of far more ships than Antony (due to the fact that Antony did not have enough oarsmen to man all his ships). Octavian could easily force Antony's ships to spread out in a line and then have his own ships surround each of Antony's and take them down.

And this is exactly what happened on the morning of September 2, 31 BCE; the Battle of Actium began. Octavian and his generals waited with his fleet a distance from the shore, while Antony went out to engage them and the fighting began. Then the day wore on and the lines naturally thinned. Cleopatra waited for the afternoon wind to shift so she could put up her sails and speed southward, a change of wind *which she expected*; it was not a stroke of luck as Plutarch would have us believe. When the time was right, her fleet of sixty ships sailed quickly through the center of the lines, and when Antony saw her make her break, he transferred from the unwieldy ship he was on to a smaller, faster galley with sails (which he conveniently had waiting nearby) and set after Cleopatra with about twenty of his own ships (at least this is the number Plutarch gives us). Plutarch claims that two-thirds of the fleet was left behind to fight on and eventually surrender (so it would suggest that far more than twenty of Antony's ships accompanied him) while Cleopatra and Antony, the Lagide treasure, and a sizeable portion of their combined fleet were safely on their way back to Egypt.

Octavian was clearly the victor of the Battle of Actium, but this did not actually mean at the time that Antony and Cleopatra were completely destroyed. Antony was still in charge of half of the Roman Empire, and Cleopatra was still in charge of Egypt. The biggest problem with their loss at Actium, however, was that word eventually got out to the client kingdoms of Egypt and of Antony that Octavian had beaten the pair, which started a rather unfortunate negative attitude toward Antony. Why would they provide more men and war matériel for the losing side at Actium? Then, as Octavian moved toward Egypt, each of these allies had to decide whether to back Antony or Octavian; since the odds seemed to be in Octavian's favor, they went with the surer bet. Like a row of dominos flicked from one end, each country fell without resistence to Octavian as he made his way toward Alexandria.

Surely Cleopatra and Antony realized how likely it was that, bit by bit, their power would erode with Octavian's advancing army. It was during this last year, as they saw ultimate defeat facing them, that they switched to Plan B before it was too late. Although there had been rumors from Rome of at least one plan to assassinate Octavian (by Marcus Lepidus, son of Brutus) and, of course, Octavian's health was still questionable (they could always hope he would just keel over and die), neither of these options seemed likely. The Roman soldiers who served Octavian and wanted their pay from an exhausted treasury might take matters into their own hands and depose their leader (which is why Octavian would have to come to Egypt and plunder Cleopatra's family treasure). Cleopatra and Antony knew they had better find a way to escape the coming wrath of Octavian, assuming bad luck did not befall him before he arrived to finish them off.

On to Plan B.

CHAPTER 15

PLAN B—THE FIRST
ATTEMPT TO FLEE EGYPT

I returned to Rome and caught a flight back to Egypt. As the plane circled for its landing in Cairo, I had to smile a bit at what Cleopatra would have thought if she knew that in 2012, Octavian could have made it to her country in just a little over three hours! In a way, perhaps, she was luckier back in 31 BCE because she would unquestionably have had a least a few months before his arrival, a few months to put together some plan of escape.

Yes, I believe she did indeed have a plan to escape from Egypt. It is this incredible plan that I feel has been completely ignored. In its place has been substituted the ridiculous story of an emotionally distraught, desperate, and hopeless queen who begs Octavian for favors and then hides in her tomb with her treasure, making idle threats. She then supposedly begs Octavian for more favors, and finally kills herself to save herself from humiliation at the hands of her Roman conqueror. For the most part, Plutarch makes both Cleopatra and Antony appear to be impotent bystanders in the months following Actium—according to him, they are weaklings who simply sit about, waiting for Octavian to do them in. Oh, yes, Plutarch does claim that they drank, partied, sighed about their situation, begged Octavian to give them a break, and groveled to Octavian to spare them. But he does not attribute to them more than a couple of pitiful attempts to stave off their demise or, should I say, give a long-serving Roman general at least some dignity before his final fall. (Note that Antony did attempt to stop Octavian's invasion from the west, and his one singular victory occurred when he prevented Octavian's men from entering Alexandria in the night.) However, there is one fascinating piece of information that Plutarch mentions, a real attempt to determine a future. Cleopatra tried to drag some ships on rollers across the desert to the Red Sea in what was ultimately a failed attempt to flee; but her enemies, the Nabataeans, burned the ships or at least some of them (the reference to this event by Plutarch is extremely limited in information). At least this is one example of Cleopatra and Antony trying to take real action. Other than that one incident, for most of the remaining nine months, Antony and Cleopatra are portrayed by Plutarch as a couple consigned to their doom, with an "eat, drink, and be merry, for tomorrow we shall die" type of attitude as the days tick down to their final moments.

Plutarch imagines Antony's state of mind: "After Antony had reached the coast of Libya and sent Cleopatra forward into Egypt from Paraetonium, he had the benefit of solitude without end, roaming and wandering about."[1] According to Plutarch, Antony was in such a terrible fit of depression that he attempted suicide: "Antony tried to kill himself, but was prevented by his friends and brought to Alexandria."[2]

Cleopatra, on the other hand, was hard at work trying to secure the future.

> Here he found Cleopatra venturing upon a hazardous and great undertaking. The Isthmus, namely, which separates the Red Sea from the Mediterranean Sea off Egypt and is considered to be the boundary between Asia and Libya, in the part where it is most constricted by the two seas and has the least width, measures three hundred furlongs. Here Cleopatra undertook to raise her fleet out of water and drag the ships across, and after launching them in the Arabian Gulf with much money and a large force, to settle in parts outside of Egypt, thus escaping war and servitude. But since the

Arabians about Petra burned the first ships that were drawn up, and Antony still thought that his land forces at Actium were holding together, she desisted, and guarded the approaches to the country.[3]

Antony continues in his depression:

And now Antony forsook the city and the society of his friends, and built for himself a dwelling in the sea at Pharos, by throwing a mole out into the water. Here he lived an exile from men, and declared that he was contentedly imitating the life of Timon, since, indeed, his experiences had been like Timon's; for he himself also had been wronged and treated with ingratitude by his friends, and therefore hated and distrusted all mankind.[4]

Cleopatra then attempted to pick up Antony's spirits:

So he might lay aside his anxieties also, he forsook that dwelling of his in the sea, which he called Timoneion, and after he had been received into the palace by Cleopatra, turned the city to the enjoyment of suppers and drinking-bouts. . . . Cleopatra and Antony now dissolved their famous society of Inimitable Livers, and founded another.[5]

And then it would seem Cleopatra also became suicidal . . .

Which they called the society of Partners in Death. For their friends enrolled themselves as those who would die together, and passed the time delightfully in a round of suppers. Moreover, Cleopatra was getting together collections of all sorts of deadly poisons, and she tested the painless working of each of them by giving them to prisoners under sentence of death.[6]

They made a last-ditch attempt to beg Octavian for mercy:

At the same time they also sent an embassy to Caesar in Asia, Cleopatra asking the realm of Egypt for her children, and Antony requesting that he might live as a private person at Athens, if he could not do so in Egypt. . . .[7]

Caesar would not listen to the proposals for Antony, but he sent back word to Cleopatra that she would receive all reasonable treatment if she either put Antony to death or cast him out.[8]

Then Octavian (also called Caesar by Plutarch) started marching toward Egypt:

When the winter was over, Caesar again marched against his enemy through Syria, and his generals through Libya. When Pelusium was taken there was a rumour that Seleucus had given it up, and not without the consent of Cleopatra; but Cleopatra allowed Antony to put to death the wife and children of Seleucus.[9]

The story of Cleopatra planning to burn all her treasures unless Octavian made a deal with her supposedly reached the general on route:

She herself, now that she had a tomb and monument built surpassingly lofty and beautiful, which she had erected near the temple of Isis, collected there the most valuable of the royal treasures, gold, silver, emeralds, pearls, ebony, ivory, and cinnamon; and besides all this she put there great quantities of torch-wood and tow, so that Caesar was anxious about the reason, and fearing lest the woman might become desperate and burn up and destroy this wealth, kept sending on to her vague hopes of kindly treatment from him, at the same time that he advanced with his army against the city. But when Caesar had taken up position near the hippodrome, Antony sallied forth against him and fought brilliantly and routed his cavalry, and pursued them as far as their camp. Then, exalted by his victory, he went into the palace, kissed Cleopatra, all armed as he was, and presented to her the one of his soldiers who had fought most spiritedly. Cleopatra gave the man as a reward of valour a golden breastplate and a helmet. The man took them, of course,—and in the night deserted to Caesar.[10]

Ah, such a tragedy unfolds for Cleopatra and Antony. But, let's stop and think about Plutarch's amazing description of Cleopatra's escape plan, how she attempted to drag her ships across the isthmus from the Mediterranean Sea to the Red Sea. What an incredible undertaking—one so spectacular, Plutarch no doubt had credible historical accounts of it having happened.

It is clear to me that this phenomenal effort to move her fleet to the Red Sea indicates Cleopatra was well aware of her predicament and was still fighting to be the mistress of her own future, something I believe she continued to attempt to orchestrate to the end. After Actium, she knew that her liaison with Mark Antony would no longer be a strong and powerful force in keeping her on Egypt's throne (unless Octavian suddenly died), that he could only aid her in some more moderate fashion, and that it would be up to her to make a drastic move if she saw Octavian heading her way. Unfortunately, Cleopatra would not know exactly when Octavian would march on Egypt, so she did not know how much time she had to take action. This lack of knowledge would have a great effect on just how she would try to escape the country.

First, we need to examine what Cleopatra would need in order to leave Egypt and survive in a foreign land for a considerable period of time. It is certain she would need a large amount of money (her Lagide treasury or at least a substantial portion of it) and a sizable number of men to protect her and it. In other words, she couldn't sail off to India or anywhere else with three ships and the contents of her treasury. She needed her fleet, her men, and her treasure.

According to Plutarch, she had at least sixty ships, a number that was surely large enough to sail the Red and Arabian Seas. But the ships were in the Mediterranean, not in the Red Sea, and that was her dilemma. There are those who believe that she might have had some ships down south at Berenice, where she sent her son Caesarion with some of the treasure, but since Caesarion was still there when Octavian sent his men to get him, he obviously didn't sail away. Also, it is unlikely that Cleopatra would have gone to the trouble of dragging any of her ships over the isthmus, over thirty miles of desert (the seas were closer together in those days than at present), if she had a reasonable number of large warships and merchant ships at Berenice.

There is a logical reason why Cleopatra might not have had so many ships on her Red Sea ports. Those Nabataeans who ended up burning up some of her ships pretty much controlled the Red Sea at the time. They were pirates who made seafaring rather challenging in those days, and we see similar activities in the same region today (e.g., the Somali pirates). There were lots of little coves and reefs along the Egyptian Red Sea shore, which limited the availability of navigable ports and provided ideal hiding places from which pirates could strike. During Cleopatra's time there were only two ports operating on the Red Sea, the one at Berenice, close to the southern border and the best location for setting off toward India; and Mersa Gawasis, the port 230 miles to the north, located just south of present-day Hurghada.

Although six caves that were carved into a coral terrace that held parts of ships and shipbuilding materials from pharaonic times were found in Mersa Gawasis in 2004 by archaeologists, it is believed these workshops were used to repair damaged ships and to recon-struct ships that were built in the shipyards of Koptos (present-day Luxor), then dismantled and carried by thousands of men on donkeys for eleven or so days through the Wadi Hammamat to the Red Sea port. There appeared to be no evidence that ships were actually being built at Mersa Gawasis or Berenice, although Strabo, the geographer, writes of a shipyard at Cleopatris (also known as Arsinoe; located at the end of the Ptolemaic Canal on the Bitter Lakes at the north end of the Red Sea) that was operational soon after Octavian took over Egypt. Once Antony and Cleopatra were taken care of and he was in control of Egypt, Octavian began preparing for an invasion of Arabia and supposedly built eighty warships and 120 transport ships for the occasion, with the help of then governor Aelius Gallus (who was the second prefect of Roman Egypt from 26 to 24 BCE, after replacing the first prefect, Cornelius Gallus [30–26 BCE]).[11]

The invasion of Arabia failed, and many of the ships sunk, but it is interesting that Strabo does say there were still 120 ships in operation sailing from the Egyptian Red Sea coast in 26 BCE.

> When Gallus was the prefect of Egypt, I accompanied him along the Nile River as far as Syene and the frontiers of Ethiopia. There I learned that as many as 120 vessels were sailing from Myos Hormos to India.[12]

Considering that just three years had passed since Rome assumed control in Egypt, I find it a bit perplexing how a shipyard and some two hundred ships were so quickly built at that Red Sea port. A trireme, one of the smallest and lightest of the warships of the period, might have taken about six thousand man hours to build; others say at least a couple of months. If the shipyard at Cleopatris was building just these types, it would have to build one trireme per week to get two hundred done in three years; or, more realistically, at one trireme every couple of months, there would only be twenty ships produced at that one Egyptian shipyard. And these would have to float around the dangerous Red Sea while waiting for the rest of the fleet to be finished. There is still the matter of building the shipyard even before building the ships, which requires bringing in the manpower and knowledge to build the ships properly and carrying all the materials through the desert as well. Perhaps it was one heck of an operation. (There are reports of Julius Caesar whipping up a large number of ships in a short time on the spot in order to invade Gaul, and there are other stories of generals putting together fleets of some sort in a limited time; how accurate or exaggerated these are is difficult to tell.) But the tale of Gallus's shipbuilding seems a bit too impressive— that he built some two hundred ships of various sizes (not only the simplest and lightest) in one brand-new shipyard established in a new land in a rather volatile area close to the crafty Nabataeans, the very enemy Rome was declaring war against.

Shipbuilding was quite a different animal in the days of ancient

Rome and Egypt. As a confirmed landlubber only having spent time on a cruise ship, a paddle boat, and an occasional sailboat with a glass of wine in one hand and a bag of chips in the other, my knowledge of how ships are put together is near zero. I can understand the concept of lashing logs together to make a raft, but beyond that, I have no real feel for the complexity of building a seaworthy ship: how much material it would take, how many men would be needed to put the ship together, and what level of skill the overseer of such a project would need to possess.

I took a trip back out to Giza, where the pyramids are, to visit one other structure at the site, the Solar Boat Museum. In a most peculiarly shaped building on the south side of the Great Pyramid is ensconced the oldest boat in the world, discovered in 1954. It was constructed forty-six centuries ago by Djederfre, son of Cheops, the pharaoh who was buried in the Great Pyramid. Now, this boat isn't theorized to have actually been a boat that was ever put into use, but rather it was constructed and then dismantled to be buried next to the king as his craft to then be reassembled in his future life. (Or it could have been a funerary boat that carried his body in the procession to the grave and then was broken down.) It was found in a pit thirty-one meters long and covered with sixteen tons of limestone blocks. It is made of cedar and, as a completed boat; I can tell you it is a stunning specimen, simply beautiful in its shape and craftsmanship. It was, indeed, a boat fit for a king to sail off into eternity.

However, putting aside my artistic appreciation for the ancient boat, I noted how intricate the boat is. It is not a really large craft, just thirty-one meters long, but it contained 1,224 pieces! And this pharaonic jigsaw puzzle took fourteen years for the reconstruction team to put together. Admittedly, the team no doubt had their work cut out for them, trying to figure out what piece went where, especially considering the parts were marked with an ancient hieratic script and they were making a boat they had never seen except in rough artistic depictions dating back to ancient times. Also, they undoubtedly were taking extreme care to put the boat together, so this was no rush job. But fourteen years and 1,224 pieces at least gave me an understanding that five unskilled men and a hammer were not going to knock together a seaworthy warship or galley or transport ship over the weekend. And Cheops's boat was quite a small, delicate thing, not a vessel meant to hold dozens or hundreds of people rowing and fighting and navigating through rough waters.

What Romans like Gallus needed for their forays and what Cleopatra needed to sail off to India were much larger and stronger constructions. From what I saw at the Solar Boat Museum, I am more likely to side with the longer time frame to construct even a trireme. Of course, the shipyard at Cleopatris may have had a number of ships being constructed simultaneously, and maybe they had an awesome contingent of manpower from the legions that were available after conquering Egypt. But I should refer to Michael Pitassi's *The Navies of Rome*, specifically to his outstanding commentary on just how many ships were able to be produced in those days; and then we can see just what the odds were of Gallus producing two hundred ships in three years on the Red Sea port at Cleopatris (Arsinoe) in Egypt.

Here is Pitassi's explanation of a claim by then ancient Greek historian Polybius that Rome built 120 ships *in just two months* (one hundred quinquerimes, four-level galleys of some 130 to 150 feet, requiring around 180 rowers; and twenty triremes, three-level galleys of 120 feet, with some 170 rowers). This was a little farther back in history, around the period between 267 and 261 BCE, when Rome had no navy and needed one to fight Carthage in the Punic Wars.

Luckily, Pitassi understands that certain claims of history must be taken with a grain of salt, allowing for gross exaggeration or misinterpretation of the writings or simply a communication breakdown between storyteller and those who later heard the tale. Pitassi's take on the matter of shipbuilding is not the only one out there, but it is a reasonable explanation that meshes well with other viewpoints I have researched on the matter of how ships are built and how long it takes to build them. I find Pitassi's analysis to be a good one with which to understand the choices of Romans and Egyptians regarding how to produce ships for use on the Red Sea.

> From 267 BC therefore, the navy was increasing its shipbuilding capacity and equally, having established such an operation, it follows that the building of warships was a continuous process throughout the coming war. From the figures that have been provided by the ancient sources, it is possible to ascertain an approximation of the production capacity for warships. By taking this larger overall view, such statements as that by Polybius that the Romans built 120 ships in two months, which on the face of it appears unlikely, can become reasonable and feasible. If one accepts the not unreasonable view that if the larger Navy Board started to increase warship building capacity in 267, when the Praefecti were appointed, and that by 265, had six yards in operation; then Polybius actually meant that it took two months to build one ship (so they were all 'built in two months,' but each), i.e., if a ship took sixty days to be built, the shipyard would at that rate, build six ships a year, half a dozen yards would build thirty-six and so on. Even if he exaggerated and it took three months to build a ship and therefore, starting in 265 BC, the 120 new ships would be all ready as they were, for use together in 261 BC. Taking the war as a whole and the ancient sources' figures for new construction (and allowing for, in addition to the 'natural' annual wastage of old ships at the end of their lives, those lost by accident or misadventure that had to be replaced) then the Romans' annual average production of new ships was about twenty-five ships.[13]

I think Pitassi's calculations tend to support my disbelief that Gallus was operating such a fantastic shipbuilding operation at Cleopatris. What seems more likely to me is that a good portion, if not all of those ships, simply sailed there from Alexandria (including Cleopatra's and Antony's remaining ships), and/or from Rome after being built in various shipyards at home or, possibly, from Koptos after being built in Egypt's own shipbuilding capital. What really strikes me, though, is the claim of some kind of shipbuilding and ship-repairing facility at Cleopatris, which leads me to think there was a reason for a shipyard to be at that location where none had been before: ships and shipbuilding materials were being transported from the Nile to the Red Sea via the Ptolemaic Canal, the canal built long ago by Cleopatra's ancestor Ptolemy II. Now the canal was supposedly in disrepair and silted up when Cleopatra came to power, but due to a sudden appearance of the shipyard at the end of it (why didn't Gallus choose Mersa Gawasis or Berenice?), it is my contention that this is fairly solid proof that the Ptolemaic Canal was operational when Octavian arrived in Egypt. And why would that be? If it had been operational upon Cleopatra's return from Actium, surely she wouldn't have bothered with her disastrous attempt to drag her ships across the Sinai Desert. A useable canal clearly would have been her first choice. Therefore, the canal was not operational *when* she returned from Actium, and so the quickest method she had at her disposal was to drag the ships across the thirty miles of isthmus desert from the Mediterranean to the Red Sea.

Let's take a look again at the time frame in which Cleopatra had to work. In September 31 BCE, she and Antony lost at Actium and sailed back to Egypt. Octavian started coming their way in the early spring. By April he was in Syria, and by July he was crossing the border into Egypt. By August 30, he was in Alexandria. Therefore, the time it actually took for Octavian to travel from Rome to Egypt was about three months. In theory, Octavian could have shown up in Egypt in December if he had rushed right off. Of course, winter was not a great time to be moving one's fleet across the Mediterranean to Egypt, but Octavian had been known to take wild risks in the past. However, I think Cleopatra would have doubted his need to hurry to Egypt, so I will accept that Cleopatra thought she had nine months to a year to work on her escape before Octavian got in her way.

So, if she wanted to flee to India, she would have to decide how she was going to get her warships and transport ships to her Red Sea port and then determine when she could leave from there. In reality, there was only one good time to sail to India, and that was the month of August (give or take a few weeks depending on the vagaries of the weather), when the monsoon winds would drive her ships east. Since shipyards were not available on the Red Sea, she couldn't just build a fleet of ships and have them waiting in the harbor for the wind to pick up in midsummer; she would have to bring the ships there.

With less than ten months to achieve her goal (she first had to return to Egypt, deal with her people, make plans, etc.), she had to choose between building brand-new ships or somehow getting her existing ships to Berenice. Could she build enough ships at Koptos, then have them dismantled, carried over to the port of Mersa Gawasis, and put back together for sailing to Berenice, all within ten months? Or could she break down her existing ships and then have them carried to the Red Sea and rebuilt, thereby saving a good bit of time? Or would she have to find some other way of getting her ships to the Red Sea?

What is interesting about the story of Cleopatra attempting to drag her ships through the desert is that she, for some reason, did indeed choose to do exactly that. Why? Her choice indicates it was not sensible to attempt to build new ships or to dismantle her old ships for some reason. If we look back at Pitassi's calculations on shipbuilding, it is unlikely that Cleopatra could build more than a half dozen ships at Koptos in such a short time frame, dismantled them, and put them back together again at Berenice or Mersa Gawasis. In fact, I think six may be way too high a number. So building, breaking apart, transporting, and rebuilding new ships was not a viable option.

Her next best choice would be to shave time off the building of the ships at Koptos by breaking down the ships already in existence. This indeed could really hurry things along, except there was one major problem. Ships that have been at sea for so long and endured quite a bit of use don't go back together again very nicely after you pull them apart. With all the warping and damage affecting the hull and the damage done while ripping the ship apart, you have a mess on your hands that isn't going to be easily reassembled in seaworthy fashion. Repairing parts of a seaborne ship is one thing; rebuilding it is another.

Which leaves Cleopatra with little choice but to move her existing ships to the Red Sea in some other fashion. Since she chose to transport them overland on rollers, the Ptolemaic Canal must not have been any use to her upon her return from Actium. Yet it seems to have been operational after her death, so why is this? It is my belief that when the simpler method (rolling ships across the desert) failed, Cleopatra had to move on to the only possibility left: reopening the canal. Now it is possible she could have been working on two plans simultaneously, making sure that if one plan failed, the other plan was already underway as a backup. This certainly is something Cleopatra likely would have done instead of putting all her eggs in one basket. When Plan A failed at Actium, she devised Plan B. When Plan B crashed and burned on the Sinai Peninsula, I believe Cleopatra already had Plan C in the works—reopening the Ptolemaic Canal.

CHAPTER 16

PLAN C—THE SECOND ATTEMPT TO FLEE EGYPT

Some may question the ability of Cleopatra to put the old canal back into operation within nine months. Could it be done? I think so, and we must keep in mind that it is possible she had already been working on the canal for months or years prior to Actium, we just have no record of it. She may have seen into the future enough to want to increase Egypt's Red Sea trade by making it easier to get ships from the Nile on to the Red Sea, eliminating the tiresome and likely expensive method of building, dismantling, and carrying newly built ships to the port and putting them back together again. Also, having a canal would make trade and pursuing various military strategies so much easier. Ptolemy II liked the idea of the canal, so I cannot see why Cleopatra sometime during her lifetime would not view its reopening as beneficial to the country. So she may have hurried it into operation in the nine months after Actium, or she may have already had it well underway when she returned to Egypt. For that matter, if it had been an unimpressive Nile inundation year when the floods were poor and there was a drought, maybe the canal was already operational but the water was simply too low at the time of her return from Actium for her ships to go through from September to December (when the water level should have been high enough). I think it most likely that the canal wasn't operational and, therefore, Cleopatra simply could not sail through it. And she couldn't repair it while the water was in the canal since the massive sludge pile would prohibit any attempt to dredge the waterway until it drained. The canal could be dredged and cleaned up from March through June when the water had finally receded.

As murky as the canal would have been for a great portion of the year, the exact months of the inundation of the Nile are murkier yet. The months when the Nile was most likely to be inundated with water seem to be from June through September, given that it takes about two months for the river to reach its highest volume of water, which means that the best time to sail one's large ships through the canal would start in August. However, because of some variation in exact inundation times and the amount of flooding, there is a possibility that the deepest waters could occur in the month of September. It is hard to say when exactly the canal would be usable. However, if Cleopatra was looking to escape Egypt via the canal and thereby use the favorable winds to get her to India, August would likely be the month she hoped the water and wind would work together to give her the best chance to escape. The difficulty for Cleopatra was not knowing ahead of time exactly what day would be the first she could safely move her ships into the canal and on to the Red Sea.

The canal is an interesting part of Egyptian history. It was an ingenious attempt by the Egyptians to bridge the Mediterranean and the Red Sea (by way of the Nile) in the only reasonable way possible prior to the building of the Suez Canal. The beginning of the canal starts thirty-nine miles northeast of Cairo, if you follow the eastern Nile branch toward the sea to the town of Bubastis, known today by the name Zagazig. I set off to see the area, knowing full well there was no canal in existence today. I wanted to stand at that spot and look eastward, to imagine the ships making their way along the canal from the Nile to Lake Timsah, where they would then turn south and sail through the Bitter Lakes to Cleopatris at the northern end of the Herooplite Gulf that leads to the Red Sea.

It is a short train ride from Cairo's main train station, Ramses, to

Zagazig, so I grabbed a taxi early in the morning to go catch one of the many trains that left fairly often heading in that direction. When I arrived, the train station was still under construction, but I managed to make my way to a ticket office where I attempted to purchase a ticket. Soon I was repeating history, struggling to locate my train platform as I had on my journey to Alexandria.

"Zagazig," I said to the woman behind the window.

"Not here. Platform 2." She waved me off.

I went to Platform 2's ticket window. "Zagazig."

"Platform 4."

I went to Platform 4. "Zagazig."

"Platform 8."

I went to Platform 8. "Zagazig."

"Platform 2." Now, I was stumped.

I tried for the next hour repeating the name of the town, pointing to the name in my guide book, scurrying back from platform to platform. I finally gave up and went to breakfast.

Sadly, I never did make it to Zagazig. Perhaps my failure to reach the canal was my way of following Cleopatra's own path through history; she never made it there, either.

The concept of a canal from Bubastis on the Nile to the Red Sea might seem like a bad idea to some: the problem being the lack of water in the canal for a number of months of the year, which would certainly make it impossible for large ships with any keel of measurable depth to pass through. Only during four months of the year, from August through November (or September through December), in accordance with the Nile inundation, would the canal fill up enough to provide sufficient depth for seagoing vessels to sail from the Nile through to the Bitter Lakes and on into the Red Sea. On the other hand, four months is better than no months for military and economic reasons, and there is certainly evidence in history that such a canal was desirable even if it had limited use and tended to silt up if it was not tended to continuously. The Wadi Tumilat, the area through which the canal was built, saw a constant flow of people and donkeys as they moved goods from the Red Sea to the Nile and vice versa. It was a practical idea to have a canal that would allow people to move goods in a much easier manner. Since Upper Egypt was a land full of canals that were traversed by shallow-bottom boats, which served as an important manner of transport in the country for centuries, it would be no surprise that the Egyptians should consider a longer and deeper canal and indeed construct one (they certainly had the man-power) along a well-traveled route that would allow for ships of all sizes—warships, large transport ships, and many smaller boats—to facilitate trade and aid in national defense.

There are a number of references to the canal being built and used prior to the reign of Cleopatra VII. It is said to have had its beginnings with Pharaoh Necho in 600 BCE, who supposedly started making the canal a reality. Apparently he did not finish it; Darius I, the Persian emperor, completed it one hundred years later in 500 BCE. It was 62 miles long (37½ miles from Bubastis to the Bitter Lakes and 24½ miles more down to Cleopatris) and 164 feet across (wide enough for two triremes to sail side by side), and it took four days for ships to make it from one end to the other. Upon completion of the canal, monuments were erected with the inscription:

A great god is Ahurumazda who has created these heavens, who has created this earth, who has created the humans, who has created the well-being for man, who has created King Darius, who has given Darius the Great Kingship with beautiful horses and men.

"I, Darius, Great King, king of kings, king of the countries of all languages, king of the wide and far-off earth, son of Hystaspes the Achaemenid. Darius King says: I, the Persian, with the Persian (soldiers), have taken Egypt. I gave the order to dig this stream from the river which is in Egypt (Piru is its name) to the River Amer Sea which comes out of Persia. This stream was dug as I have ordered, and the vessels journeyed on this stream from Egypt to Persia, as I have ordered."[1]

Interesting as it is that the canal was constructed and was operational, what is of even more significance is the statement of

Greek historian Diodorus Siculus (first century BCE) that the canal was managed by Ptolemy II and was very active, a major traffic artery for the next two centuries.[2] In fact, he states that Darius I actually did not finish the canal because he feared the saltwater of the Bitter Lakes would come into the canal and back into the freshwater Nile and so he gave up completing it; and that it was actually Ptolemy II who figured out that a lock was needed, and he constructed one on the eastern end, which made the canal a workable waterway. Ptolemy II made the port that the Romans later used at Cleopatris (also known as Arsinoe).

> An artificial canal leads from the Pelusian arm to the Arabian Gulf and the Red Sea. The first attempt to construct this was made by Necho, the son of Psamtik; The Persian Darius continued the work up to a certain point, but, finally, did not finish it, as he was told that the piercing of the isthmus would cause an inundation of the whole of Egypt, it being proven to him that the Red Sea was more elevated than Egypt. Later Ptolemy II finished the canal, and ordered a lock constructed with much artifice to be built at the most appropriate place. This he had opened before and closed quickly after every passage, thus never leaving it open longer than was necessary. The canal is called Ptolemy after its builder, and at its exit lies a city called Arsinoe.[3]

There is further commentary stating that parts of the canal were blocked by sand during Cleopatra's life and that it was the Roman emperor Trajan (98–117 CE) who cleared the silt and put it back into use. Hadrian, the next emperor, dredged it also and sent his fleet through to the Red Sea to conquer Nabatea and kept it functional as well during his reign (117–138 CE).[4]

So the canal seems to have been used for many a year from the time of Darius I (or at least Ptolemy II) well into the Roman Era, which proves to me that there is no reason to believe Cleopatra could not have had the canal in use during her reign or was not attempting to put it into use at the time of her death. The simple fact that a few years after her death, two hundred Roman ships appear at the canal's eastern end attests to my theory of Cleopatra likely having the canal operational and ready for use in moving her ships to the Red Sea.

But then the question would be, if this is so, why did she waste time dragging her ships over the Isthmus, and why didn't her ships ever make it to the Red Sea before Octavian invaded Egypt? I believe the problem lies not in Cleopatra's failure to have the canal finished in time, but in that she had to wait until the Nile inundation filled the canal satisfactorily enough to get let ships through.

In other words, Cleopatra really needed Octavian to stay away from Egypt until August. If he had left Rome a month later, history might have turned out very differently.

CHAPTER 17

A MOTIVE FOR THE
MURDER OF CLEOPATRA

I returned to Alexandria. As I stood on the dock staring past the colorful fishing boats floating tranquilly in the harbor, I thought of Octavian over on the other shore in Italy. Cleopatra must have stood on this very same spot wondering just how soon her enemy would push off his shores and come to destroy her. Cleopatra knew that, like a cancerous brain tumor that needed to be cut from his head, Octavian would need to remove her from his mind and his world with a swift and lethal blow.

The motive for Octavian's murder of Cleopatra is quite clear. This woman dared to create an heir with Julius Caesar (whether or not that heir was truly his biological child); joined with his enemy, Antony, to wage battle against him; and, most outrageously, continued to mock him with her existence and her incredible wealth. And, even though Cleopatra and Antony were badly beaten at Actium and fled to Egypt in mid-battle, Octavian knew she would never give up. She might retreat temporarily, but she would never surrender. If she fled, she would be back. He would have to march on Egypt and destroy her, along with her Roman general and her royal line. Only in this way could Octavian ever hope to be the last man standing and in total control of the Roman Empire.

Back in Egypt, after she failed to drag her ships across the Sinai

Desert to the Red Sea, Cleopatra could do nothing but wait and hope that the Nile inundation would come before Octavian did. Meanwhile, she continued building her Caesarium and taxing her people. She didn't let on that as soon as the canal waters rose, she would be absconding with her fleet and her treasure; it wouldn't do her any good if word got out that she expected to lose the war if Egypt was invaded.

It might seem that she was deserting her people like a captain jumping a sinking ship and leaving his men aboard (as some say she and Antony did at Actium), but staying with her people only to be humiliated and then executed while the conqueror took control of her entire military and all her riches would hardly do much for the country anyway. It is far better to retreat for the time being, allow the victor to quietly take control of your country and then return with a vengeance when the time is right and win back your land. Cleopatra's plan to leave was not one of cowardice; it was simply expedient. In fact, many of the Ptolemies—and even Cleopatra herself—had left Egypt when someone had managed to take over the throne and the ruler's life was threatened. They fled, they waited, they gathered forces, and they returned when the time was right to recapture their title of pharaoh. If one simply allowed oneself to be killed, the dynasty might end right there, but if one survived to fight another day, the Ptolemaic line would continue. Cleopatra seemed to be behaving as any Ptolemy would.

Then Cleopatra received horrific news. Octavian was on his way even though winter was barely over. Unless he was detained along the way or took ill, he would reach Egypt before the Nile floods. If he arrived before August, her only hope would be that her general at Pelusium could withstand a siege that might keep Octavian busy long enough for the rains to come and the Nile to rise; and then she could rush her fleet to the canal and get through it before he was any the wiser. I am sure she wished she could have already had her fleet in place on the Nile where the canal begins, waiting for the moment the waterway filled sufficiently, but the Nile route was most likely one that Octavian would choose to advance his armies toward Alexandria (as did Alexander before him), and it would end Cleopatra's plans if she were caught like a sitting duck with her fleet bunched up at the canal entrance.

Apparently, either her general sold out, gave up, or simply could not withstand Octavian's forces. Pelusium fell in a day. Plutarch writes:

> Accordingly, the war was suspended for the time being; but when the winter was over, Caesar again marched against his enemy through Syria, and his generals through Libya. When Pelusium was taken there was a rumour that Seleucus had given it up, and not without the consent of Cleopatra; but Cleopatra allowed Antony to put to death the wife and children of Seleucus.[1]

Plutarch certainly got a dig in at Cleopatra, insinuating that she purposely had her general give up Pelusium in order to gain favor from Octavian and then was so nasty that she had his family murdered to make it look like he had betrayed her and not the other way around. I doubt that this was at all true, considering how important it was to keep Octavian occupied at the border and that Cleopatra knew full well that no favors were going to sway Octavian from having her eliminated. More likely, the claim that she murdered Seleucus's family is a Plutarch fabrication, or it could be that Cleopatra was really angry at Seleucus for doing such a bad job of protecting the border. It could also be that Seleucus simply surrendered to save his own skin, which would have unquestionably sent Cleopatra over the edge.

Octavian was in Egypt prior to the Nile inundation. Now Cleopatra's position had become dire. Yet all hope was not lost, even if her odds of success were increasingly bleak. Cleopatra still saw a glimmer on the horizon, and that was carrying out Plan C by staging Actium Two at Alexandria. By using the strategy that allowed Antony and Cleopatra to escape Actium with a good portion of their fleet, Cleopatra hoped a replay of that maneuver might allow her to sail to the canal and out of Egypt.

While Cleopatra was waiting in Alexandria for the floodwaters to rise and Octavian was almost at the eastern border of Egypt, Antony had rushed over to the western border, to the fort of Paraetonium (today's Marsa Matrouh), 149 miles west of Alexandria, to try to keep his legions from defecting and to prevent Roman general Cornelius Gallus from entering the country.

> Gallus afterwards accompanied Octavianus [Octavian] to the battle of Actium, B.C. 31 when he commanded a detachment of the army. After the battle, when Octavianus was obliged to go from Samos to Italy, to suppress the insurrection among the troops, he sent Gallus with the army to Egypt, in pursuit of Antony. In the neighbourhood of Cyrene, Pinarius Scarpus, one of Antony's lieutenants, in despair, surrendered, with four legions, to Gallus, who then took possession of the island of Pharus, and attacked Paraetonium. When this town and all its treasures had fallen into the hands of Gallus, Antony hastened thither, hoping to recover what was lost, either by bribery or by force; but Gallus thwarted his schemes, and, in an attack which he made on Antony's fleet in the harbour of Paraetonium, he sunk and burnt many of the enemy's ships, whereupon Antony withdrew.[2]

The battle didn't go well for Antony, so he returned to Alexandria to do what he could to protect the city and implement Plan C's Actium reenactment. It's important to point out, however, that Suetonius's description of Gallus's sinking or burning many of Antony's ships is not repeated anywhere else nor is there any particular number of ships documented as having been destroyed. This detail is important because if Cleopatra and Antony's Plan C was to work, a combined Roman and Egyptian fleet would have to confront Octavian's ships as they did at the first battle of Actium. Antony's ships had to engage Octavian's while Cleopatra's ships waited to sail off when the battle was at its height. Without evidence to the contrary, and recalling the fact that Gallus possessed some two hundred ships to attack Arabia a few years later, I speculate that Antony may have lost some ships in his attempt to stop Cornelius Gallus at Paraetonium, but he did not lose his entire fleet. In fact, there is some corroboration of this in Plutarch's description of the final Alexandrian battle. He writes: "At daybreak, Antony in person posted his infantry on the hills in front of the city, and watched his ships as they put out and attacked those of the enemy."[3]

His ships. Not Cleopatra's. Of course, this could just be poor writing on the part of Plutarch, but then the very next description of what those ships did seems to validate that he was indeed speaking very specifically of Antony's fleet:

> . . . and as he expected to see something great accomplished by them, he remained quiet. But the crews of his ships, as soon as they were near, saluted Caesar's crews with their oars, and on their returning the salute changed sides, and so all the ships, now united into one fleet, sailed up towards the city prows on.[4]

Now, just a bit further on in Plutarch's rendition of that day, he does have Antony suspecting Cleopatra of stabbing him in the back and ordering the surrender of her navy in the Alexandria harbor, but I find it rather interesting that, if this were true, shouldn't we have Plutarch saying that Antony saw *Cleopatra's* ships go out toward the enemy and *Cleopatra's* ships salute Caesar's crews with their oars? No, Plutarch specifically states that they were Antony's ships, which is one reason he was so shocked; his ships would be under his command and his command was to engage Octavian's fleet in battle.

It is important to establish that Antony did still have enough of a fleet to at least attempt to engage Octavian's fleet and that it was his fleet that was heading out to meet with Octavian's. So where was Cleopatra's fleet? It may have been positioned behind Antony's, closer to the shore, and simply isn't mentioned because her ships never moved out of place. I will return to that last battle of Alexandria in a bit. For now, I simply want to establish that Antony had failed at the western border and returned to Alexandria with what remained of his fleet. Meanwhile, Octavian had just taken over Pelusium, and the month of July was not starting off well for Cleopatra.

She needed four more weeks, at least, to get her ships to the canal. At that point in time, the ships were likely with her in Alexandria, because if they were down in Memphis in the harbor waiting for the canal to fill, it wouldn't make sense that Cleopatra was in Alexandria when Octavian arrived there, and he would have seen her fleet while making his way to the city.

We really do not know, however, exactly by what method Octavian arrived at Alexandria or how long it took him. Since he entered the city on August 1, one can guess that he might have taken four weeks or more to march his army through the Nile delta. What little is written about these events comes, again, from Plutarch, who states that "at the same time [whilst Cleopatra was repeatedly sending him messages asking for mercy and likely determining his progress in her direction] that [Octavian] advanced with his army against the city."[5]

One might think that Octavian didn't need to have that big of an army, and he didn't need a fleet since he moved in from the east along the coast. But I think there is good reason to believe he at least had a reasonable number of legions with him and likely a fleet, or at least part of his fleet, to bring along food and water, especially since they traversed the Sinai Peninsula from Gaza to Pelusium. This is a rather unpleasant and treacherous stretch for an army to cover, but it would have been foolish to embark upon such a march without having a way to supply the soldiers with food and drink. A good description of how Octavian likely proceeded with his legions comes from the description of Alexander the Great's own travels along this route:

> Thus, the army will have journeyed from Gaza to Pelusium sometime in October, if not earlier. Of all the months of the year, September and October, are absolutely the worst to travel in the Sinai. Rains do not begin here until November, and the few wells along the coast, which are often too brackish to drink in any case, would be dry or virtually dry just before the onset of the rains. The coast of Sinai from Gaza to Pelusium is entirely covered with sand dunes, and the army would

have to march along the shore wet by the ocean lest the horses and wagons sink in the sand. There is no vegetation along the coast from Raphia to the Bitter Lakes. Even if supplies were collected at Gaza, the rations would not last more than four days. The fleet sailed alongside the army by the coast, and they undoubtedly set up magazines of provisions before sailing on to Pelusium. Notably, the march passed without incident, and Alexander covered the 127 miles in only seven days—undoubtedly to conserve provisions.[6]

It makes sense that Octavian also would have his fleet alongside him to carry provisions for his men as they traveled to Gaza and then Pelusium. The next question is, after Pelusium fell, by which route did Octavian proceed to bring his army to Alexandria? Although there is some possibility that he somehow went due west across all the Nile branches, using bridges and whatever roads existed, there is nothing in the literature that speaks of any particularly direct route straight to Alexandria (at the Canobic mouth) from Pelusium (at the Pelusiac mouth). According to the description by Strabo of the delta area between Pelusium and Alexandria, during the Nile inundation the land would be comprised of a marshy mishmash of elevated land areas and small canals to navigate from one area to the other.

These then are two mouths of the Nile, one of which is called the Pelusiac, the other the Canobic and Heracleiotic mouth. Between these are five other outlets, some of which are considerable, but the greater part are of inferior importance. For many others branch on from the principal streams, and are distributed over the whole of the island of the Delta, and form many streams and islands; so that the whole Delta is accessible to boats, one canal succeeding another, and navigated with so much ease, that some persons make use of rafts floated on earthen pots, to transport them from place to place. But at the time of the rising of the Nile, the whole country is covered, and resembles a sea, except the inhabited spots, which are situated upon natural hills or mounds; and considerable cities and villages appear like islands in the distant prospect.[7]

Composed of a mass of rivers, lakes, and canals, it isn't the easiest region in which to travel, especially if the waters are rising well in a good Nile inundation season. The more suitable route to Alexandria for Octavian to take in the summer would be from Pelusium, down the eastern branch of the Nile to Memphis, and then up the western branch of the Nile to Alexandria. Following this route, the army would have a far easier march, and the ships could float alongside them until they reached their destination. Alexander himself marched his troops along this 250-mile route. No general with knowledge of the Egyptian delta and the Nile inundations would take his army due east in the summer from Pelusium if he wanted his forces to reach Alexandria successfully.

If Octavian took the Nile route, he would have prevented Cleopatra's early departure from Alexandria. If she took her ships on the Nile from Alexandria down to Memphis and then up to Bubastis to the canal, she would surely run into Octavian. Alternately, she could sail straight to Pelusium, which would take her only a few days, but then there she would be marooned with no way to enter the canal until the Nile inundated properly. We don't know if Octavian left some of his fleet at Pelusium to prevent any of her ships from passing eastward or entering the Nile at the Pelusiac mouth, but it makes sense for him to set up a blockade at that location. We don't know if he did have some of his fleet come directly against the wind toward Alexandria, but there is nothing written of an early arrival of any ships before Octavian entered the city with his troops. Certainly, Antony went that exact westerly direction in order to get to Paraetonium in late June, so it is hard to say what military decisions might have been made necessary, even if they were not the preferred method of operation.

I want to note, for those who might question the ability of Cleopatra to take her fleet in the Pelusiac mouth or the Canobic mouth, that either was equally possible. The Nile had seven major arms reaching the Mediterranean in ancient days, but it was these two that had mouths that were wide enough for large ships to pass through. There were harbors at Memphis and Koptos, locations where ships were built and stationed. And it is written that along with much trafficking of goods between the Red Sea and the Nile ports, naval ships also moved from those locations to the Mediterranean, and invading armies moved their ships from that sea down the Nile. In his travels down to Heliopolis, fifth-century BCE Greek historian Herodotus noted this at the mouth of the Nile:

> First when you are still approaching it in a ship and are distant a day's run from the land, if you let down a sounding-line you will bring up mud and you will find yourself in eleven fathoms. This then so far shows that there is a silting forward of the land.[8]

Suffice it to say, Cleopatra was in Alexandria, apparently with her fleet. Octavian was coming her way from the east with his troops and fleet, and Gallus was converging from the west with his troops and fleet and might already have been in Alexandria blocking the port. The Nile inundation, however, was about four weeks away, which meant that Octavian would be arriving in Alexandria just about the time the waters reached a high-enough level to open the canal for business. Cleopatra had only one option—Plan C's Actium Two. She would have to duplicate the maneuvers of Actium, have Antony's fleet engage Octavian's, and then, hoisting their sails, her fleet would move out quickly. Her fleet would sail through or behind the line of battle to the east, and then turn down the western branch of the Nile, the one Octavian had just come up. She would sail her fleet through the Canobic mouth and move quickly down to Memphis and up to Bubastis, a trip that would take about four or five days (based on the recorded travels of Herodotus). As her fleet veered to the east behind the lines of battle, her flagship at the front, she could only hope that as many ships as possible would make it out of the harbor and follow her, those in the back giving battle if necessary to allow those at the front to make their escape. The same would be true on the Nile and in the canal; the ships in the rear, if necessary, could stop and block the route and protect the fleet, allowing the ships at the front more time to put distance between themselves and any pursuers. With the element of surprise, the advantage of a head start, and the likelihood that Octavian would think she would sail down to Koptos or Thebes and move overland toward Berenice or south into Nubia rather than turning north toward the canal (which she would hope he was not aware had been cleared), she might make it to the Red Sea with the majority of her fleet and men and make a successful run for India.

Meanwhile, she would not want Octavian to catch wind of her plans or have any suspicions that she might flee. If he got the notion that she might have some sort of escape plan, it is possible he would investigate and take extra precautions to block any exit from the country. There is a chance that this is why Plutarch has her sending messages back and forth to Octavian, begging for his mercy, and then threatening to burn all the treasure while hiding in her tomb in Alexandria:

> She had a tomb and monument built surpassingly lofty and beau-
> tiful, which she had erected near the temple of Isis, collected there
> the most valuable of the royal treasures, gold, silver, emeralds,
> pearls, ebony, ivory, and cinnamon; and besides all this she put there
> great quantities of torch-wood and tow, so that Caesar was anxious
> about the reason, and fearing lest the woman might become des-
> perate and burn up and destroy this wealth, kept sending on to her
> vague hopes of kindly treatment from him, at the same time that he
> advanced with his army against the city.[9]

Cleopatra may have created this "desperate plan" as a distraction so she could move portions of the Lagide treasury to Berenice or Memphis—to be picked up on the way to India—without Octavian realizing what she was doing. Since Cleopatra was still in Alexandria when Octavian arrived, we must surmise that the inundation was slow in coming. Clearly, the most she succeeded in accomplishing with her messages, if there was any truth to their existence, was to appear not to be planning to flee Alexandria.

It would be a bold plan, a desperate plan, and it could work if all the breaks fell her way. Cleopatra surely hadn't had much good luck since Octavian came on the scene, but luck can always change. It even seemed that a good omen occurred the night before her plan would have to be enacted. Plutarch might have been indulging in his usual dramatic overkill, but his description of Antony's successful defense of Alexandria on July 31, 30 BCE, if it were true, might have given Cleopatra a dash of hope: "But when [Octavian] had taken up position near the hippodrome, Antony sallied forth against him and fought brilliantly and routed his cavalry, and pursued them as far as their camp."[10]

Unfortunately, what little luck she might have had in her favor seemed to run out on the morning of August 1.

CHAPTER 18

THE UNFORESEEN
MURDER OF ANTONY

I found myself a seat on Saad Zaghloul Square underneath the statue of the early twentieth-century Egyptian statesman and nationalist, which had a soaring base with his figure on top and was built on the exact spot where Cleopatra's great Caesarium once stood. It was later known as the Temple of Augustus because Octavian completed the unfinished structure after the death of Cleopatra. The statue rests near the shore of the Mediterranean with the royal docks and palace nearby. Once Cleopatra's Needles, three fine red-granite obelisks that she had moved from Heliopolis to adorn her grand temple, stood here overlooking the great harbor (until 1877, when they were transported across the sea to London, Paris, and New York). No doubt two of the obelisks stood on either side of the entranceway to the Caesarium just as two obelisks stood guard at the doors of the temples of Luxor, Karnak, and Dendera.

> The first major building to be completed under the Romans was the Caesareum. On the sea-front between the Emporium and the little promontory on which Antony built the Timoneion, Cleopatra had started building a splendid temple in honour of Julius Caesar. She did not live to finish it, and it was completed by Octavius and known as the Caesareum. At the entrance, facing the sea, were two obelisks, brought from Upper Egypt.[1]

The description of the Caesareum is of a magnificent temple:

> It stands situate [sic] over against a most commodious harbour, wonderfully high and large in proportion, an eminent seamark full of choice paintings and statues, with donatives and oblations in abundance, and beautiful all over with gold and silver, curious and regular in the dispositions of the parts, with galleries, libraries, porches, courts, halls, walks, groves, as glorious as expense and art could make them, the hope and comfort of sea-faring men coming in or going out.[2]

It is extremely important to discern whether Cleopatra was holed up in a tomb or a temple because that location's very architecture can indicate where it was located and what Cleopatra saw as its purpose for August 1, 30 BCE. Before the days of the Ptolemies, in the Old and New Kingdoms of Egypt, two types of temples were built, cult temples and funerary temples (a fancy name for tombs). The cult temples were massive complexes located in town, in locations where the people could visit them regularly to worship their gods and their pharaohs; Luxor, Karnak, Dendera, Philae, and downtown Alexandria were homes to these lavish complexes. Tombs (funerary temples) were usually off in the desert, built into mountains or hills outside of town, so it took effort to reach them (and since they were sealed once the body was ensconced in them, the tombs rarely served much purpose).

No structures built by the Ptolemies currently exist, so we cannot differentiate between their temples and tombs (I will call the funerary temples "tombs" to make it simple). History, however, records Cleopatra's great Caesarium as being right in town at the harbor; and outside of town is a burial ground, a place known as the Al Qabbari Necropolis, which was discovered by forensic anthropologists of the Centre d'Études Alexandrines, directed by Jean-Yves Empereur. Mummified skeletal remains dating back to the Hellenistic era (323–146 BCE) in forty-two collective burial chambers were found by accident during road construction just west of the city in 1999. There is another tomb in the town of Stagni, only 350 yards west of the Al Qabbari burial chambers, which are actual aboveground chambers carved into the large rock. Here we find a big stone cube with just one sealed entrance containing a chamber and a number of small rooms (it has subsequently been removed from the rock and stands freely in a garden at the Kom el-Shuqafa catacombs). The subterranean Macedonian Alabaster Tomb, likely built around 300 BCE and uncovered in 1907 in El Shatby, Egypt, lies east of modern downtown Alexandria and only a few blocks east of the ancient royal palace. The existence of this tomb might indeed indicate that there was a royal cemetery closer to town than others in Egypt. However, the location of this underground tomb is to the east of Cape Locias, so while it is close to the sea, it is not on a harbor or near the docks as the Caesarium is, the location that approximates where Plutarch places Cleopatra's mausoleum.

One thing is clear from exploring each and every one of the tombs (funerary temples): namely, not one of them has windows to look out of, to haul bodies through, or to allow light and air inside. Tombs were sealed boxes, sometimes a number of sealed boxes, that occasionally had passageways leading to the sealed boxes. Only someone carrying a torch could find his or her way, and then for only a short time since the air supply was limited. The tombs were dark graves meant to keep mummified bodies intact and their valuables for the afterlife safe from grave robbers.

Therefore, tombs had no windows. In fact, Macedonian tombs, which the Ptolemaic tombs were modeled after, were blocks of stone with an arched roof, the entire structure being covered over with dirt to bar the entranceway. But Plutarch says that the edifice in which Cleopatra had locked herself had windows, along with some other very odd features for a tomb. Here is the very illustrative part of Plutarch's story about Cleopatra and her sojourn in the mausoleum, a portion of his narrative that is full of fascinating and curious details.

At daybreak, Antony in person posted his infantry on the hills in front of the city, and watched his ships as they put out and attacked those of the enemy; and as he expected to see something great accomplished by them, he remained quiet. But the crews of his ships, as soon as they were near, saluted Caesar's crews with their oars, and on their returning the salute changed sides, and so all the ships, now united into one fleet, sailed up towards the city prows on. No sooner had Antony seen this than he was deserted by his cavalry, which went over to the enemy, and after being defeated with his infantry he retired into the city, crying out that he had been betrayed by Cleopatra to those with whom he waged war for her sake. But she, fearing his anger and his madness, fled for refuge into her tomb and let fall the drop-doors, which were made strong with bolts and bars; then she sent messengers to tell Antony that she was dead. Antony believed that message, and saying to himself,

"Why doest thou longer delay, Antony? Fortune has taken away thy sole remaining excuse for clinging to life," he went into his chamber. Here, as he unfastened his breastplate and laid it aside, he said: "O Cleopatra, I am not grieved to be bereft of thee, for I shall straightway join thee; but I am grieved that such an imperator as I am has been found to be inferior to a woman in courage."

Now, Antony had a trusty slave named Eros. Him Antony had long before engaged, in case of need, to kill him, and now demanded the fulfilment of his promise. So Eros drew his sword and held it up as though he would smite his master, but then turned his face away and slew himself. And as he fell at his master's feet Antony said: "Well done, Eros! though thou wast not able to do it thyself, thou teachest me what I must do"; and running himself through the belly he dropped upon the couch. But the wound did not bring a speedy death. Therefore, as the blood ceased flowing after he had lain down, he came to himself and besought the bystanders to give him the finishing stroke. But they fled from the chamber, and he lay writhing and crying out, until Diomedes the secretary came from Cleopatra with orders to bring him to her in the tomb.

Having learned, then, that Cleopatra was alive, Antony eagerly ordered his servants to raise him up, and he was carried in their arms to the doors of her tomb. Cleopatra, however, would not open the doors, but showed herself at a window, from which she let down ropes and cords. To these Antony was fastened, and she drew him up herself, with the aid of the two women whom alone she had admitted with her into the tomb. Never, as those who were present tell us, was there a more piteous sight. Smeared with blood and struggling with death he was drawn up, stretching out his hands to her even as he dangled in the air. For the task was not an easy one for the women, and scarcely could Cleopatra, with clinging hands and strained face, pull up the rope, while those below called out encouragement to her and shared her agony. And when she had thus got him in and laid him down, she rent her garments over him, beat and tore her breasts with her hands, wiped off some of his blood upon her face, and called him master, husband, and imperator; indeed, she almost forgot her own ills in her pity for his. But Antony stopped her lamentations and asked for a drink of wine, either because he was thirsty, or in the hope of a speedier release. When he had drunk, he advised her to consult her own safety, if she could do it without disgrace, and among all the companions of Caesar to put most confidence in Proculeius, and not to lament him for his last reverses, but to count him happy for the good things that had been his, since he had become most illustrious of men, had won greatest power, and now had been not ignobly conquered, a Roman by a Roman.

Scarcely was he dead, when Proculeius came from Caesar. For after Antony had smitten himself and while he was being carried to Cleopatra, Dercetaeus, one of his body-guard, seized Antony's sword, concealed it, and stole away with it; and running to Caesar, he was the first to tell him of Antony's death, and showed him the sword all smeared with blood. When Caesar heard these tidings, he retired within his tent and wept for a man who had been his relation by marriage, his colleague in office and command, and his partner in many undertakings and struggles. Then he took the letters which had passed between them, called in his friends, and read the letters aloud, showing how reasonably and justly he had written, and how rude and overbearing Antony had always been in his replies. After this, he sent Proculeius, bidding him, if possible, above all things to get Cleopatra into his power alive; for he was fearful about the treasures in her funeral pyre, and he thought it would add greatly to the glory of his triumph if she were led in the procession. Into the hands of Proculeius, however, Cleopatra would not put herself; but she conferred with him after he had come close to the tomb and stationed himself outside at a door which was on a level with the ground. The door was strongly fastened with bolts and bars, but allowed a passage for the voice. So they conversed, Cleopatra asking that her children might have the kingdom, and Proculeius bidding her be of good cheer and trust Caesar in everything.

After Proculeius had surveyed the place, he brought back word to Caesar, and Gallus was sent to have another interview with the queen; and coming up to the door he purposely prolonged the conversation. Meanwhile Proculeius applied a ladder and went in through the window by which the women had taken Antony inside. Then he went down at once to the very door at which Cleopatra was standing and listening to Gallus, and he had two servants with him.[3]

I pulled out from my briefcase the photos I had taken while visiting the temples of Luxor and Karnak and the Temple of Isis on the island of Philae. As I looked over the photos, I saw windows, four windows high up on the front-facing pylon walls at Luxor, a double row high up on the pylons at Karnak, and a few on the pylon walls of the Temple of Isis. It is clear that these windows were perfectly stationed on the outer walls (the walls that protected the inner buildings and grounds of the temple) on either side of the huge door between the pylons that opened into the inner sanctuary.

I had to snicker a bit at this point as I reviewed the placement of the windows in these temple pylons. They were about four stories high. Is it really believable that Cleopatra, a woman of nearly forty years who (for a lifetime) had her every need catered to by her servants, that she and two handmaidens actually had the strength to haul a dying Antony, a strong warrior of some weight, up four stories on a rope? For that matter, why in the world would they do such a cruel thing, making him endure such bruising and scraping along the pylon walls? Why not simply open the door?

Speaking of doors, it seems a bit odd to me that the door to the tomb Plutarch describes would be bolted from the inside. Did the dead of the day actually lock themselves in, or was an innocent person always placed in the tombs with the dead to throw the sealing bolt? In fact, from what I have been able to gather, both Egyptian and Macedonian tombs had heavy doors placed in the doorframes that were the openings to the tombs, and then the doors were sealed, either by granite plugs and wax in the spaces around the doors or by building walls of heavy limestone brick on the outside of the doors, and burying the tombs under dirt the rest of the way.

On the other hand, there were priests inside religious *temples* (not tombs), and they did bolt and unbolt the doors to the sanctuary on a regular basis.

> The common form of Egyptian bolt for a two-leaf door is a piece of metal or wood flat on one leaf and rounded on the other which slides in two staples on one leaf and in one or two on the other. An examination of door-frames in the temples shows clearly not only that vertical bolts were used which engaged into the sill and the lintel, and bolts for single-leaf doors engaging in the jamb, but that the doors could be barred from the inside, recesses into which the bar was slipped was not uncommon for temple doors.[4]

So Plutarch's mentions of both windows and a bolted door lead me to believe that we are indeed looking at a cult temple as the location where Cleopatra spent her last few days until she was captured. If her son, Caesarion, made a stop on his way to Berenice at the temple of Dendera, a temple on the Nile thirty-seven miles north of Luxor, he would be at the only site in Egypt where depictions of the queen and Caesarion, as coregents, remain to this day on the outer rear wall. The temple itself is the most complete building of its type still standing—as close a construction as one can find in Egypt that would be similar to the magnificent Caesarium in Alexandria, and its structure tells us a lot about the building Plutarch is actually speaking of when he describes the "tomb" Cleopatra was hiding in.

Upon entering the Dendera site, one passes through what is left of the pylons at the front of the sanctuary, just the doorframe. Then there is a long space that would have been the open forecourt, and then one enters the magnificent hypostyle hall, a huge interior with massive pillars that support the roof, which still actually exists at Dendera. University of Bologna professor Sergio Pernigotti describes temples of ancient Egypt quite well; the following depicts as exactly as possible what Dendera must have looked like, and no doubt how the Caesarium would have appeared as well.

> The Egyptian temple, as we know it from the beginning of the second millennium to the Ptolemaic and Roman Periods, was of a standard type, regardless of size. Whether large (in some cases, very large) or small, it always contained the same elements, linked to one another in an almost unvarying scheme. The temple was sited in a vast area surrounded by a wall of unbaked, and often impressively large, bricks. This wall sometimes enclosed less important religious buildings, as well as other structures, also built of unbaked brick, such as service facilities, warehouses, and the homes of the priests, other temple functionaries, guardians, and administrative personnel.
>
> The temple itself was a long building composed of a series of sections in which the roof gradually became lower and the floor higher, until the chapel was reached. The chapel contained the tabernacle holding the image of the god to whom the temple was dedicated. Anyone entering the temple passed through the monumental gate at the same level as the first pylon, moving from the bright sunlight of the open forecourt through the shadows of the hypostyle hall, and into the increasing darkness of the rooms leading to the sanctuary and of the rooms that sometimes surrounded it.[5]

The forecourt offered a fine location for Cleopatra to actually make a fire if she wanted to pretend to burn up her treasure or, in my opinion, to send up smoke as a signal for the battle to begin (and to make Octavian believe she was actually still in the temple when, in fact, she would be sailing out of the harbor). I had walked through the stunning hypostyle hall of the Dendera temple complex, explored the underground tunnels where Antony's son no doubt would have attempted to hide once the Caesarium was breached, and up to the roof where I could stand and view the landscape for miles around and, where Cleopatra on her roof at the Caesarium, could view progress of her plan of action. I also noted that with so large a complex, with so many rooms, corridors, and cubbyholes, Octavian would have had to embark upon a lengthy search of the place to ensure that Cleopatra had not hidden anything useful inside, like poison. For a tomb, yes, he could easily check the few empty rooms and see that nothing was tucked away inside, but a temple would take days to search. He would have to station guards inside with Cleopatra and her handmaidens if he wanted to ensure that they had nothing inside that they could use in a lethal manner.

After being able to experience the Dendera, a structure so much like the Caesarium, it is easier to understand what actually occurred on the grounds of the temple when Cleopatra's plan fell apart.

Let me stop here to recall the part of Plutarch's story in which he claims Antony stabs himself, and the Roman general and Cleopatra are reunited at the "tomb."

Antony supposedly has just seen the navy surrender and suspects Cleopatra has betrayed him. Cleopatra is terrified of Antony's anger, so she runs into her tomb, lets fall the drop-doors, and bolts them. Then she sends word to Antony that she is dead. Antony decides to kill himself as well. He takes off his breastplate and asks his slave Eros to stab him. Eros can't bring himself to do it, and instead kills himself. Then, Antony, feeling bested by his slave in courage, runs his sword through his belly and drops on the sofa. He doesn't die right away, but is bleeding profusely and, somehow, Cleopatra finds out what has happened and sends his men to carry him to the tomb; yet, when they arrive, she won't open the door. Instead, she drops ropes down from a window, and she and her ladies haul him up. Meanwhile, Antony's bodyguard Dercetaeus runs Antony's sword over to Octavian and tells him Antony is dead.

There is quite a bit of nonsense in Plutarch's creative writing, but let me focus here on the demise of Antony. Having already established that Cleopatra expected no favors from Octavian, I hardly think surrendering to him would serve much purpose. But Plutarch says she does this behind Antony's back, betraying him and then hiding in her tomb, behind heavy, bolted doors because she was so frightened of his anger. This is a laughable story. Why would she worry about Antony's anger and not Octavian's? And what of the burning of the treasure? Wasn't that the reason she was locked up in the tomb? A convoluted and unconvincing story it is that Cleopatra surrendered, hid, and then sent over to Antony a phony story of her death. Then, forgetting Cleopatra's supposed betrayal and feeling anguished over the fact that the women he loves is dead, he commits suicide (although not immediately successfully). Yet, when he hears Cleopatra lied to him about being dead, he wants to be with her, to die in the arms of the woman who has been horribly disloyal to him. Meanwhile, Dercetaeus, his bodyguard, runs off to Octavian with Antony's sword to prove he was dead even though the surrender had already occurred.

My head is spinning at Plutarch's contorted logic. I find the idea of Cleopatra sending over false stories of her death and Antony subsequently committing suicide highly improbable. It is far more likely that Antony's men realized it was going to mean their annihilation to fight Octavian, so in desperation they did what they had to do: they assassinated their general. Then, they surrendered to Octavian as most everyone else had already done. When the deed was accomplished, the sword was brought by Dercetaeus to Octavian to prove Antony had been dispatched. The same message was delivered to the harbor, and the men on Antony's ships raised their oars and conceded to Octavian's fleet. Where, exactly, Antony would have been murdered that morning—on the top of the Paneium overlooking Alexandria, or in his quarters, or outside the temple while en route to say good-bye to Cleopatra and the children—is of little importance, but the likelihood that the assassination was premeditated prior to the exact moment is something to strongly consider. Men do what is expedient, and Antony's desire to fight, while it served his purposes (to save his children and Cleopatra and to be his final moment of glory), would have been suicide for the Roman soldiers.

If Antony was not murdered outside the door of the temple, but taken down at another location, he was likely brought to Cleopatra to let her know the battle, and her plan to escape, was over and finished. If so, perhaps Antony's men felt some remorse over killing their leader and thought it would at least be right to bring him to the queen. Then again, perhaps they disliked the queen enough to wish to dump Antony's body at her door to let her know they held her responsible for his demise.

At the moment Antony was struck down, Cleopatra was most likely either on the roof of the temple or at one of the windows. Her men were on guard at the door, and other men were standing ready in the open forecourt to light a fire. The forecourt of an Egyptian temple is a huge open space with all the air in the world to get a blazing fire started and unleash a towering plume of smoke. From her high vantage point in the temple, Cleopatra would have seen her doom sealed. She would see Antony murdered (if it happened as he was coming to say farewell and take her and the children to her ship), and she would have known immediately that the plan was blown. Or, if he was murdered elsewhere, she would have observed the ships surrendering and turning back. With a dying or deceased Antony now lying in front of the temple, she simply would have ordered her men to unbolt the front door and bring him in. No elaborate methods of receiving her husband would have been necessary.

When Octavian's man Proculeius was sent to capture Cleopatra, he likely just put a ladder up to the window. Now it is possible, if the building was still under construction, that he came up through some scaffolding. No doubt he came with a swarm of men to capture Cleopatra alive and to stop her from setting any fires that might destroy her considerable treasure. Clearly, no fire was ever set, so there was likely no treasure there to burn up (she had probably already removed it from Alexandria). The queen was trapped, her last hope of escape extinguished.

CHAPTER 19

THE CAPTURE OF CLEOPATRA

I sat in a chair in front of a shabby little café on the Corniche. I remembered my visit to the temple at Dendera, and how I looked up at the ceiling with its soaring columns embracing the roof and I wondered how it would feel to be Cleopatra standing among all that magnificence and knowing that such grandeur was something I actually lived, that the whole of the country saw me as more than a mortal, saw me as a goddess, saw me as a savior. Then, as I had walked deeper and deeper into the Dendera temple, I could feel a sense of isolation. Is that how Cleopatra felt when all the splendor was to be taken from her, cutting her down to size, to that of a simple human being? The crushing weight of defeat and despair that must have pressed down upon Cleopatra as she sat next to the body of her husband and the huddled forms of her crying children must have been unbearable. Perhaps, in an odd twist of fate, the grandeur of the temple that surrounded her and once made her feel superior now made her feel small, weak, and insignificant.

Or possibly the coolness of the stones around her shot their chill into her heart, freezing the blood in her veins, turning her into an ice queen for her last, final stand against Octavian. Of the ancient authors, none painted a particularly emotional scene on the part of Cleopatra, save Plutarch, who described the queen as highly distraught and hysterical, so much so that she inflicted injury upon herself in order to counteract the emotional pain she felt inside.

204   THE MURDER OF CLEOPATRA

And when she had thus got him in and laid him down, she rent
her garments over him, beat and tore her breasts with her hands,
wiped off some of his blood upon her face, and called him master,
husband, and imperator. . . .
[H]er breasts were wounded and inflamed by the blows she gave
them. Because of her grief and pain—for her chest was inflamed and
lacerated where she had beaten it.[1]

Even at a time when her world collapsed around her and hope
had been extinguished, would Cleopatra fall apart, or would she hold
herself together, carrying her pharaonic superiority and pride to the
bitter end? I believe that Cleopatra's high level of narcissism would
not have allowed the world to see her shaken or crying or humbled. I
find Plutarch's description of Cleopatra's behavior unseemly for such
a queen; that she would abuse herself in such a fashion was more
likely a dramatic story than a reality.

Two issues must be examined concerning Cleopatra's self-abuse:
how common was it for the women in the ancient world, specifically
Egypt and Greece, who lost their husbands to injure themselves physically in their grief? And, second, was Cleopatra the type of woman
to do so?

There are quite a number of writings, including the Bible, which
cite woman and men beating themselves upon their breasts as a sign of
mourning.[2] Hairpulling and wailing were common as well. Mourning
was to be a public display, though, showing others the importance of
the person who died and the level of grief those remaining felt for the
loss of their loved one. Much of the mourning process was communal
and served as a group bonding experience.

Sometimes the act was more of a political statement, and pro-
fessional mourners were hired to add to the numbers of bereaved,
thus raising the importance of the deceased. How often the phrase
"beating one's breast" actually meant inflicting damage is questionable because little was written about resulting injuries. Therefore,
"beating one's breast" is most often construed as a public display,
rather than actual self-abuse.

Beating of the breast is primarily an Eastern mourning activity and is a common form of expression in Greece and Egypt. Ancient Egyptian tombs even show art depicting women beating on their breasts in front of mummies, with one such work showing blood dripping from a woman's breast onto the body of the deceased.[3]

Therefore, Plutarch's story of Cleopatra grieving in such a fashion was not at all beyond reason.

However, was it probable? There is no evidence in Cleopatra's past behavior that she was prone to histrionics. When Julius Caesar was murdered, there was no mention of Cleopatra abusing herself. When Cleopatra and Antony barely escaped with their lives from Actium, it was Antony who fell into a depression and mistreated himself physically with alcohol. Cleopatra always held her head high and pressed on.

There are two reasons for "beating one's breast" after the death of someone important. First, it would be the public display to generate communal cohesiveness and a political show. Antony's death occurred at a time and place where a display of extreme grief by Cleopatra would serve no purpose to the community. No one except her children, maidservants, and a contingent of guards would have witnessed such an act and, therefore, the "breast beating" would serve no purpose in any communal or political sense.

Second, such a show would be commensurate with the depth of emotion one would feel for the loss of a loved one. Since Cleopatra spent little time with Antony in their last year together and not even all that much in the many years prior, nor did she seem to express much passion for him, it is difficult to believe that this man—who had just failed her yet again, and who likely cost Cleopatra both her life and her sovereignty—was going to awaken much anguish in her. The only anguish Cleopatra likely felt was for the tragic failure of her attempt to save herself, her children, and Egypt. While she might be terribly upset at the turn of events, because the practice of breast beating is a public mourning ritual for the dead, she would not likely have engaged in such abuse as a personal reaction to bad news.

One also wonders if the reports of such public displays ever offered any proof of the level of harm the women did to themselves; I could find none. I conducted role-play to put myself through an experience of the sort to see what it felt like, physically and emotionally. Role-play is an important part of crime reconstruction. How will we be able to determine if some behavior could truly be an element of a crime if we are not sure it is even possible or plausible? My role-play educated me quite a bit. I found that pummeling one's breasts is incredibly awkward and required a wide arc of one's fists with quite a bit of force in order to actually land a solid blow that causes pain and bruising. Because it requires much energy and a feeling of foolishness ensues quite quickly, I concluded that one would indeed have to be experiencing hysterical grief to keep up such a ridiculous activity or one must be earning a tidy sum for the performance.

Actual laceration of the breasts in order to draw blood is even more difficult. This requires first tearing away of all the outer clothing and then clawing with great pressure to even get a good scratch—and then one must be standing in public half-naked. All in all, in a crazed emotional haze, it would be far easier to abuse one's face and rip one's hair out. It occurred to me that supposed public displays of grieving for a dead ruler or important relative may be more a mock attack on oneself with a great deal of screaming and crying to make the assault seem agonizing. Since oftentimes this was paid work, it would behoove the actresses to put on a good show but not cause serious damage to themselves; to do otherwise would rather make the earnings not worth the effort.

Another proof that Cleopatra did not abuse herself is actually contained within a contradiction just paragraphs away in Plutarch's rendition of events when, according to his account, Octavian sends his man Proculeius to capture Cleopatra before she can set fire to the treasure. While I will discuss the matter of how Cleopatra ended up in the hands of Octavian a bit later in the analysis, it is first important to establish that Cleopatra did no harm to herself. Plutarch writes of when Proculeius slipped into the "mausoleum" and came up behind Cleopatra,

. . . whereupon the queen turned about, saw Proculeius, and tried to stab herself; for she had at her girdle a dagger such as robbers wear. But Proculeius ran swiftly to her, threw both his arms about her, and said:

"O Cleopatra, thou art wronging both thyself and [Octavian], by trying to rob him of an opportunity to show great kindness, and by fixing upon the gentlest of commanders the stigma of faithlessness and implacability."

At the same time he took away her weapon, and shook out her clothing, to see whether she was concealing any poison. And there was also sent from [Octavian] one of his freedmen, Epaphroditus, with injunctions to keep the queen alive by the strictest vigilance, but otherwise to make any concession that would promote her ease and pleasure.[4]

Would not Proculeius, in seeing a bloodied Cleopatra, knife in hand, already believe she had stabbed herself? Would he not check for such wounds? Would he, if he wanted her to stay alive, not inform Caesar immediately that she was suffering from bruises and gashes on her breast from her own abuse? Yet he apparently notices none of these things, nor does he call for medical assistance. He also never notes that she has exposed either of her breasts for examination. It is only later that the issue of these supposed injuries to Cleopatra's breast arises again. This glaring omission could simply be an oversight by Plutarch, or it could be a story of self-abuse later fabricated as an explanation for the injuries Cleopatra exhibits after being in Octavian's custody. The next part of the story concerning Cleopatra's capture and incarceration suggests that the injuries were sustained after she was put under his guard.

After a few days [Octavian] himself came to talk with her and give her comfort. She was lying on a mean pallet-bed, clad only in her tunic, but sprang up as he entered and threw herself at his feet; her hair and face were in terrible disarray, her voice trembled, and her eyes were sunken. There were also visible many marks of the cruel blows upon her bosom; in a word, her body seemed to be no better off than her spirit.[5]

We must return to Cleopatra's state of mind and her choice of strategy at this dire moment when we examine how she came under Octavian's control and what transpired between them. Once it was clear to Octavian that Antony was dead, for he had received the proof by Dercetaeus's delivery of Antony's sword, Plutarch writes:

After this, he sent Proculeius, bidding him, if possible, above all things to get Cleopatra into his power alive; for he was fearful about the treasures in her funeral pyre, and he thought it would add greatly to the glory of his triumph if she were led in the procession. Into the hands of Proculeius, however, Cleopatra would not put herself; but she conferred with him after he had come close to the tomb and stationed himself outside at a door which was on a level with the ground. The door was strongly fastened with bolts and bars, but allowed a passage for the voice. So they conversed, Cleopatra asking that her children might have the kingdom, and Proculeius bidding her be of good cheer and trust Caesar in everything.

After Proculeius had surveyed the place, he brought back word to Caesar, and Gallus was sent to have another interview with the queen; and coming up to the door he purposely prolonged the conversation. Meanwhile Proculeius applied a ladder and went in through the window by which the women had taken Antony inside. Then he went down at once to the very door at which Cleopatra was standing and listening to Gallus, and he had two servants with him. One of the women imprisoned with Cleopatra cried out, "Wretched Cleopatra, thou art taken alive."[6]

And Cassius Dio, the only other ancient historian to write of this event, says:

And so Antony died there in the embrace of Cleopatra; she felt confident about Octavian and made it clear to him right away what had happened, but she did not completely trust that she would suffer no harm. Therefore, she remained inside so that, even if nothing else should save her, she could obtain amnesty and her kingdom by exploiting Octavian's fear of losing her treasure. Even then, amid such calamity, she was so mindful of her sovereignty that she preferred to die with her name and status intact rather than to live as a private citizen. To be sure, she also had fire for her treasure and for herself asps and other reptiles, which she had tested on men to determine how each of them killed. Octavian was eager to control her treasury and to take her alive and lead her in his triumph, but having given her, in some sense, his word, he did not want to seem to have her as a prisoner taken against her will. So, he sent to her Gaius Proculeius, an equestrian, and Epaphroditus, a freedman, with instructions detailing what should be said and done. They met with Cleopatra and, while discussing some reasonable options, suddenly grabbed her before completing the negotiation.[7]

The ancient authors tell a very odd story of Cleopatra's lockdown in the "mausoleum," or temple, as I have determined. Let's pretend for a moment that the story is true, that Cleopatra did indeed plan to destroy her treasure in desperation.

A fire is not an instantaneous affair. It requires quite a bit of work to start it, stoke it, and build it up to an all-consuming furnace that would have the power to destroy such a quantity of goods as the Egyptian royal treasury is described to have contained. Are we to believe that Cleopatra and her ladies stayed alone in this massive edifice with a mountain of treasure amid the logs and pitch with no one else to assist them in putting this plan into action? We are speaking of the queen of Egypt, who had gone into battle with men and always had her guards and protectors at her disposal. Would not then Cleopatra bring a contingent of men with her into the temple to guard her and to fight anyone who attempted to enter? Wouldn't she, if she were truly planning to set a fire, set her men to build and tend the blaze? Are we to believe she was so foolish and impotent a queen that she must manage it herself with just a couple of middle-aged women to assist her in such a monumental task? Would she simply stand by the door and trade foolish talk with Octavian's men, handmaidens listening at her side, while knowing that at any time his army could attack and be inside the building within minutes? All of this seems highly unlikely.

Neither would Octavian waste time with negotiations if he believed the coveted Lagide treasure might be inside the temple. Once he was able to move on the city with the knowledge that Antony was dead and the enemy had surrendered, it would not be long before his men would be at the temple to storm it and capture both Cleopatra and her treasure. Wasting time in foolish negotiations would only delay his attempt to protect and seize the treasure and capture Cleopatra alive. If by this point he realized that no treasure was in the temple, he would still want to move just as quickly to take Cleopatra, and all others who might have vital information, into his custody. He was also eager to find Caesarion and, and as part of his plan to destroy the Egyptian royal line, eliminate him.

Large as the temple was, it was sensible that Cleopatra and her personal guard would move into the depth of the temple while her men attempted to prevent Octavian's soldiers from entering. This would prevent her death in the assault and allow her the opportunity to set the stage for the moment when she would come face to face with her enemy.

Inevitably, Cleopatra would lose this standoff. Once she had lost control of the temple and had been captured by the forces of Octavian, where would he keep her sequestered? There are two stories concerning this matter:

From Plutarch we have a piece of the story with information that appears to be missing. First, in the passage that follows, he writes of the moment when Proculeius took the dagger from Cleopatra's possession in the mausoleum (as he has stated earlier, this is where she had hidden herself).

And there was also sent from [Octavian] one of his freedmen, Epaphroditus, with injunctions to keep the queen alive by the strictest vigilance, but otherwise to make any concession that would promote her ease and pleasure.[8]

Yet later Plutarch writes:

[Octavian] had resolved to send off her and her children within three days. After Cleopatra had heard this, in the first place, she begged [Octavian] that she might be permitted to pour libations for Antony; and when the request was granted, she had herself carried to the tomb, and embracing the urn which held his ashes, in company with the women usually about her . . .[9]

Plutarch does not tell us where Cleopatra is but says she must be carried to the mausoleum. But surely she cannot be in the mausoleum, or this transport would not be necessary. Plutarch fails to include in his tale any information about what transpired between the time Epaphroditus is sent to watch Cleopatra and allow anything she would like for her comfort (in the mausoleum) to the point in the story when she is obviously returning to the mausoleum. Either she was actually in the temple or palace where she was confined for a period and then brought to the mausoleum, or she was in the mausoleum, brought elsewhere, and then returned.

Ancient Roman historian Florus explains:

When she despaired of convincing the Princeps [Octavian] and realized that she was spared only for display in his triumph, she took advantage of a rather lax guard and escaped to the mausoleum (this is what they call the royal tomb).[10]

Cassius Dio goes further in describing her captivity:

Then they took her to the palace, but did not remove any of her accustomed retinue or attendants, in order that she should entertain more hope than ever of accomplishing all she desired, and so should do no harm to herself.[11]

It makes sense that Cleopatra was taken from the temple and removed to the palace. Indeed, Octavian wanted to calm the public at that point, since the Alexandrians were known to be a rather volatile citizenry. To keep Cleopatra in the temple under guard makes it quite clear that Octavian means to depose the queen and seize the Egyptian throne for himself. On the heels of the devastating defeat of the country, it behooves him to have an interim period to calm the people and give them some solace in the safety of their queen. Bringing her to the palace allows Octavian to appear generous and willing to negotiate.

Plutarch gives us this picture of Octavian's attempts to win over the public following the death of Antony and the capture of Cleopatra:

> And now [Octavian] himself drove into the city, and he was conversing with Areius the philosopher, to whom he had given his right hand, in order that Areius might at once be conspicuous among the citizens, and be admired because of the marked honour shown him by [Octavian]. After he had entered the gymnasium and ascended a tribunal there made for him, the people were beside themselves with fear and prostrated themselves before him, but he bade them rise up, and said that he acquitted the people of all blame, first, because of Alexander, their founder; second, because he admired the great size and beauty of the city; and third, to gratify his companion, Areius.[12]

So it would seem that Cleopatra was brought back to the palace and kept under guard. Although there is a claim she was to be kept comfortable and allowed anything that she desired for her happiness, Plutarch's description of her time in captivity hardly seems one of luxury and well-being; Cleopatra is wearing prison garb, sleeping on a pallet bed on the ground, and is a physical mess.

And while in this miserable state, Plutarch writes that Cleopatra "welcomed it as an excuse for abstaining from food and so releasing herself from life without hindrance."[13]

It would seem at odds with the queen's stubborn character to survive all difficulties and to fight for her country and her son's right to the throne for her to then starve herself to death. Furthermore, for this monarch who had always used her beauty and her charms to manipulate men and who was accustomed to the wealth and power of her position to suddenly refuse lodgings in the finer rooms of the palace in favor of a simple mat on a hard floor is highly improbable. And for her to refuse to dress in royal attire, preferring to don the simple tunic of a slave is inconceivable.

The setting of Cleopatra's incarceration within her own palace resembles far too closely a jail with all the accoutrements of a prisoner's life: barren cell, hard sleeping surface, prison uniform, and very little food. Add to this the marks of assault on Cleopatra's body, and the cell becomes a torture chamber. While Octavian was putting on a pretense of kindness and humility in the square in Alexandria, he was likely having his men torture Cleopatra to gain information as to where she had secreted the Lagide treasure and where Caesarion, next in line for the Egyptian throne, was hiding out.

The abuse to her body is evidence of the custom of Roman scourging. Similar to the torture of Jesus, Cleopatra likely endured the Roman whips—leather strips with metal ends. Women were not exempt from such beatings. With arms tied above their heads or held out from their bodies, the whipping would be executed on the back of the prisoner by the torturer. Although most of the damage would be to the upper back, the leather strips can wrap around the body and cause damage to the chest area. A few errant strokes might cause injury elsewhere on the victim.

Plutarch describes that upon finding Cleopatra's body after her "suicide by asp," some claim to have seen two light and indistinct punctures on Cleopatra's arm.[14] Admittedly, this is probably just embellishment from Plutarch to explain that Cleopatra used a cobra to kill herself and there had been some evidence of snakebite. But, if Cleopatra were redressed in lavish clothing befitting a queen following her demise, anyone viewing her body would see little of any evidence of torture except for, perhaps, an accidental mark or two on her arms one could attribute to another cause. If Plutarch is relating a true story, Cleopatra's breasts were already mutilated, so it would make little difference if her back were likewise afflicted. Either she was dressed as to cover all the damaged areas of her body, or nobody outside of Octavian's circle saw and reported any trauma Cleopatra had suffered.

If Cleopatra was not one to "beat her breasts," and there is little evidence that there is any truth in this claim that she was, then one wonders why the story of such damage to her breasts exists. The only plausible explanation is that she was tortured for information. While the public outside held out hope that Octavian would be merciful to their queen, his men were likely inflicting their cruel form of torture upon her.

There is one final comment made by Suetonius about Cleopatra's last days that is most interesting: "The younger Antony (the elder of the two sons by Fulvia) Octavian dragged away from the statue of the Deified Julius, where he had taken refuge . . . and killed."[15]

Plutarch says of this moment:

> As for the children of Antony, Antyllus, his son by Fulvia, was betrayed by Theodorus his tutor and put to death; and after the soldiers had cut off his head, his tutor took away the exceeding precious stone which the boy wore about his neck and sewed it into his own girdle; and though he denied the deed, he was convicted of it and crucified.[16]

Antyllus was not one of the children for whom Octavian would be inclined to have mercy. He was the 100 percent Roman son of Antony by his Italian wife, Fulvia, and keeping him alive could one day cause problems for Octavian. He was also not a small child who could easily forget the past and be molded by Octavian to blindly follow him. It was better to dispose of him than allow him to one day take revenge for his father's death.

The Deified Julius statue would most likely have been in the Caesarium, the temple in which I believe Cleopatra had ensconced herself; one more bit of proof that the mausoleum was not the location of Cleopatra's showdown with Octavian. Since her children were with her and were preparing to leave the country, it only makes sense that the young Antony (Antyllus) was with her, too. When the Roman soldiers breached the building, Antyllus's only hope would be to hide in the bowels of the religious rooms or the crypts where the religious items were stored and hope not to be found, later to escape when all was quiet. Whether he was simply discovered by the soldiers and killed or he was given up by his teacher who knew of secret rooms within the temple is questionable. What is assuredly true is that Cleopatra retained her poise and dignity even as she was dragged away and imprisoned.

One can take from the tale of Plutarch that Octavian wanted to keep Cleopatra "safe" and "secure" and that he was genuinely stunned to find that she had snuck in a snake and committed suicide, that her death was the last thing he would want because this prevented him from being able to then bring Cleopatra back to Rome and parade her in his triumph. Yet there are a number of reasons why Octavian would actually prefer her dead (once he knew where her treasure and her son were stashed).

The primary reason would simply be that Cleopatra would always be a danger to him if she were alive somewhere in the world. Just like "dead Caesars" were better than live ones, so were dead Ptolemies. Octavian was a very calculating political player, and leaving a queen on the chessboard is simply a sign of a poor game player. Also, he was well aware that the last time a Ptolemy was dragged through Rome in a triumph, in 46 BCE, when Julius Caesar marched Cleopatra's sister Arsinoe proudly through the streets, the citizens ended up feeling sorry for the girl and pressured Caesar into releasing her, which he did. Octavian did not want public sympathy to build around Cleopatra. Finally, Octavian needed a smooth transition in Egypt from centuries of Ptolemaic rule to Roman rule; humiliating the Egyptians by degrading their beloved queen of the last two decades and treating her like an animal would not have been a good move. And, of course, there was always the risk of Cleopatra escaping somewhere on the way back to Rome, and that simply was not a risk Octavian was willing to take. No, Octavian wanted Cleopatra dead, but only after he had the information he wanted and then only in a way that would be the most beneficial to his future plans. He played his hand brilliantly.

Therefore, Plutarch's tale does not seem to be the most likely scenario of how Cleopatra and Antony met their respective ends. As a profiler, I put together all the evidence and created a reconstruction of the last days of their lives, a dramatic replay of history that will be a more accurate recounting than the scenario Plutarch has left us.

CHAPTER 20

THE RECONSTRUCTION

As the sun slowly rose behind the encampment of Octavian, exposing one rectangle of cohort after the other like rows of playing cards dealt out across the long table of the Alexandrian plain, Antony climbed the circular stairs to the top of the Paneium. This odd cone of a hill was only one of two places in the city high enough to view the entire area, and from here Antony could survey the situation that awaited him that day.

As soon as he reached the top, he wished he had come alone. The half dozen men who had accompanied their leader up the hill fell silent behind him as if their windpipes had suddenly paralyzed. Before them lay a stunning panorama of Roman power stretching back upon land and sea until the images mercifully became difficult to make out in the dim light of the early-morning sky.

After taking in the fleets on the north side of the city and the army directly in front of him to the east, Antony passed his gaze over the canal and Lake Mareotis on the south side. He could see the line of supply ships Octavian had moved alongside his troops that were moored on the north side of the canal beginning at the front of the encampment. The lake itself held no opposition ships, just merchant vessels and pleasure barges lined up at the docks and a number of small Egyptian triremes cautiously patrolling the harbor, keeping their watch of Octavian's movements from a distance.

Then he looked over toward the sea; there Antony could see the line of Octavian's ships waiting for battle far outside the harbor in the sea and, just outside the reefs of the harbor, his own ships in a line facing them. Inside the harbor sat Cleopatra's ships, sails on board, waiting for the battle to begin, the signal for the ships to move forward and slip through the channel, to raise the sails, and let the northwesterly winds move them swiftly to the Canobic mouth of the Nile. As soon as he escorted Cleopatra and the children to the docks and gave the word, Cleopatra's men would light the fire at the Caesarium, and when the smoke went up, his forces would begin the battle. The fleet of Egyptian ships carrying Cleopatra and the children would slip away. As long as Octavian's forces were engaged in battle, like at Actium, Cleopatra would have a head start on her way to the Ptolemaic Canal, and Octavian would not be able to pursue the fugitives quickly enough to stop them.

The sights before them did not inspire Antony's men. Their eyes took in the mass of men on the battlefield, the size of Octavian's cavalry moving into their positions on the flanks of the infantry, and the array of warships aimed at a far smaller number of ships of Cleopatra and Antony's much-reduced navy. A creeping dread spread collectively through their limbs. Their own infantry stood like statues on the low hills in front of the gates like an early-afternoon shadow of the troops facing them.

"Is it worth it, Antony?" asked Dercetaeus.

Antony turned and faced his men. They were the best of his cavalry. He had asked a lot of them in the past, and they had always come through for him. Even after Actium, they still stood by him.

"My friends." Antony reached out his large hand and gently placed it on Dercetaeus's right shoulder. "Our fight is not over until we have vanquished the enemy or he, us. At Actium, we separated our forces so as to have a chance at returning to battle, and this is the battle we saved ourselves for. I am sending Cleopatra and my children away, but I am remaining here with you, as my place is with my men. I do not care for my safety but for victory or an honorable death."

The men remained silent and Antony could feel their commitment wavering.

"Come, men!" Antony exhorted. "We are warriors! Let us take to our places and give Octavian his due! Our infantry and fleet await the signal. Come let us hurry to the Caesarium, get Cleopatra and the children to their ship, and have the fire lit. As soon as the smoke starts upward, we will begin our battle! Last night we were victorious in routing their cavalry, and by Hercules, today we shall be victorious again!"

Antony grinned at Dercetaeus, clapped him once on his shoulder, and waved for his men to follow him. He hurried down the steps to the men and horses below, mounted his steed, and led the way to the temple.

The glorious Caesarium overlooked the Great Harbor. As he approached its walls, a bit of melancholy swept through Antony. Cleopatra had put a great deal of care and artistry into designing this beautiful tribute, and he had enjoyed strolling through its gardens. It wasn't yet finished, and neither he nor Cleopatra would likely ever see its completion. He felt at least a comforting bit of satisfaction at the thought of what would go through Octavian's mind when he saw the smoke billow up! His treasure, his treasure! All his future riches going up in smoke! How he would spur his men to attack, his eyes glued to his prize, his aim to storm the city and save his booty.

And, meanwhile, Antony gloated in his revelry, Cleopatra would be sailing off down the Nile; and when Octavian reached the Caesarium, he would find nothing among its ashes but charred wood.

They had arrived at the door of the monument, and Antony dismounted from his horse. He turned away from his steed, and as he did, he felt an agonizing blow to his midsection. His knees gave way and he felt himself sink to the ground. He looked up and saw Dercetaeus, a sword in his hands bent from the effort of thrusting it underneath the mail, and Antony's blood dripping from it. Behind him, Antony saw his men standing with their heads bowed.

He looked up and he saw tears on Dercetaeus's cheeks.

"Why?" he managed to gasp. "Why?"

"Because this is folly, Antony, and we will fight for a purpose, but we will not fight to our deaths just for the life of your Egyptian queen. We are still young, Antony, and we don't need to make the last hurrah of an old soldier. But," said Dercetaeus, his voice breaking, "we will make sure all of Rome knows that you chose an honorable death and this is what will be related."

Dercetaeus leaned over Antony's body and grasped the handle of the leader's sword. He pulled it from its sheath, scraped the flat side of the blade along the blade of his own bloody sword, and backed away from his dying commander. The blood of the great Roman on his own weapon would mean only one thing: he died an honorable death in the best tradition of his people.

A wave of anguish passed over Antony as he watched the men remount their horses, and dust choked him as the hooves kicked up the loose sands from the ground as they passed by. Then it became unnaturally quiet. He lay frozen and unmoving until he heard a cry. He grunted with the effort as he rolled his body over and gazed toward the top of the monument, the rising sun blinding him from behind the building. He could see a bobbing of heads at the window high up on the pylon left of the monument's gate, and he knew that Cleopatra had been watching.

❖

Cleopatra felt time come to a crushing halt. Just a short while ago, minutes had been speeding by as she stood at the top of the temple and watched her plan fall into place. First she had seen the gates to the city open and the infantry flow out onto the ground in preparation for the attack on Octavian's forces. Her fleet, sails tucked on board, was stirring with the morning light and the men were readying themselves at the oars to take the ships to the harbor entrance. Antony had sent the cavalry into their positions and went with his small group of men to view the situation. It was at that moment that Cleopatra felt she would come out of this desperate circumstance with hope for the future, both for herself, for her children, and for her country.

Then Cleopatra felt her lungs struggle for air as the scene below her transmogrified into a disaster, an unstoppable drama that took only seconds but played out in agonizing slow motion far below her. She could do nothing to change its outcome. But she could see what Antony had not: the stepping back of his men and Dercetaeus drew his sword and the violent thrust of the sword into Antony's abdomen, the sturdy Roman sword penetrating an armor rarely breached by an enemy's sword.

She watched as Dercetaeus galloped off with the cavalry back toward the gates of the city. She knew he was off to make his deal with Octavian, to show him the evidence of the demise of Antony, and to facilitate a complete surrender to the enemy. Meanwhile, the others of the cavalry raced off across the Heptastadion over to Pharos, where a signal to Antony's men would be shortly given. She realized then that the plan to surrender had already been in effect before the sun even rose, that no smoke signal from the top of the temple would have had any effect on Antony's men.

She gazed down at the fallen figure lying alone on the ground, the stunned Egyptian guards still frozen at the gate, and she felt a wave of revulsion. During the last year Antony had lost one ally after the other, battle after battle. Now, when he had the chance to prove himself a man and a true general, he lost the command of his men. She wished that she would have had the option of choosing Octavian over Antony, for then, she had no doubt, she would have been the coruler of an Egyptian-Roman empire, or at least the ruler of a still-powerful country.

But, unfortunately, Cleopatra had little choice in the matter. Rome had been split between the two men and she had to choose a side; Antony was the needier of the two and the more manageable.

Now he lay dying at the foot of the temple, and Cleopatra's dreams were dying with him.

❖❖❖

Antony lay on his side where his cavalrymen had left him, and now the guards at the door were gathered around him.

"Bring him in," shouted Cleopatra from above, and she hurried down the stairs to instruct her men inside the temple to unbolt the large front door. Two guards had lifted up Antony and, as they came through the door, Cleopatra waved them on toward the inner rooms of the temple. The door was closed behind Antony and his bearers, and the bolt dropped back into place, securing the temple for at least a small measure of time.

Cleopatra turned and followed the soldiers to the inner sanctum, where they gently lay Antony down upon a richly upholstered bench. The children had caught a glimpse of the glum procession as they passed through the second courtyard and came running to their father's side.

"Father!" cried Antyllus. "What happened?"

Antony could scarcely see his son through his blurring vision.

"Antyllus." Antony attempted to reach out and touch his son's head, but fell back with the slight effort. "Antyllus."

Tears streamed down Antyllus's cheeks and he shifted from foot to foot, his agitation increasing as blood seeped out from under Antony's armor and began to drip from the bench to the floor beneath.

"Father! Open your eyes!" Antyllus beseeched Antony. Antyllus suddenly looked only a boy, not the almost-man who had stood proud at his coming-of-age ceremony just months ago.

The twins kept their distance, hugging the waists of Cleopatra's handmaidens, who stroked their hair and patted their heads, bent over and whispered in their ears, offering what little comfort they could under such horrible circumstances.

Cleopatra grabbed Antony by both shoulders and shook him. "Antony! Antony!" If she could only get a strong-enough response, if the wound wasn't that deep, if she could rouse him quickly enough, bandage him, and send him back to his men before they went over to Octavian, if she could just . . .

Antony's lips did not move in response, and his breathing had become barely perceptible.

The last foolish flicker of hope blew out, and Cleopatra felt a wave of nausea overtake her. She stepped away from Antony. He was beyond help and, therefore, he could be of no further use to her.

Antyllus looked from his father to Cleopatra, desperation etched on his face. He knew what his father's death meant.

"You made me stay!" he accused Cleopatra. "You let Caesarion go, but you made me stay!"

Cleopatra looked at him dispassionately. "It was your place to stay. Your father didn't run away, nor did I. We did what we must, and Caesarion did what was required of him. He did not want to leave."

Antyllus's eyes darted toward the front door of the temple and up at the walls surrounding him. "I can make a run for it."

Cleopatra laughed. "A run for it? Where do you think you can run with that face of your father's and thousands of Roman soldiers between you and the border of Egypt?" She narrowed her eyes at him. "You can act like a man, Antyllus. You can stay and fight with our soldiers when Octavian's men come over the walls of the temple."

Antyllus turned away from her and sank to his knees by his father's side. He grabbed his father's hand, but then pulled his own away quickly. Antony was dead.

Cleopatra climbed up the circular stairs to the roof over the hypaethral room. From here she could see all of Alexandria—her Alexandria. She felt a terrible pain as she watched the fleet sail out of the harbor and the ships raise their oars in unison, signaling her navy's surrender to the enemy. Then the two fleets merged, and like the wave of a tsunami, one large mass rolled over and came back toward the docks.

The gates were now open at the front of the city, and she no longer could tell which side was which. She laughed ironically when she remembered that the only ones left on her side where the men with her at the temple. And, she wondered, how long would they put up even a minimal fight to turn back Octavian's men? An hour? A few minutes? It was not as if anyone believed they could hold out for long. For that matter, even if they could, they would run out of food and be starving to death by the end of one week's time.

Cleopatra wished only for some manner of resistance, just to let Octavian know her people were not traitors like Antony's Romans; that they would be willing to die for their queen. Such a show might be in her favor. Octavian might realize the depth of her countrymen's loyalty for her and conclude that allowing her to rule might be to his advantage.

Besides, she still had her treasure. She could offer to send it to him bit by bit in exchange for her life and her sovereignty. Meanwhile, if she could indeed get her men to put up a fierce fight when Octavian made his attempt to breach the temple, she could buy more time for Caesarion to leave Berenice; at least he would still be free.

Motion from the hills in the front of town caught Cleopatra's eye; a long trail of horses, Octavian's cavalry, and a portion of his infantry were billowing into the city like the smoke that was supposed to go up from inside the Caesarium that morning. The swath of dark, sleek horses with their silvery rows of helmeted riders retraced the same path Antony took earlier that day as he led his men to the temple and himself to his death.

Cleopatra let out a long rush of air, not realizing she had been holding her breath. It was time to go exhort her men to fight for her, for Egypt, for pride. She would let them know Octavian was the type to leave no Egyptian soldier alive who didn't come to him at the earliest opportunity. Perhaps she could spur them on to fight with all they had.

She suddenly heard shouting from below, from in front of the temple. There was a rising commotion, and she felt some satisfaction in knowing she was still being defended.

The sounds of battle were short-lived, and there was quiet once again on the street below. One of her guards came up the stairs, bowed stiffly in front of her, keeping his eyes low.

"Octavian asks you to open the door and save your men. He says he will do what he can for you and your children."

Cleopatra snorted. "Tell him if he dares to climb these walls, the fire shall be lit and all his treasure will be lost." At this point, Octavian might truly believe she was holding out to the last moment. She might as well play along, as she had no other options left except for her men to try to hold on while the Romans swarmed up scaling ladders and descended into the temple.

The guard bowed quickly and went to deliver her message. Cleopatra followed him down the staircase and went to speak to her commander in charge of the temple brigade.

She met his eyes directly. "Will you be giving fight or turning tail like Antony's men?"

The commander was a man of exactly Antony's age, and he knew the fears of men younger than he. He smiled broadly at Cleopatra, as if he was actually enjoying the day.

"My men will do as I command, and I will do as you command."

Cleopatra nodded. "Very well. I expect the Romans will be assaulting us from all sides, over the walls and through the windows. We should have burnt all our damn ladders! I am sure, by now, they have procured them from our construction sites."

Cleopatra hoped he would fare better than Antony at encouraging his men to engage in battle. She had planned to give a rousing speech herself, but then thought better of it. She had lost so much of her command that a woman giving orders at this time might not be the best course.

Cleopatra stepped close to the commander and let tears come into her eyes.

"Do this for me, this one last time." She made herself tremble and look a bit confused. "My children, I must go to my children." She touched his arm gently as she turned away, and then she ran off softly across the courtyard and disappeared into the darkened chamber.

Octavian did not take the bait. He struck immediately. Cleopatra did not know if he feared that she would indeed light the fire, attempting to destroy the Lagide treasure, or if he simply did not wish to barter with her. The ploy had been worth trying, regardless. Now Octavian wanted Cleopatra and the Lagide treasury in his hands without any more delay.

The "battle" lasted for less than twenty minutes, but Cleopatra's guard did not disgrace themselves. Only Antyllus turned out less than a general's son, and, instead of joining the others in protecting the temple, he turned and ran farther into the temple corridors, hiding out in a crypt that he hoped would be overlooked until some unknown time when he might slip out unseen.

Proculeius, Octavian's right-hand man, made his entrance as soon as his men had quelled the small rebellion and the door was unbolted. He made his way past the large pile of logs and found his eyes searching between the timbers for any sign of the Egyptian wealth Octavian so dearly coveted. He stepped over the bodies of the faithful Egyptian soldiers and the last of the unfortunate Roman infantrymen who lost their lives on a day that began as one meant for celebration.

The beauty of the temple was not lost on Proculeius even as he viewed the brutal results of warfare within its walls. He could see, at that moment, why the Egyptian queen would fight so hard for her country, and why Antony should be so taken by this Alexandrian splendor. The soaring pillars with the geometric shapes and bright colors, the intricate motifs, put Roman architecture to shame. The immense flourishes of gold adorning the interior and furnishings were dazzling, and the quantity of it, astonishing.

He was stopped in the hall by one of Cleopatra's servants.

"Cleopatra awaits you," he informed Proculeius, motioning the astounded Roman to enter into the most spectacular of its worship rooms. The woman had nerves of steel!

Proculeius went forward, surrounded by guards on all sides, expecting an ambush. But when he entered the room with his men, his footsteps echoed in the silence. There were but four bodyguards, two standing rigidly on either side of a pedestal intended for displaying the god of the temple. There Cleopatra sat, the woman who had turned the heads of two great Roman rulers, waiting calmly for

Proculeius to approach her. She was stunningly beautiful. It was hard to believe that this was a woman defeated, about to lose her country, about to lose her life.

Cleopatra smiled warmly at the Roman. "You must be Proculeius. Antony has told me you are an honorable man, and since you have been sent by Octavian, I can believe this is an auspicious sign of his good intentions." Cleopatra nearly coughed when she spoke those words, knowing Octavian hated her and would do only as much as he might be forced into acquiescing. As for Antony, his understanding of human nature left much to be desired. Proculeius was likely a two-faced bastard.

But the emissary smiled graciously in return. "Indeed, Madam."

Cleopatra waved her arm in a semicircle in the direction of the immense fire materials in the courtyard. "Have you seen the treasure, Proculeius?"

"I saw nothing, Madam, but the tower of wood logs."

"Quite right, Proculeius," Cleopatra agreed. "I had never planned to destroy my treasure or this beautiful temple. It would be such a waste for everyone, and I haven't the heart to do such a horrid thing."

She could see the man was puzzled. She laughed.

"The treasure, Proculeius," she said, "is not here. I removed it long ago, keeping it safe for its proper disbursement. Please inform Octavian that I wish to continue to handle the affairs of Egypt, under his dominion, and I will be sure to deliver the monies as is needed to pay whatever debts he has incurred during these last difficult years. His soldiers and the people of Rome need not suffer any longer."

Cleopatra went on. "My son, Caesarion, is no longer in the country. He will remain outside Egyptian borders as long as Octavian does not feel he has a place in the governance of this region."

Cleopatra fixed her eyes on some spot past Proculeius's left ear.

"Tell Octavian that I wish to move forward. Antony is dead; his fight with him is over. Like my neighbor, King Herod of Judea, I have no ill will toward Octavian. Herod was loyal to Antony, as was I, and when Antony failed him, did not hesitate to transfer his loyalty to Octavian, and so will I."

Proculeius wasn't quite sure why Cleopatra was saying this to him. He found himself nearly agreeing that she should be spared and Octavian should be thankful to her for her willingness to cooperate.

What magnificent will! What confidence! Did Octavian hate her because she was truly evil, or because he saw himself in her reflection and he could not tolerate seeing a woman as his equal in that unbiased mirror?

Proculeius admired the queen; of this, he was sure. He actually felt a bit peeved that he had never been a guest in her country or enjoyed the queen's magnanimity.

He realized Cleopatra had not looked back at him. The audience with the queen was over. She, the prisoner, had dismissed her jailer.

Proculeius bowed and strode out of the temple.

Octavian did not take the news well. He had Cleopatra's treasurer brought to him and demanded to know where the Lagide treasury had been hidden.

Seleucus remained silent.

Octavian had him tortured. Still Seleucus said nothing.

Octavian's patience was at an end. He had been away from home a long time. He had business to take care of, and Cleopatra was impeding it. Unlike Proculeius, he hardly believed Cleopatra's assertion that she and Herod were of the same mind-set. Herod could be bought. Cleopatra would never consider herself subservient, no matter how convincingly she played the part. If ever she found an opportunity to carve out her own destiny, she would do so, and Octavian wasn't about to hand her the knife. Even though she actually had cooperated with the Romans for the last two decades, he just didn't trust her.

"Bring me Cleopatra," ordered Octavian.

The Alexandrians were beginning to ask about the fate of their queen. They had seen the skirmish at the temple and now saw the Roman guards replace the Egyptian force on the perimeter of the temple complex.

"Escort the twins, the family servants, and Cleopatra in a tight formation three men deep. Let the populace see them through the soldiers, but be sure there are no gaps that would allow for any escape or a sudden hero from the crowd to break through the line and try to save them. I want no drama," he warned. "It should appear that the queen is being allowed to return to the palace while government matters are being worked out."

Octavian paused.

"Antyllus is not to leave the temple. Finish him and make sure he is not recognizable. Put a Roman uniform on him and bring him out among the bodies of the dead soldiers."

Antyllus did not survive the hour. He was found crouching among the deity's ceremonial crockery in the middle of the row of crypts where he had once gotten in trouble as a boy for playing hide-and-seek.

He was pulled from the chamber, and with a flash of a blade, Antyllus's head left his body. It was hidden in a bag, and when the boy was removed from the temple in military dress, he appeared as another anonymous soldier who had died for his Rome.

The march from the Caesarium Temple to the palace past the stares of her countrymen was a crushing humiliation, but Cleopatra's head remained high. As she nodded her greetings, she looked up and saw the horrified looks of her people as they leaned from windows and stood upon any rise of land or structure to get a glimpse of their queen. When she arrived at the palace steps, the rectangular formation surrounding her little party opened up at the front and allowed them to pass through the open doors of the main hall. At least she was permitted to enter her previous home gracefully, almost as an honored guest rather than as a closely guarded prisoner of war.

The show of civility was fleeting. As the doors closed behind her, her children were sent with their caretakers in one direction and Cleopatra and her handmaidens were taken to a far room in the palace that had served Cleopatra quite well when she wished to keep a political prisoner close by. Now the tables were turned and she was locked in the room with her two ladies.

The room had been swept clean. Before Cleopatra was locked in the cell with her ladies, their clothes were removed, and their bodies checked for weapons and hidden poisons. All three women were handed simple slips to wear in their confinement.

When evening came, the guards returned and removed the hand-maidens. Cleopatra was left alone. She hadn't eaten since leaving the Caesarium, and hunger was beginning to trouble her. She had little time to dwell on the sensation. The door to the small chamber opened, and a man of slight stature entered with three larger men who hung back and closed the door gently behind them. The most muscled of the entourage held his arm close to his side, his fist closed around a handle from which sprouted long leather straps that reached the floor.

The lead man, his chiseled face devoid of expression, placed a slim sheaf of papyrus papers, a small container of ink, and a quill on the floor in front of the bed on which Cleopatra was sitting.

"Write a list. Octavian wants a full report on the locations of your treasure."

Cleopatra ignored the request.

"Tell Octavian that I will only release the treasure if I continue to be its comptroller."

"Octavian commands you to write and will not take no for an answer." The man's face remained a stone.

"He will get no other answer from me."

Cleopatra kept her gaze steady as she faced her inquisitor.

The man stepped back and motioned for the three men to come forward. A smile imperceptibly played on his lips.

"They will change your mind."

Cleopatra knew what the men could do, two holding her arms immobile, the third wielding his whip. But she was still queen, the immortal Isis, and the great Cleopatra.

"Never."

The men moved in, and the whip fell upon her.

Three days passed with no food and no water, only the daily visits from the three men and their instrument of persuasion.

On the fourth morning, Cleopatra lay unmoving on her cot, angry welts crisscrossing her back, her breasts, and her shoulders, with a few stray marks on her arms where the whip had veered off course. Her face was untouched but drawn, and her eyes were shadowed underneath from agonizing pain and exhaustion. Fever raged in her body, the result of untended infections in the mangled flesh of her torso.

She was brought a guest—her treasurer, Seleucus.

Standing haggardly in the doorway, bent with the pain he too suffered at the hands of Octavian's torturers, he gasped when he saw Cleopatra.

He turned with rage toward the Romans.

"How could you?" he bellowed at them with contempt. "She is the pharaoh, the great goddess Isis, the Mother of Egypt!" His eyes were tormented with the vision of his fallen Cleopatra.

"Bastards! Enough! I will tell you what you want to know."

He covered his eyes to block out the sight of the ravaged queen, and then cupped his hands over his ears when he heard her cry out as he hobbled away, "No! No! You fool! You mustn't tell him!"

Cleopatra moaned as the door slammed shut. What a pathetic, gutless man! How could he give in just at the sight of her, as if she hadn't borne all the pain for a purpose? Now the weakling, the only other being in Alexandria who knew the locations of the treasure, had given away her kingdom, her one last bit of power.

She sat silently in her empty cell, waiting for the arrival of her death. She knew when the door opened, Octavian would not be standing there. He would come neither to ask her for her last wishes nor to gloat. He was not the type of man either to feel the need to do the right thing or to waste time rejoicing over the extermination of an annoying insect. She knew she would be dispatched without ceremony, she and her country, into the footnotes of Roman history.

She heard their steps and she saw two soldiers enter through the door of her cell. She rose unsteadily to her feet, nodded, and turned silently away from them, clasping her hands behind her back. A shadow, an arm, a bit of pressure to her neck, and the pharaonic era was over.

CHAPTER 21

OCTAVIAN'S TRIUMPH

It has been quite a journey since my first visit to Egypt in 2003 for the filming of *The Mysterious Death of Cleopatra*. I have traveled through the ancient world of the pharaohs and visited their cities, their temples, and their tombs. Today I board a small local bus, filled entirely with men, to my final destination, an archeological site called Tapasoris Magna, thirty miles west of Alexandria. I have in my hand a note from Dr. Zahi Hawass, to show to the archeologist managing the dig for Dr. Hawaas and the Dominican archeologist Kathleen Martinez, who believe Cleopatra may have been buried in a tomb in the desert, away from the prying eyes of the Alexandrian mob.

While on the bus, I read the final words of Plutarch on the days following the deaths of Cleopatra and Antony.

As for the children of Antony, Antyllus, his son by Fulvia, was betrayed by Theodorus his tutor and put to death; and after the soldiers had cut off his head, his tutor took away the exceeding precious stone which the boy wore about his neck and sewed it into his own girdle; and though he denied the deed, he was convicted of it and crucified. Cleopatra's children, together with their attendants, were kept under guard and had generous treatment. But Caesarion, who was said to be Cleopatra's son by Julius Caesar, was sent by his mother, with much treasure, into India, by way of Ethiopia. There Rhodon, another tutor like Theodorus, persuaded him to go back, on the ground that [Octavian] invited him to take the kingdom. But

233

while [Octavian] was deliberating on the matter, we are told that
Areius said:—

"Not a good thing were a Caesar too many."

As for Caesarion, then, he was afterwards put to death by
[Octavian], —after the death of Cleopatra; but as for Antony,
though many generals and kings asked for his body that they might
give it burial, [Octavian] would not take it away from Cleopatra,
and it was buried by her hands in sumptuous and royal fashion.

But [Octavian], although vexed at the death of the woman,
admired her lofty spirit; and he gave orders that her body should
be buried with that of Antony in splendid and regal fashion. Her
women also received honourable interment by his orders. When
Cleopatra died she was forty years of age save one, and had shared
her power with Antony more than fourteen. Antony was fifty-six
years of age, according to some, according to others, fifty-three.
Now, the statues of Antony were torn down, but those of Cleopatra
were left standing, because Archibius, one of her friends, gave
[Octavian] two thousand talents, in order that they might not suffer
the same fate as Antony's.

Antony left seven children by his three wives, of whom Antyllus,
the eldest, was the only one who was put to death by [Octavian]; the
rest were taken up by Octavia and reared with her own children.[1]

So the brutalized Cleopatra is strangled and quietly removed
to a sealed tomb to spend eternity with her Roman consort. With
all-out war averted with the surrender of Cleopatra and Antony's
forces and the cleverly concocted story of Cleopatra's iconic suicide
released to the public, the country passes quietly into the hands of
the Roman conqueror. There is no citizen revolt. Once the Lagide
treasure is safely in hand and the last Ptolemy, Caesarion, the alleged
son of Julius Caesar, is located down in Berenice and eliminated,
Octavian's major problems are solved. He is the undisputed ruler of
the Mediterranean world; he had money to pay his troops and make
his country wealthy; and he would never have a Ptolemy challenge
him again. *This* was Octavian's Great Triumph.

I arrived at the site of Tapasoris Magna and was greeted by the archeologist and given a tour of the ruins. I asked if there had been any proof yet that this was the burial site of Cleopatra and Antony, and he told me that, in spite of many interesting artifacts indicating this was clearly a temple of importance, including a number of coins bearing Cleopatra's head that had been found and a necropolis that had been uncovered behind the temple, there was not yet proof that this was Cleopatra's and Antony's final resting place. So the mystery of where they are buried continues.

AFTERWORD

WHAT THIS NEW VIEW OF CLEOPATRA MEANS TO WORLD HISTORY

One week before the Egyptian Revolution of 2011, I walked across Tahrir Square, the site of the massive protest, eating an ice cream, totally unaware of the unrest about to explode. Cairo is a bustling city, but it suffers from years of oppression, unemployment, and the suppression of women, albeit to a lesser degree than some of the neighboring countries. It had been over two thousand years since Cleopatra, a woman, ruled Egypt; and rarely have women held such lofty positions of power since her day. I wondered just how much the people here in modern Egypt and elsewhere actually know about Cleopatra VII, the tough and amazing woman who ruled successfully for nearly twenty years under conditions that would have been trying for any ruler, let alone a female, which was quite an amazing feat. Understanding just how brilliant and determined the last pharaoh was should be an inspiration to girls and women everywhere. Since females have been noticeably absent from power positions in the history of humankind, a clearer portrayal of a woman of Cleopatra's caliber should be a great addition to our knowledge of world politics and sociology.

No longer seen as merely a seductive, overly emotional woman who made poor choices and ended up cowering in her tomb, Cleopatra can now take her rightful place as a political figure with brains and brawn, equal to any man of her time or in any century thereafter.

NOTES

CHAPTER 2: THE PHANTOM COBRA

1. E. A. Wallis Budge, *The Egyptian Sudan: Its History and Monuments*, vol. 2 (Philadelphia: Lippincott, 1907), p. 211.

2. Cleopatra VII's mother was Cleopatra V, and her sister, Cleopatra VI. Joyce Tyldesley, *Cleopatra: Last Queen of Egypt* (New York: Basic Books, 2008), p. 27.

3. Rosalie David, *The Ancient Egyptians: Beliefs and Practices* (Portland, OR: Sussex Academic Press 1998), p. 148.

4. Plutarch, *Lives*, vol. 9, *Demetrius and Antony, Pyrrhus and Gaius*, trans. Bernadotte Perrin, Loeb Classical Library (Suffolk, UK: St. Edmundsbury Press, 1920), p. 307.

5. Ibid., p. 325.

6. Ibid., p. 329.

7. Cassius Dio, *Roman History*, trans. Earnest Cary and Herbert B. Foster, Loeb Classical Library (Boston: Harvard University Press, 1917), p. 39.

8. Suetonius, *The Twelve Caesars*, trans. Robert Graves (Harmondsworth, UK: Penguin, 1957), p. 51.

CHAPTER 3: THE STAGE

1. Strabo, *The Geography of Strabo*, vol. 3, trans. Hans Claude Hamilton and William Falconer (London: G. Bell & Sons, 1889), pp. 228–31.

2. Jean-Yves Empereur, *Alexandria Rediscovered*, trans. Margaret Maehler (New York: George Braziller, 1998), p. 112.

3. Franck Goddio started his explorations underwater in Alexandria in 1992. After nearly three thousand dives in 1996, he had found enough archeological evidence to declare that he had found Cleopatra's palace under the Mediterranean waters off the shore of the city. Laura Foreman, *Cleopatra's Palace* (New York: Discovery Books, 1990), pp. 168–70.

4. There are a number of discussions as to what happened to the library of ancient Alexandria, but I find Parenti's argument the most sound. Michael Parenti, *The Assassination of Julius Caesar: A People's History of Ancient Rome* (New York: New Press, 2003), pp. 155–57.

CHAPTER 4: THE MAKING OF THE QUEEN: PART ONE

1. N. G. L. Hammond, *The Genius of Alexander the Great* (Chapel Hill: University of North Carolina Press, 1997), p. 40.

2. J. G. Manning, *The Last Pharaohs* (Princeton/Oxford: Princeton University Press, 2010), p. 1.

CHAPTER 5: THE MAKING OF THE QUEEN: PART TWO

1. Plutarch, *Lives*, vol. 9, *Demetrius and Antony, Pyrrhus and Gaius*, trans. Bernadotte Perrin, Loeb Classical Library (Suffolk, UK: St. Edmundsbury Press, 1920), p. 197.

2. Ibid.

3. Ibid., p. 193.

4. Cassius Dio, *Roman History*, trans. Earnest Cary and Herbert B. Foster, Loeb Classical Library (Boston: Harvard University Press, 1917), p. 169.

5. Plutarch, *Lives*, p. 197.

CHAPTER 7: CLEOPATRA VII BECOMES QUEEN

1. Prudence J. Jones, *Cleopatra: A Sourcebook*, Oklahoma Series in Classical Culture, vol. 31 (Norman: University of Oklahoma Press, 2006), p. 56.

2. Plutarch, *Plutarch's Lives*, ed. Arthur Hugh Clough and trans. John Dryden, Modern Library Classics (New York: Modern Library/Random House, 2001), p. 231.

3. Jones, *Cleopatra*, p. 56.

4. Gaius Suetonius, *The Twelve Caesars*, trans. Robert Graves (Middlesex, UK: Penguin Books, 1957), p. 17.

CHAPTER 8: JULIUS CAESAR

1. Plutarch, *Plutarch's Lives*, ed. Arthur Hugh Clough and trans. John Dryden, Modern Library Classics (New York: Modern Library/Random House, 2001), pp. 165–67.

CHAPTER 9: MARK ANTONY

1. Plutarch, *The Makers of Rome: Nine Lives*, trans. Ian Scott-Kilvert (New York: Penguin Classics, 1965), p. 291.

2. Ibid., p. 285.

3. Ibid., p. 282.

4. Quoted in Prudence J. Jones, *Cleopatra* (London: Haus Publishing, 2006), p. 84.

5. Ibid.

CHAPTER 10: OCTAVIAN

1. Gaius Suetonius, *The Twelve Caesars*, trans. Robert Graves (Middlesex, UK: Penguin Books, 1957), pp. 81–82.

2. Ibid., p. 86.

3. Gaius Suetonius, *Lives of the Caesars*, trans. Catherine Edwards (New York: Oxford University Press, 2000), p. 85.

4. Ibid., p. 78.

5. Suetonius, *Twelve Caesars*, p. 26.

6. Ibid., p. 68.

CHAPTER 12: THE ROAD TO ACTIUM: PART TWO

1. Anthony Everett, *Augustus* (New York: Random House, 2006), p. 96.

CHAPTER 13: THE ROAD TO ACTIUM: PART THREE

1. Plutarch, *Lives*, vol. 9, *Demetrius and Antony, Pyrrhus and Gaius*, trans. Bernadotte Perrin, Loeb Classical Library (Suffolk, UK: St. Edmundsbury Press, 1920), p. 195.
2. Cassius Dio, *Roman History*, trans. Earnest Cary and Herbert B. Foster, Loeb Classical Library (Boston: Harvard University Press, 1917), pp. 25–27.
3. Plutarch, *Lives*, p. 263.

CHAPTER 14: ACTIUM

1. Plutarch, *Lives*, vol. 9, *Demetrius and Antony, Pyrrhus and Gaius*, trans. Bernadotte Perrin, Loeb Classical Library (Suffolk, UK: St. Edmundsbury Press, 1920), pp. 267.
2. Ibid., p. 270.
3. Ibid., p. 272.
4. Ibid., p. 275.
5. Ibid., p. 277.
6. Ibid., p. 279.
7. Ibid.
8. Ibid., p. 281.
9. Ibid., p. 282.
10. Ibid., p. 283.
11. Ibid., p. 284.
12. Ibid.
13. Ibid., p. 285.
14. Ibid., p. 287.
15. Ibid., p. 288.
16. Ibid., p. 289.
17. Ibid., p. 291.
18. Ibid.
19. Ibid., p. 292.
20. Ibid., p. 294.

CHAPTER 15: PLAN B

1. Plutarch, *Lives*, vol. 9, *Demetrius and Antony, Pyrrhus and Gaius*, trans. Bernadotte Perrin, Loeb Classical Library (Suffolk, UK: St. Edmundsbury Press, 1920), p. 297.

2. Ibid.

3. Ibid.

4. Ibid., p. 303.

5. Ibid.

6. Ibid., p. 305.

7. Ibid.

8. Ibid., p. 307.

9. Ibid.

10. Strabo, *The Geography of Strabo*, vol. 3, trans. Hans Claude Hamilton and William Falconer (London: G. Bell & Sons, 1889), pp. 228–31.

11. Ibid.

12. Michael Pitassi, *The Navies of Rome* (Woodbridge, UK: Boydell Press, 2009), pp. 48–49.

13. Ibid.

CHAPTER 16: PLAN C

1. Vincent Scheil, "Inscription de Darius à Suez," *BIFAO* 30 (1931): 297, cited in "Ancient Egypt: An Introduction to the History and Culture of Pharaonic Egypt," last modified May 2009, http://www.reshafim.org.il/ad/egypt/timelines/topics/canals .htm (accessed November 20, 2012).

2. Diodorus Siculus, *Historical Library*, vol. 1, chap. 33, trans. Julius Friedrich Wurm, quoted in "Ancient Egypt: An Introduction to the History and Culture of Pharaonic Egypt," last modified May 2009, http://www.reshafim.org.il/ad/egypt/ timelines/topics/canals.htm (accessed November 20, 2012).

3. Ibid.

4. Ibid.

CHAPTER 17: A MOTIVE FOR THE MURDER OF CLEOPATRA

1. Plutarch, *Lives*, vol. 9, *Demetrius and Antony, Pyrrhus and Gaius*, trans. Bernadotte Perrin, Loeb Classical Library (Suffolk, UK: St. Edmundsbury Press, 1920), p. 307.

2. William Smith, ed., *Dictionary of Greek and Roman Biography and Mythology* (Boston: Little, 1880).

3. Plutarch, *Lives*, p. 311.

4. Ibid., p. 310.

5. Ibid., p. 307.

6. Donald W. Engles, *Alexander the Great and the Logistics of the Macedonian Army* (Berkley: University of California Press, 1978), p. 60.

7. Strabo, *Geography*, vol. 3, book 17, trans. William Falconer (London: G. Bell & Sons, 1903), p. 223. Available at http://rbedrosian.com/Classic/Strabo.html.

8. Herodotus, *Histories*, cited in "Ancient Egypt: An Introduction to the History and Culture of Pharaonic Egypt," last modified May 2009, http://www.reshafim.org.il/ad/egypt/geography/ (accessed November 20, 2012).

9. Plutarch, *Lives*, p. 307.

10. Ibid.

CHAPTER 18: THE UNFORESEEN MURDER OF ANTONY

1. Strabo, *The Geography of Strabo*, vol. 3, trans. Hans Claude Hamilton and William Falconer (London: G. Bell & Sons, 1889), pp. 228–31.

2. Ibid.

3. Plutarch, *Lives*, vol. 9, *Demetrius and Antony, Pyrrhus and Gaius*, trans. Bernadotte Perrin, Loeb Classical Library (Suffolk, UK: St. Edmundsbury Press, 1920), pp. 314–17.

4. Somers Clarke and R. Engelbach, *Ancient Egyptian Construction and Architecture* (New York: Dover Publications, 1990), p. 160.

5. Sergio Pernigotti, *The Egyptians*, ed. Sergio Donadoni (Chicago: University of Chicago Press, 1990).

CHAPTER 19: THE CAPTURE OF CLEOPATRA

1. Plutarch, *Lives*, vol. 9, *Demetrius and Antony, Pyrrhus and Gaius*, trans. Bernadotte Perrin, Loeb Classical Library (Suffolk, UK: St. Edmundsbury Press, 1920), p. 307.

2. Gerhard Kittel and Gerhard Friedrich, *Theological Dictionary of the New Testament*, vol. 1 (Grand Rapids, MI: Eerdmans, 1977), p. 453.

3. Somers Clarke and R. Engelbach, *Ancient Egyptian Construction and Architecture* (New York: Dover Publications, 1990), p. 169.

4. Plutarch, *Lives*, p. 317.

5. Ibid., p. 323.

6. Ibid., pp. 316–17.

7. Cassius Dio, *Roman History*, trans. Earnest Cary and Herbert B. Foster, Loeb Classical Library (Boston: Harvard University Press, 1917), pp. 25–27.

8. Plutarch, *Lives*, p. 318.

9. Ibid., p. 325.

10. Quoting Florus from *Life of Antony* in Prudence J. Jones, *Cleopatra: A Sourcebook*, Oklahoma Series in Classical Culture, vol. 31 (Norman: University of Oklahoma Press, 2006), p. 170.

11. Dio, *Roman History*, p. 34.

12. Plutarch, *Lives*, p. 319.

13. Ibid., p. 322.

14. Ibid., p. 330.

15. Suetonius, *The Twelve Caesars*, trans. Robert Graves (Middlesex, UK: Penguin Books, 1957), p. 51.

16. Plutarch, *Lives*, p. 321.

CHAPTER 21: OCTAVIAN'S TRIUMPH

1. Plutarch, *Lives*, vol. 9, *Demetrius and Antony, Pyrrhus and Gaius*, trans. Bernadotte Perrin, Loeb Classical Library (Suffolk, UK: St. Edmundsbury Press, 1920), pp. 321–33.

BIBLIOGRAPHY

Abbot, Jacob. *Cleopatra*. Fairfield, IA: First World Library, 2005.

Appian. *The Civil Wars*. Translated by John Carter. London: Penguin Group, 1996.

Ashton, Sally-Ann. *Cleopatra and Egypt*. Oxford, UK: Blackwell Publishing, 2008.

Atiya, Farid. *Cheops' Solar Boat*. 2nd ed. Cairo, Egypt: Farid Atiya Press, 2009.

Baines, John, and Jaromir Malek. *Cultural Atlas of Ancient Egypt*. New York: Checkmark Books, 2000.

Baker, Simon. *Ancient Rome*. London: BBC Books, 2006.

Bard, Kathryn A. *An Introduction to the Archeology of Ancient Egypt*. Malden, MA: Blackwell Publishing, 2008.

Bass, George F., ed. *A History of Seafaring*. London: Omega, 1974.

Beard, Mary. "Cleopatra: From History to Myth," *Guardian*, March 18, 2003.

Bongioanni, Alessandro, and Maria Sole Croce, eds. *The Illustrated Guide to the Egyptian Museum in Cairo*. Cairo: University of Cairo Press, 2001.

Bradford, Ernle. *Cleopatra*. London: Hodder and Stoughton Limited, 1971.

Brooklyn Museum. *Cleopatra's Egypt: Age of the Ptolmeies*. New York: Brooklyn Museum, 1988.

Burstein, Stanley M. *The Reign of Cleopatra*. Norman: University of Oklahoma Press, 2004.

Caesar, Julius. *The Civil War*. Translated by John Carter. Oxford, UK: Oxford University Press, 1998.

Dio, Cassius. *Roman History*. Translated by Earnest Cary. Loeb Classical Library. 9 vols. Harvard University Press, 1914–1927. Available at http://penelope.chicago.edu/Thayer/E/Roman/Texts/Cassius_Dio/home.html.

Casson, Lionel. *The Ancient Mariners*. Princeton, NJ: Princeton University Press, 1991.

———. *Ships and Seamanship in the Ancient World*. Princeton, NJ: Princeton University Press, 1971.

Chavaeu, Michael. *Cleopatra: Beyond the Myth*. Translated by Cornell University Press. Ithaca, NY: Sage House, 2002. Originally published by Editions Liana Levi, 1998, Paris, France.

Clarke, Somers, and R. Englebach. *Ancient Egyptian Construction and Architecture*. New York: Dover Publications, 1990.

Dando-Collins, Stephen. *Cleopatra's Kidnappers: How Caesar's Sixth Legion Gave Egypt to Rome and Rome to Caesar*. Hoboken, NJ: John Wiley & Sons, 2006.

Davis, John D., and Henry Snyder Gehman. *The Westminster Dictionary of the Bible*. London: Westminster Press, 1944.

Dillon, Matthew. *Girls and Women in Classical Greek Religion*. New York: Routledge, 2003.

Donadoni, Sergio, ed. *The Egyptians*. Chicago: University of Chicago Press, 1990.

Dueck, Daniela, Hugh Lindsey, and Sarah Pothecary. *Strabo's Cultural Geography: The Making of a Kolossourgia*. Cambridge: Cambridge University Press, 2005.

Empereur, Jean-Yves. *Alexandria*. New York: George Braziller, 1998.

———. *Alexandria Rediscovered*. New York: George Braziller, 1998.

Engels, Donald W. *Alexander the Great and the Logistics of the Macedonian Army*. Los Angeles: University of California Press, 1978.

Everett, Anthony. *Augustus*. New York: Random House, 2006.

Flamarion, Edith. *Cleopatra: Life and Death of a Pharaoh*. New York: Harry N. Abrams, 1993.

Foreman, Laura. *Cleopatra's Palace*. New York: Random House/Discovery Books, 1990.

Forster, Edward M. *Alexandria: A History and a Guide*. Garden City, NY: Anchor Books, 1961.

Foss, Michael. *The Search for Cleopatra*. New York: Arcade Publishing, 1997.

Freedman, David Noel, Allen C. Myers, Astrid B. Beck, eds. *Eerdmans Dictionary of the Bible*. Grand Rapids, MI: William B. Eerdmans Publishing, 2000.

Freeman, Charles. *Egypt, Greece, and Rome*. New York: Oxford University Press, 1996.

George, Margaret. *The Memoirs of Cleopatra*. New York: St. Martin's Press, 1997.

Gohary, Jocelyn. *Nubian Monuments on Lake Nasser*. Cairo: American University in Cairo Press, 1998.

Gohary, Said. *The Twin Tomb Chapel of Nebnefer & His Son Mahu at Sakkara*. Cairo: Supreme Council of Antiquities, 2009.

Goldsworthy, Adrian. *Antony and Cleopatra*. New Haven, CT: Yale University Press, 2010.

———. *Caesar: Life of a Colossus*. New Haven, CT: Yale University Press, 2006.

Grant, Michael. *Cleopatra*. Edison, NJ: Castle Books, 2004.

———. *From Alexander to Cleopatra: The Hellenistic World*. New York: Collier Books, 1982.

Green, Peter. *Alexander to Actium*. Berkeley: University of California Press, 1990.

———. *The Hellenistic Age*. New York: Modern Library, 2007.

Gurval, Robert Alan. *Actium and Augustus*. Ann Arbor: University of Michigan Press, 1995.

Hammond, N. G. L. *The Genius of Alexander the Great*. Chapel Hill: University of North Carolina Press, 1997.

Harris, W. V., and Giovanni Ruffini. *Ancient Alexandria between Egypt and Greece*. Netherlands: Brill Academic Publishers, 2004.

Hawass, Zahi, and Franck Goddio. *Cleopatra: The Search for the Last Queen of Egypt*. Washington, DC: National Geographic Society, 2010.

Hazzar, R. A. *Imagination of a Monarchy: Studies in Ptolemaic Propaganda*. Toronto: University of Toronto Press, 2000.

Holbl, Gunther. *A History of the Ptolemaic Empire*. Translated by Tina Saavedra. New York: Routledge, 2001.

Hughes-Hallet, Lucy. *Cleopatra: Histories, Dreams, and Distortions*. New York: Harper & Row, 1990.

Jones, Prudence J. *Cleopatra*. London: Haus Publishing, 2006.

———. *Cleopatra: A Sourcebook*. Norman: University of Oklahoma Press, 2006.

Kantouris, Costas. "Archaeologists Find Massive Tomb in Greece," *USA Today*, February 12, 2006.

Kemp, Barry J. *Ancient Egypt*. 2nd ed. New York: Routledge, 2006.

Kerisel, Jean. *The Nile and Its Masters: Past, Present, Future*. Rotterdam, Netherlands: A. A. Balkema, 2001.

Kittel, Gerhard, Gerhard Friedrich, and Geoffrey William Bromiley, ed. *Theological Dictionary of the New Testament*. Vol. 1. Grand Rapids, MI: William B. Eerdmans Publishing, 1985.

Kleiner, Diane E. *Cleopatra & Rome*. Cambridge, MA: Belknap Press, 2005.

Lewis, David. *The Cambridge Ancient History*. Cambridge: Cambridge University Press, 1994.

Lindsay, Jack. *Cleopatra*. New York: Coward McCann & Geoghegen, 1970.

Louis, Henry. *Handbook of Gold Milling*. Charleston, SC: Nabu Press, 2011. Originally published 1984 by Macmillan.

Manning, J. G. *The Last Pharaohs*. Princeton, NJ: Princeton University Press, 2010.

Marlowe, John. *The Golden Age of Alexandria*. London: Victor Gollancz, 1971.

McCullough, Colleen. *Antony and Cleopatra*. London: Harper Collins, 2007.

———. *Caesar: A Novel*. New York: Avon Books, 1997.

———. *The October Horse*. New York: Pocket Books, 2002.

Millmore, Mark. *Imagining Egypt: A Living Portrait of the Time of the Pharaohs*. New York: Black Dog & Levanthal Publishers, 2007.

Murray, Margaret A. *The Splendour That Was Egypt*. London: Sidgwick and Jackson, 1949.

Parenti, Michael. *The Assassination of Julius Caesar: A People's History of Ancient Rome*. New York: New Press, 2003.

Parkinson, Richard. *Pocket Guide to Ancient Egyptian Hieroglyphs.* New York: Barnes & Noble Books, 2003.

Pitassi, Michael. *The Navies of Rome.* Woodbridge, UK: Boydell Press, 2009.

Plutarch. *Lives.* vol. 9. *Demetrius and Antony, Pyrrhus and Gaius.* Translated by Bernadotte Perrin. Loeb Classical Library. Suffolk, UK: St. Edmundsbury Press, 1920.

———. *Plutarch's Lives.* Edited by Arthur Hugh Clough. New York: Modern Library, 2001.

———. *Plutarch's Lives.* Vol. 2. Edited by Arthur Hugh Clough. Translated by John Dryden. New York: Modern Library, 2001.

Pollard, Justin and Howard Reid. *The Rise and Fall of Alexandria: Birthplace of the Modern World.* New York: Penguin Books, 2007.

Potter, David. *Emperors of Rome: The Story of Imperial Rome from Julius Caesar to the Last Emperor.* London: Quercus, 2007.

Preston, Diana. *Cleopatra and Antony.* New York: Walker, 2009.

Ramage, Edwin S. *The Nature and Purpose of Augustus' "Res Gestae."* Stuttgart, Germany: Franz Steiner, 1987.

Roller, Duane W. *Cleopatra.* Oxford: Oxford University Press, 2010.

Rosalie, David. *Discovering Ancient Egypt.* London: Facts on File, 1994.

Ruffle, John. *The Egyptians.* Oxford, UK: Phaidon Press, 1977.

Saunders, Nicholas J. *Alexander's Tomb: The Two Thousand Year Obsession to Find the Lost Conqueror.* New York: Basic Books, 2006.

Schiff, Stacy. *Cleopatra: A Life.* New York: Little, Brown, 2010.

Suetonius, Gaius. *Lives of the Caesars.* Translated by Catherine Edwards. New York: Oxford University Press, 2000.

———. *The Twelve Caesars.* Translated by Robert Graves. Middlesex, UK: Penguin Books, 1957.

Severy, Beth. *Augustus and the Family at the Birth of the Roman Empire.* New York: Routledge, 2003.

Sharp, S. *The History of Rome from the Earliest Times to the Conquest by the Arabs.* Vol. 2. Harvard/George Bell & Sons, 1885.

Shipley, Graham. *The Greek World after Alexander.* New York: Routledge, 2000.

Shorter, Alan W. *Life in Ancient Egypt.* London: Purnell & Sons, 1937.

Southern, Pat. *Augustus.* London: Routledge, 1998.

Spalinger, Anthony J. *War in Ancient Egypt.* Oxford, UK: Blackwell Publishing, 2007.

Staccioli, R. A. *Rome: Past and Present.* Rome, Italy: Vision, 2008.

Stannard, Dorothy. *Insight Guide to Egypt.* Maspeth, NY: Langenscheidt Publisher, 1998.

Starr, Chester G. *The Influence of Sea Power on Ancient History*. Oxford, UK: Oxford University Press, 1989.

Strabo. *Geography*. Vol. 3. Translated by William Falconer. London: G. Bell & Sons, 1903. Available at http://rbedrosian.com/Classic/Strabo.html.

Toledo, Jose Sanchez. *Imperium Legions*. Madrid, Spain: Andrea Press, 2004.

Tyldesley, Joyce. *Cleopatra: Last Queen of Egypt*. New York: Basic Books, 2008.

Venit, Marjorie Susan. *Monumental Tombs of Ancient Alexandria: The Theater of the Dead*. Cambridge: Cambridge University Press, 2002.

Vinson, Steve. *Egyptian Boats and Ships*. Buckinghamshire, UK: Shire Publications, 1994.

Wachsmann, Shelley. *Seagoing Ships & Seamanship in the Bronze Age Levant*. College Station: Texas A & M University Press, 1998.

Weigall, Arthur E. P. B. *The Treasury of Ancient Egypt*. London: William Blackwood & Sons, 1911.

Welsh, Frank. *Building the Trireme*. London: Constable, 1988.

Wertheimer, Oskar von. *Cleopatra: A Royal Voluptuary*. Philadelphia, PA: J. B. Lippincott, 1931.

Wilkinson, Toby. *The Rise and Fall of Ancient Egypt*. New York: Random House, 2010.

Winks, Robin. *The Ancient Mediterranean World*. Oxford, UK: Oxford University Press, 2004.

INDEX

ABOUT THE AUTHOR

PAT BROWN has a master's degree in criminal justice from Boston University. She is the chief executive officer of the Sexual Homicide Exchange (SHE), a nonprofit criminal-profiling and investigative organization offering pro bono services to families and law enforcement to solve cold homicide cases throughout the United States and Canada (www.SHEprofilers.com); the president/consultant of the Pat Brown Criminal Profiling Agency, which provides crime-scene analysis and behavioral profiling to prosecutors, defense attorneys, and international clients (www.patbrownprofiling.com); and a well-known crime commentator on television shows such as *Nancy Grace, Jane Velez-Mitchell,* the *Today* show, the *Early Show, Inside Edition, Fox and Friends, Larry King Live,* and *Geraldo at Large.* She is the author of *How to Save Your Daughter's Life; Only the Truth; The Profiler: My Life Hunting Serial Killers and Psychopaths;* and *Killing for Sport: Inside the Minds of Serial Killers.* She also developed the first criminal-profiling certificate program in the United States for Excelsior College.